BOUNDLESS

CAROLYN DAWN FLYNN

BOUNDLESS

atmosphere press

Published by Atmosphere Press

Library of Congress Cataloguing-in-Publication Data

ISBN 979-8-89132-482-4

Flynn, Carolyn Dawn. Boundless
1 - Flynn, Carolyn Dawn
2 - Motherhood - United States - biography
3 - Motherhood - New Mexico - biography
4 - Family relationships - United States - biography
5 - Journalism - United States - biography
6 - Journalism - New Mexico - biography
7 - Journalism - New York - biography
8 - Spirituality - United States - biography
9 - Spiritual life - United States - biography
10 - Title

Cover design by Felipe Betim

Reprint of David Whyte's poem, "Just Beyond Yourself", is used with permission from David Whyte/Many Rivers.

The names of some of the characters in this book have been changed for privacy reasons.

Atmospherepress.com

For my little stars,
who are big stars now

Just Beyond Yourself

Just beyond
yourself.

It's where
you need
to be.

Half a step
into
self-forgetting
and the rest
restored
by what
you'll meet.

There is a road
always beckoning.

When you see
the two sides
of it
closing together
at that far horizon
and deep in
the foundations
of your own
heart
at exactly the same time,
that's how
you know

it's the road
you
have
to follow.

That's how
you know
it's where
you
have
to go.

That's how
you know
you have
to go.

That's
how you know.

Just beyond
yourself,
it's
where you
need to be.

– David Whyte, from *The Bell and the Blackbird*

part one

-

Songs of Innocence

DEAD ON ARRIVAL

JANUARY 2001

WE ARE A STREAK OF RED on a desolate horizon. The twins and I are speeding down Interstate 25 in an ambulance. Above us, sirens scream, filling my ears. To the city, we are a jagged flash to underscore a blood-red sunset on the Sandia Mountains. To us, we are inside this blanch-white sarcophagus of tubes and wires racing down a highway, trying not to die.

My babies are eighteen months old. They are rushing us to a hospital. I say this in my mind to sear it into me. This. Is happening. Through the scratch-crackle of the radio, voices of dispatchers and paramedics speak in a frantic staccato code. I grasp that they are trying to figure out which place will take my babies first: Lovelace Northeast Heights? University of New Mexico, with its child trauma unit? Finally, a decision. "Lovelace Gibson," the dispatcher says. "They are ready to receive them."

Lovelace Gibson, where the twins were born. I draw Grace a little nearer to me. Both babies are cold as quartz. When I look into Paul's eyes, they are gray flint. His pupils are disappearing into a tiny black hole. "Don't leave, little stars," I whisper.

Two paramedics monitor their heart rates and their oxygen, green and blue lines missiling across two screens. "They give them Narcan," the one with the glasses turns to me and says. "That's what they do."

Ash. Activated charcoal. And Narcan. The drug they give people who overdose on opioids. They will fill them with ash. Like they are urns.

All I knew was I had arrived at the babysitter's house to pick up the twins and found ambulances parked at the curb. When I crossed the threshold, I saw one paramedic holding Grace in his lap as another flashed a penlight in her eyes. Paul was tethered to a heart monitor, sensors pasted to his bare chest. "They climbed out of the playpen where they were napping. I'm sorry! I am so sorry!" the babysitter had said when she greeted me at the door. She told me the twins had ingested a prescription morphine derivative that she had left uncapped on the nightstand. "I don't even know for sure they ingested it," she added, her afterthought and nothing I could hear. My babies were descending into deep sleep right before my eyes as though under the ghost spell of another shore. The tender, rose-infused cheeks that had just that morning nestled at my breast were crumbling into ashes, so light they could slip through my fingers.

Before I could spring into panic, the babysitter clasped my forearm, pinning me in place. "Stay strong for the twins," she said. "Right now they need every ounce of you."

In a flash, I had snapped into fierce warrior mode. No time to cry, only seconds to fight for their lives.

The ambulance surges forward. "What happens?" I ask the paramedics. "When we get there."

That morning my husband had said he didn't want to work on our marriage. "We must do everything we can to save this," I had said. "For them." I pointed to the crib they shared. "This. Is not worth saving," he said and stormed out of the house. I had gathered the twins, their lunches, and their sippy cups. I had barred the tears into a frozen place behind my eyelids and dropped the twins off at day care.

"Do they pump their stomachs?" I want this poison out of them. I want to believe modern medical technology has solutions for this.

"With the activated charcoal," the paramedic with the glasses says, "they don't pump their stomachs. The Narcan intercepts the receptors in the brain. And the charcoal is like ash. It absorbs the narcotic. It has to pass through."

Paul grows cold to the touch. His skin feels clammy. We are still twelve miles away. Fifteen minutes. I reach to swaddle the blanket around my son.

"Stay awake, little stars," I whisper to him, then turn my face to Grace. "Stay alive. It's worth it."

Arrived. A team in blue pounces on my babies. Seconds only, then Narcan, activated charcoal, heart rates normal. They are still conscious.

"They're dead."

My husband bursts through the automatic doors.

"No, they're alive." I look away. I reorient my gaze to the twins, Paul with a glassy gray-eyed stare. Grace's eyelids flutter.

Just then, Grace jolts from her gurney and erupts a spew of ash. My husband and I stand in awe like we're watching an ancient volcano on Santorini. Just two years ago, we'd been on our honeymoon in Greece, walking the tunnels of Akrotiri. Frescoes, pottery, a once-teeming marketplace, all preserved beneath the ash. The center of the island had fallen into the sea and disappeared. The ring of land that remained had been buried in ash. For the first time today, our eyes meet. We immediately turn away to look at the same thing. Grace heaves sheets of cinder and lava from the back of her throat. Her plum-colored Baby Bum playsuit turns black, leaving a swath of charred earth. As I dab at her chest with a white towel to absorb the slag, I think it is the most beautiful thing I've ever seen.

Paul never spews. He just absorbs it.

After three hours of observation in the ER, the doctors decide it is best to admit the twins so they can be monitored all night. They transfer us to the pediatric ward. There, attendants affix portable heart monitors to each twin's back. Settled in our room, I notice there is no heartline on Paul's monitor. Too weary to panic, I call the techs.

"Oh, just needs a new battery," the tech says and walks off to find some AA batteries.

I am not going to sleep tonight if whether they live or die depends on fresh batteries. My husband is quickly asleep in the hospital bed to my left. I roll my bed next to the twins' cribs, so I can wake up every thirty minutes and peer over the rail to watch them breathe. I cup my hands to their tender cheeks as I watch the green line, heart rate; the blue line, oxygen; the yellow line, respiration. Monitors hold the room in an eerie stream of never-ending light.

INTO THIS SAME WING OF THE HOSPITAL I had come after a positive pregnancy test, two months after my second miscarriage, and because I had been high-risk, they had done an ultrasound at six weeks. For this third baby, my faith was wobbly. I would not let myself imagine a face, fingers, a heartbeat for her. Not yet.

"You have two babies in there," the ultrasound tech had said.

"Two," I had said as though I was learning the word for a number in a new language. "Twins?"

"Twins," she had said. "Do you want to hear the heartbeats?"

Yes, I did. The heartbeats sounded like two whispering voices threading their way through a line hot-wired to the outer edges of the universe. As if that wire had tapped into a percussive tribal chant, a vigil dance to hold life and call rain and catch light.

"That is the sound of life," she said.

I hadn't thought life would sound like that, that a heartbeat would have a voice. Or voices. But they did.

The technician explained that when the sensor picked up a heartbeat six weeks in, 98 percent of those pregnancies come to term—her words for "the mother doesn't lose her babies." Two months before, I had miscarried. One year to the day before that, I had miscarried. Both times, the blood spilled out of me, emptying my womb. But this news was good. I let this fact settle in me like rich sediment. Like a river finding a place to bank itself. To become a riverbank.

So there will be two, arriving together.

THAT VIGILANT NIGHT in the pediatric ward, my husband stone-cold asleep, the three of us, mama and two babies, slipped into a fetal rhythm. I could find sleep only in the space between their heartbeats. The twins' heartbeats snuck in underneath mine, and together we beat in perfect peace. This is what I once was able to give my two babies but never again could give them, the sanctity of my womb, the shared heartbeat of knowing you are completely cared for. There, in our fetal constellation, all systems of my body had orchestrated themselves to a single point of orientation, the sustenance of two small lives. My blood had hummed through my body, delivering nourishing oxygen and amino acids. My blood had a destination and a purpose.

If they were going to stay alive, I was grateful, but I didn't know where we could go from here. The only thing I knew to do was keep vigil and listen for what would come next. God certainly had my attention now. The Irish poet John O'Donohue tells a story about three harps. One harp is bigger, the other two are smaller. When the harpist strikes a chord on the big harp, it infuses the two smaller harps with the grandeur and beauty of its resonance. As Big Harp, my task is to send out enough tuneful spirit for Baby Harp One and Baby Harp Two to come into harmony with the sudden twinge of being alive. Could I? This felt frightening, that I might lose both of them, all at once, as suddenly as they came to me. I quivered at the thought that they were ashes already.

two

No Time to Cry

BEFORE THE SUN SEEPED THROUGH the open sky, night-shift nurses who had been invisible all night burst in and swept through our room, disconnecting tubes and monitors. We can go home today, they told us, barely glancing at the actual patients in their side-by-side cribs. Sleepless me wobbled out of the bed. As I folded their clothes, I kept my eyes on the twins, now not tethered to any electronic marker of life. I lifted the Baby Bum onesie bearing the charred path of Grace's rejected poison and held it before me. I tucked it into the diaper bag.

"We'll have to pick up my car at the babysitter's," I reminded my husband. He looked perplexed. "*We* came here by ambulance."

He called the babysitter and blared assurances to her. No harm, no foul, the twins are fine, he said into the phone with booming confidence, though the pediatrician had yet to come answer our medical questions. By the time the doctor arrived, it was midmorning, well past our daybreak alert. We were advised to watch for signs of non-cardiogenic pulmonary edema, fluid in the lungs, or any sort of acute respiratory distress. "It's watch and wait," the pediatrician said.

"Are we watching for something that is *likely* to happen?" I asked, which got no real answer. *When will we know we're out of the woods?*

We were catapulted out of a hospital into nothing. We returned by the same route we came, up the interstate. As we strapped the twins in the car seats, snowflakes flurried around us. I looked to the eastern horizon, the mountain stone gray and pink beneath murky clouds. I looked across to my husband. His eyes were sober cold. His eye color was hazel, and once I had found warmth and spark there. I had credited his recessive genes for the stroke of luck that the daughter we chose to name Grace ended up with green eyes. But now he was looking nowhere, somewhere past us, beyond the place where the Sandias gave way to hills of piñon and juniper rolling north to Santa Fe.

"You do know that our children almost died," I said. "You do know we're lucky." *You know how close we were to unlucky. To tragic. To unthinkable.*

"They didn't die, though," he said.

The snow clouds that wreathed the foothills were a rare and chilling sight, holding the mounds of the low hills beneath a gray cloak. I shivered a little. The bean sí of Irish lore abides in the tumuli that dot the Irish countryside. She arrives to herald the death of a family member. Today we had sent her back to the mounds of earth and stone and death, away from us.

I turned a bright face to the twins in the back seat. "It's snowing." I pointed to the snowflakes landing on the glass window. "See. They have all kinds of shapes."

At the babysitter's house, my husband jumped out of the car and rushed to hug her. "An honest mistake," he said. Part of me was grateful he said it, something necessary to go on. Part of me wondered why he said it again and again, as though the most consuming thought was his concern for her guilt or worry. Hello, I am the mother.

As my husband drove off in his car, the babysitter reached into the minivan to touch the twins' outstretched hands. I see her as a mother, confirming: Yes, they are alive. This is when I understand. It was true they did not die. Another truth has come alongside to live next to this: From here on, it will only be the slow death.

Back at the house, my mother had been waiting through a vigilant night, praying prayers that were always better and clearer than mine. It happened she was visiting from Kentucky. Here she was with a cup of tea and a board book, the provenance of all that had gathered in me to be summoned into the motherhood, now a providence in my fragile hour. She welcomed the twins into her arms. She directed me to the couch, then let the twins pile on me as I read *My Mama is a Llama*. They pressed their faces to my chest. Their giggly voices rang through the house.

When my husband arrived a few minutes later, he announced, "I'm going to take a nap." He turned to me. "Maybe take a bubble bath."

This would be his only concession to my struggle.

I agreed, and my mother took my place. Paul tunneled into her like now that he had found her, he would never need to find his way out. Grace tilted her head so that her cheek touched my mother's. She beamed at me as I headed toward the bubbles.

Immersed in a cumulus of warm white water, I considered I could just kick through my grief, the way I have always done. I could scream at it. I could rent my clothes in the most biblical display of despair. I could argue with it, a position I find a better fit, as a skeptical and curious journalist who always tests her truths. Soap clouds, easy to sweep aside.

I did not want a bubble bath. I leapt out of the tub like the water had scalded me. Every idea I had about how soothing such a spa moment ought to be, every super-woman dictum I ever had about how self-care is where it's at, every magazine article I had ever assigned to a freelance writer for the girl getaway issue— ab-so-lute-ly wrong. The cure was husbands who supported their wives, and children who were safe and didn't die.

I burst from the bathroom wrapped in a towel and fell into my mother's arms. "What kind of God would do this?" The wrathful Old Testament guy was not my Guy—I am a progressive Christian in the contemplative tradition and a practitioner of mindfulness meditation. Our way of being in the world is love, not wrath. But He was acting like That Guy.

She let me vent. She let me lament. She did not hold me back.

Though she was a wife of a Baptist deacon, she did not quote Bible verses that reminded me that my questions had stepped out of the bounds of all the ways patriarchy wanted me to understand who God was. How dare I ask such questions? As my mother held me, I understood that as a mother, I had the perfect right to ask. Our unspoken mother code.

"OK, I get it. You have the immense power to give life. Awesome, God!" I said. "And take life away. Is this You doing that?" This felt like a swift blow to two innocents. I looked at the calm face of my mother. "Is *this* who God is?"

The day after my second miscarriage, I had made myself stop. I had taken a rare day off work at the city's daily newspaper, where I was in senior management. I had stood at the sandy crest of our property by the fire pit, looking out to the Sandia Mountains. I had fervently entered a day of prayer and contemplation. Out of my grief, I had promised God I would do anything, whatever it took, to bring those two lost babies back. One month later, the twins were conceived. I thought I'd heard an answer, a promise.

Now I wailed. "You promised to protect these children," I cried. "And I believed you."

My mother held me in her arms. "I don't trust you anymore," I said to my compassionate and universal God. "I think you are cruel. And capricious."

When we lament, we are finally honest. We are, at last, vulnerable.

The psalms are the literary structure of shared lament, expressions of solidarity that pre-date the printing press. They are ecstatic expressions—experiential, kinetic, performative. They are akin to the whirling dervish of Sufism, the vocal ritual art form of the Irish keen. In Psalm 22, the poet David writes, "I am poured out like water/And all my bones are out of joint/My heart has turned to wax/It has melted within me." This one struck me as more authentic than anything I ever remembered about conversations I'd had with God throughout my life. This psalm expressed raw, unearthly emotion. *I cry out by day, but you do not answer,* the psalmist wrote. *I cry out by night, but I get no rest.* I was in a new conversation now. But did I want to have it?

MY HUSBAND EMERGED to see me crying. The twins had resumed telling each other their stories, simple stories about simple people that circulated around the yellow Little Tikes house with the arched pink door and mint green window. They giggled as they chased each other to the sink with white, plastic faucets and pretended to rinse lemon-yellow saucers, confident that adult humans would come together and make dinner for them. Our gaze crossed the room, forming a safe and definite X at the place where the twins pretended, played house. I did not look at him. He did not look at me. We fed the twins and put them to bed.

He asked me to meet him at the bonfire. I arrived as he sipped Côtes du Rhône and roasted salmon on the grill. I approached the fire. "I know what we're fighting for but I don't know if I'll ever understand what we're fighting about," I said. I knew I was going to have to leave, but I could not just yet. Inside, the twins were sleeping in the same crib, their breathing rhythmic, heartbeats aligned.

three

RAUCOUS DEPARTURES

I lie under a starlit sky
And the seasons change in the blink of an eye
I watch as the planets turn
And the old stars die and the young stars burn
– Lord Huron, "Lonesome Dreams"

DECEMBER 2016

IN THE BOSQUE ALONG THE RIO GRANDE, I heard a fluttering above the gray thatch of bare trees. A skein of snow geese broke and swooped down to fields of broken winter grass. The place I stood was the place of recognition, their meetup point. Thousands of miles they had logged, calling themselves away from home territory, Alaska, the Canadian Arctic, frozen places. This river had been a heartline south to their winter home. For days, they will gather here.

I edged closer to listen to the clamor. In their disharmony, I heard a refrain that told me I stood between the end of something and the beginning of another thing. It was winter, a season of listening. I lifted my eyes and trained my gaze on the copper trees at a dusky opening in the woods. Our photographer stood ahead of me, waiting. Her camera began whirring and clicking. Emerging from the bronze trees were the twins, striding side by side, shoulder aligned with shoulder. Grace wore spry maroon Keds, pearly tights with heart-shaped black dots. Paul wore a burnished black jacket and a gingery soul patch. Above us, new arrivals of snow geese eagerly called out, "Here, here," announcing familiar land-marks. The twins walked until they stopped at a cascade of golden leaves. Grace mounted a fallen cottonwood and tugged her denim jacket as the camera shutter released a froth of sound. Their senior photos. The photographer asked the usual question. "Where will you go?"

MARCH 2017

THIS QUESTION RINGS OUT A CRY OF DISRUPTION through a whole season. It asks me to tell you a story I am not ready to tell. How do I begin telling you the story about my babies leaving me? It is the story that has loomed at the edges of the story I had been telling about my life all along. A story I never wanted to tell. Which is an ironic thing for a journalist to write. All my life, I have been asking other people to tell hard stories.

Come spring now, and the ending begins to arrive one late afternoon. Down in the Rio Grande Valley, the snow geese gath-ered once again, only now their song was sudden, and it was urgent. It was a new season, the season of fertile confusion. I came home as a blue-aster sky filled with the cawing of raucous departures. Around my house, baby quail skittered along behind their mothers and fathers, brushing fan paths in the sand. Sparrows sang sweet songs from the cottonwoods, hopping on heart-shaped leaves. The stucco glistened in the slanting sun, and I took my place at the door, waiting. I am the light at the window, a perfect rectangle of amber glow that frames a cinnamon reed shade you can roll up with a string. I stand in the frame now. From the road, you may see I am home and draw a certain centrifugal comfort while the mur-murs and shouts of burgeoning lives spring about you in the wild yonder. From there, I look so necessary. I look the perfect pic-ture of stability, the one who holds the whole orchestra together, never misses a beat. It was nearing sunset, the hour when the sun slips fast out of the day and spring reverts to winter. Daylight time would teeter like this for another week. And then the twins circled swiftly to my house, stopping so sharply that the gravel crunched in the sand.

"Mom!" Paul said, hooking me into a bracing hug. He dropped the car keys and tossed a book on the counter. I bent to see the title: *Gödel, Escher, Bach: An Eternal Braid.* "I had my MIT interview."

We were eight weeks out from the twins' choosing colleges, but only rarely was there this kind of excitement. This all-consuming occupation usually had a drag on it. But today, the interviewer had begun his conversation with Paul by talking about string theory, which had sent Paul deeper into the bookstore where they met for coffee. There, next to the string-theory books, he had found this one. "Everyone calls it GEB," he said, his eyes sparkling. "These are the earliest ideas about cognitive science that are informing artificial intelligence today." The author had won a Pulitzer, his father a Nobel, legacy stuff. The subtitle referred to the Eternal Golden Braid, which was described as a metaphorical fugue on minds and machines in the spirit of Lewis Carroll.

"It's a braid of questions about consciousness, thinking, and creativity," Paul said. "He uses logic, art, puzzles, and music theory to explain how consciousness emerges from the thinking system that supports it."

"Where does Lewis Carroll come in?" I asked.

"That is what I have to find out."

Hello, meet my son.

"Hi, Mama," Grace said, casting herself into my arms like a trapeze artist catapulting herself across a void. I was reminded that I was her safety net.

Grace's ukulele swung down from her shoulder, bumping my arm, and I felt the flash of her brilliant defiance, how determined she was never to be categorized, how fierce she was to have her voice heard. She was a gentle songwriter with a woeful voice and someone with a single point of focus that all who are still here to catch a breath must be cared for.

Hello, meet my daughter.

Hello, meet ambition. Hello, meet happiness. We wanted both. I wanted the twins to know opportunity. I wanted them not to censor their desire. At the same time, I wanted to protect them from the danger of desire, which can crush us. Sometimes, this conversation got raucous, precisely because it was so unwanted and wanted just the same. This was the delicate hour when college talk could easily become room-emptying talk.

"Here, let's watch the sunset," I said because that was our coming-home ritual. Sometimes I called us the house of two sunsets.

I just have to etch it here, along the crimson light before it fades on the mountain: For seventeen years, I have watched and waited, and they have lived.

IF THIS WERE THEIR STORY AND NOT MINE, it would follow the senior-year trope of high school musicals, where everything is on the line—your entire future!—and you're just trying to fall in love and pick a college. Everyone is asking you to tell the story of your whole life ahead of time.

This is the No. 1 reason that most conversations with the twins hit blind alleys. Every time, I am tossed next to the trash cans, calling up to my vanishing children on the fire escape as rats rattle metal cans. When two-thirds of my family leaves—hard stop— am I to be left with only my vanishing journalism career? Once there had been dinners with Gloria Steinem and special investigations on domestic violence—now I was barely alive in a dying industry. My career may end, not at a shattering-the-glass-ceiling peak but a free fall. All I had was shards of unanswered questions. And a strange sense of recklessness that left me unrecognizable to myself. My life in mid-sentence.

If this were my musical, some delicate percussion, maybe the swish of snare drum, maybe the sorrowful tear of a timpani, would cue me to turn to the song of my looming loneliness. I would dejectedly kick the can and turn back to the open street where I must live now. The danger was I would get swallowed in street bustle before I even began to sing.

Ah, but the real danger: I am not free to sing until I know the twins are singing. For that, I must take you back two years when the twins were fifteen.

A POUNDING, POUNDING, POUNDING thudded through the house. It shook the walls as I sautéed snow peas in the wok. No longer could I ignore the beat of the war drums. I strode down the hall to Grace's room and swung open her door. My teenage daughter was drubbing nails into the wall, rearing back with the hammer like it was a Lincoln Log-splitting axe. When I swiveled to look at her wall, I saw it was studded with roofing nails, the hardest, most penetrating nails from our toolbox. She gritted her teeth as she bound her fingers in green yarn and wrapped strands of fiber in and around the nails to form letters. I locked eyes with her and she stopped. We both turned to the message floating up from the white wall like an Eight Ball warning: Try Dying.

Not "die trying," which would have been an affirmation of ambition and perseverance that could be a cutesy, crafty wool-spun internet meme motivating young hearts onward to a successful life. These wrappings my daughter had pinned to the wall spelled "T-R-Y D-Y-I-N-G," just try it, a defiant invitation to death. It chilled me.

Now I knew. All three of us had felt the pull into the conversation with the slow death, the one where you know what's coming, you just don't know when. I'd lost my father, suddenly, as a young woman, nearly the way I'd lost my children before they could even talk. I'd lost my mother slowly. Which was the way I'd been losing myself. What I knew was: I wasn't going to lose the twins. Not again. No.

That year my mother died, and the twins had written reams of poetry. Grace had written songs like "R.I.P," which stood not for a tombstone inscription but Red Imaginary Payphone, a desperate message in a bottle cast out across the ocean of the internet to someone who Hope believed would understand but who Reality understood was just red and imaginary. When I listened to her song, it was delicious. Her voice was exquisite and heartbreaking in a way that made me want more of it and less of it at once. Her song, it was about the disconnect, the problem of our age. My daughter had named it: people who saw only screens and not real people with faces and voices. She had sung about standing right in front of someone who would not see her or hear her. "We throw our wishes away/at the astronaut café," she sang. "We fly away through a sky that tastes like mint." Her song was so "Lucy in the Sky with Diamonds" that I could remember my own ninth-grade descent into the existential abyss. I had lived into enough territory beyond ninth grade that I could know that year had not been my undoing but my becoming.

I looked my daughter deep into the eyes, and I wondered if we even agreed on what we were trying to do together.

PARTS OF THEIR CHILDHOOD will never get on this page. That's because there are two narrators. I am only one of them, but we feel the same. We want them here and alive. After that proclamation on the wall, I'd enrolled the twins in a better school, academically rigorous but more importantly, a place where they could be seen. "She can't breathe there," I'd told their father. She won't live unless we change this, I didn't say.

Despair had always lurked at the edges of the twins' lives as children of divorce. Months after that day, when as toddlers, they came to the brink of death, they arrived at All Angels Episcopal Day School. They were toddlers just beginning to master language and identity—*they were toddlers who had just NOT DIED*—this was how I saw them. And this is how they saw themselves, a pair of two-year-olds who had spent every waking moment of their lives together, shared the crisis of birth, and even the crisis of death. Standing at the edge of the playground, with its brightly painted Lego-colors fire poles and swing sets and tire swings, desert sand glittering all around, they quietly announced themselves to their new teachers and schoolmates as they tried to decide who would be their real friends, they had said, holding hands, "We're divorced."

The truer way of saying that was "we're divorc-*ing*." Though the divorce papers had been stipulated, stamped, and signed by a judge fifteen years ago, the final decree on what had happened had never come. We had accomplished a modicum of co-parenting functionality but never emotional closure. Here comes the end of court-ordered custody. Here looms the emotional culmination of the one true thing we've shared and always will share: These two people will now go live their lives beyond our beautiful mess.

IN THE RIGHT HERE, RIGHT NOW of the year of Where Will You Go, the twins and I stood in a calming silence as the sunset descended around us. In Albuquerque, New Mexico, the most mysterious element in our domain is the sky. Its presence is everywhere, these questions, too, all around us and above us, prisms that hold the light and bend it to a mountain. The sky is our ally because it has much bigger fish to fry. It's not that the sky doesn't care about our problems—it's just that our problems are so solvable from its perspective. First, we looked east as a watermelon pink washed over the mountains, glowing on the peaks and trickling down into the deep blue folds of the foothills. Then we turned west as the sun blazed through clouds, yellow as a field of

Tuscan sunflowers. It is a sunset in two movements.

Sitting on the west-facing porch, I pointed to the evening star as it rose. Hello, meet spring of senior year. Hello, meet the razor edge of the future.

"Tell me more about MIT," I said.

Hello, meet hope. Hello, meet worry. Hello, meet the keen edges of every conversation we have now. They won't tell me they are frightened about the future. They will tell me they are being brave. They won't tell me that most conversations with me cancel out their conversations with their father—and vice versa. They won't describe how our sharp swords hold them in a delicate maze.

For the past two years, we had been churning out college essays, including two killer applications, one to MIT (Paul), the other to Tulane University's neuroscience program (Grace). Some seventeen-year-olds sought validation through the mirror of college acceptance, some through unlimited sexual conquest—or both. Some through an inner guidance system, hopefully, provided by a loving parent, or even two. The twins seemed to be a mix that was dominated by "loving parent" but could be especially validated by "MIT said yes."

"I've been calculating the odds about whether I have a chance," Paul said. "If they only have, say, two slots for students from New Mexico, that means I'm competing with seventeen-year-olds out of a pool of a population of two million, about 44,000 people. Not that many people. If we assume most of the applicants are from the Albuquerque-Santa Fe corridor, that's the seventeen-year-olds out of only one million people. About ten thousand. Fewer people. Then we have to earn the ACT score to get in. Smaller pool." He turned to me. "I think it's me and six people."

"And you probably know them," Grace said.

"Mom, I really want this," Paul said.

Want this. Really want this. This was the unvoiced desire I had already heard beneath every essay he'd ever written. Many friends and sisters will say how remarkable the twins are at achieving things. Some who are mothers of not-studying teenagers will lament that their own seniors are not trying harder, not willing to work through the confusion of the future. I cannot voice the real stimulus because it would mean disclosing our poverty. The twins want a better future because they know where the edges are. They know they could tip over. There is a reason that two of the past five presidents have been sons of single mothers. It's because their single mothers knew that at any moment, their children could fall off the edge of the earth.

Once, I had proclaimed our house the "Be Who You Are House." I had mainly said this to walls and doors, my voice most likely shrill, trying to penetrate the gypsum and wood they had put between them and me, just so they could think this one out. Come ninth grade, the twins had fortressed their rooms to find out who they were, mainly, it seemed, through YouTube and GitHub. Before that it had been One Direction (thankfully, only briefly) and Powder Toy, the online physics game. Before that, Coke or Pepsi: Which One Are You? and Nerf Gun Club obstacle courses we set up at the park, in that time long, long ago when the twins still wanted to live in an analog universe, and not Minecraft, where their screen names were Banana Sky and Snowfire. So a flash or two later after their birth and near-death at eighteen months, we had blasted through free-falling at the Tower of Terror in Disney World (when they were six), trekking up the spiral towers at La Sagrada Familia in Barcelona (when they were nine) to this. Now seventeen years had passed since these two creatures had emerged from me, whole, via the modern Western medicine phenomenon of the Caesarean section, so that they were born one minute apart, really, only forty-five seconds. They had spent nearly every day of their lives together except for four weeks Grace had spent in a summer college-prep art program at Lesley University, living in a dorm right at the doorstep of Harvard, and then Paul and I had whisked ourselves to Boston for her art show and to tour Harvard, MIT, and Berklee College of Music, just to see if we saw who we were, if we saw a future in any of those places.

We had been having these conversations—just not with each other. The twins had been furiously writing college essays, with me as their editor. They'd been having conversations with gatekeepers, an array of people eager to peer into their future, expecting them to describe their lives ahead of living them.

"It would be fantastic if you got into one of your 'reach' schools," I said. "But remember, what you're really trying to do is build a happy life. What you're really looking for is the place where you can be who you are."

I delighted in their reaching for it at the same time I knew I was reaching for the end of us. I found something animating in this potent desire of theirs. It was the sense of being alive, and not dead.

I turned my face to Grace, who had engaged in the patient and delicate work of crafting a path for herself, when Paul's path in computer science had been so painfully obvious. She'd chosen neuroscience and music, a major in psychology that would lead her to the work where her interests in integrative therapies such as nature immersion and mindfulness and music could forge a path forward—and make her decent money.

Paul anticipated the conversational pivot and said, "I think you've done an amazing job of figuring it out, Grace."

"I agree," I said. "You took the time you needed to center and dig through the confusion." Knowing I risked the scatter, I said, "I'm proud of you."

I threw myself into this risky territory because I love their wit and brilliance, their thirst to create a life that's uniquely their own. My role as mother has been vista gatherer and sounding board as I've listened to a ferocious accumulation of preferences. What they don't want is denounced loudly; what they do want is announced early and often but always changing. Not always do they say what they really want. Often, if I've failed to calibrate the time limit on these conversations, they can tilt into sudden nihilism. All things family can be scorched into existential meaninglessness by a single errant extra word.

"Thank you, Mom," Grace said, taking the compliment. "But I don't have time to think about this now."

FROM GRACE'S ROOM, I heard as she ran through "Riptide" by Vance Joy, an urgently strummed song that pushed all this away with force. From Paul's room, I heard the flow of "Canon in D" on guitar. Sitting alone on the porch as night avalanched into the house, I sighed, my night music. *You knew this year would be painful.* My personal vow had been to be emo-diverse—to feel it all, even the conversations that end in annihilation. Without meds, unlike most of America. Just feel it. All the highs, all the crying-on-the-floor moments. With meditation and an ounce or two of faith that there was something higher than me, something that thought with a better mind and activated a deeper heart. I called her all-loving God, and I meant the all-loving part. I also meant the "her," because I needed God to be whole, both he and she, wise protector and fierce nurturer. Mindfulness practice had trained my brain, rewired it. So had the pure, unrefined love of motherhood. It would be hard to say which had built more resilience.

Senior year was building to a crescendo, and all three of us knew what was on the horizon: Two of us were leaving. The twins had emerged from their mid-teen cocoons and announced the answer to who they were: Someone who goes to college somewhere else.

Clearly, it was time for a road trip.

BECAUSE ON THESE WESTERN HIGHWAYS between New Mexico and Arizona are where I have always figured everything out, the road rumbling beneath my wheels, music cranked up and a wide blue horizon. Because there is so much potential to be unleashed, only an endless stretch of highway could hold us. Because as the poet David Whyte writes, we are appreciators of horizons, whether we reach them or not. Because we don't know everything yet. We don't know if Grace will go to Tulane or Willamette or University of Colorado in Denver. We don't know if Paul will go to Carnegie-Mellon or British Columbia, Stanford or MIT. Maybe Arizona State University or maybe right here at the University Near Mom, also known as the University of New Mexico, this place which would be nearly free but a decision on the front end of their lives to clip their wings. They are planning to go farther than that.

Because they make it clear they are tired of my parenting. I haven't halted climate change or racial injustice or gender inequality and I cannot explain why, if I have had so much more time to fix the world they're entering, it is not right. Because my wisdom will always be thirty-eight years behind the world they live in now. Because they like to argue, and I do too. Yet they don't like to argue, and I never know which mood it is because moments of sweet connection can back flip into scorched-earth airings of grievances, and then I'm the empty, ravaged village lost in the smoke of a war I never declared. Because someday I will die, and in the end, they will walk all of this alone.

Because this felt like dying.

I returned to my commitment to emo-diversity, recalling the lines from the Rumi poem that began, "I lived for hundreds of thousands of years as a mineral and then I died and was reborn as a plant." His soul lives as a plant, dies, and is reborn as an animal, then lives as an animal reborn as a human being. The poem lands on "What have I ever lost by dying?" I didn't know the hereafter of the empty nest, only that while I was still animal, vegetable, mineral, person, mother, human, I wanted us to give these last days our full presence. However, as they faced the barrage of big questions, I seemed to have only one: "Am I supposed to die now?" Am I animal, vegetable, mineral, nothing?

"We could see Carlsbad Caverns," I suggested the next night

at dinner, coming much from the same department as my father once did, that you must know your own backyard before you leave it. The year I turned fourteen, he had plodded a Winnebago Chieftain up our driveway past my mom's post at the kitchen window, and we had rushed to the carport, watching with squinted eyes and decidedly affected teenage smirks. He announced we were going to see the world. "Florida!" one sister had said. "Canada!" I had said because I wanted to go to another country, and that was the closest one. But he had insisted we tour all the sparkling blue lakes, laurel-scented mountains, and outdoor summer theaters of Kentucky before we set out on RV adventures to Disney World and Niagara Falls.

Just like my father before me, no measure of enthusiasm I could heft into my voice was making a difference with the twins. Neither had made eye contact. It was one of our rare moments seated at the dinner table, despite my ardent efforts to preserve that icon of Americana once known as the family dinner. Across from me, Paul scooped up a last bite of romaine, feta, and spanakopita. Red onions and Kalamata olives from the Greek salad had already been rejected, stacked on the high rim of the green glass plate to announce preferences. We had sat down ahead of Grace, who had ignored a dozen calls to dinner, nine more than I should have issued. Is it so hard, really, to eat when someone feeds you?

"White Sands, maybe," I said, thinking of the crystal-white dunes raked by the desert wind, the feeling of being nowhere. They had detonated the first atomic bomb there. "It could be nice to see your own state before you head off on your college adventure."

This corny thought drew only some barely grunted "mehs," and I had to admit that the sorry little Airbnbs in Alamogordo reminded me why I'd never explored southern New Mexico, even though I'd lived here twenty-five years. Honestly, it had been a quarter of a century. If I'd wanted to go there, I would have done it by now.

The geography of New Mexico was not the issue at hand, not what concerned me. The real issue was that I might lose their hearts. Had I laid the foundation? Had it been undermined by their father or the culture? Had it been weakened by my own all-too-apparent flaws? Was this solid?

The risk of alienation had been an ever-present factor in the fifteen years since I left their father. Though courts had entered in as a voice of restraint, the battlespace had moved to their hearts and minds. We'd lived at the borderlands of despair, but to the world, all outward signs pointed to repaired lives. No one had split the atom, and there was not an unstable atom at the core—because the courts had pronounced it so. That had not been my lived experience. We could see the whisk of death when it rushed past in an ambulance but not when it was a child clinging to his mother's ankles, trying to protect her with his small body.

The question they got asked every day was "Where will you go?" But the real question I had was "Where will you come when you come home?" Would they know where they belonged?

Late that night, each of us cocooned into our rooms, I stumbled upon a story in *The Washington Post*. The desert in Anza-Borrego park in southern California was blooming like never before. What had prompted this breathlessness? Extraordinary rains. Not since 1999—it was not lost on me, not since the year the twins were born—had the wildflowers burst forth like this. Poppies, desert five-spots, stream orchids, ghost flowers. Oh, I wanted to see a ghost flower.

As I clicked through a slide show of California hillsides blanketed in bursts of orange and purple flowers, I envisioned the three of us, one last family spring break. We would make a short stop in Phoenix to see Grace and Paul's godparents and my writer friends Maureen and Dennis, then cross the creosote desert where the ocotillo bloom like temple oranges, and the Joshua trees twist and bristle but secretly delight that they have their own special habitat. What sealed the deal was Palomar Mountain Observatory, home of the Hale telescope. On this one fact, I won the twins over, and that was that.

four
The Cage, It Called

WE DROVE OUT OF THE CITY, climbing Nine Mile Hill on Interstate 40, pressing steadily upward to the Continental Divide, where West really becomes West, the place from which all rivers flow one direction or another. This is where the waters choose their ocean—Pacific or Atlantic. Hawks glided high above us, etching north across the azure sky. I pressed the Prius due west, crossing beneath them to form an X. I appreciated how definite this was. Combined, land and sky, we had made a mark.

Soon we crossed the Rio Puerco and entered the badlands, blood-stained and chalky white cliffs. We passed through To'hajiilee, a broken-off piece of the Navajo nation, formed during the Long Walk, the forced relocation of the tribe in 1864. It was said that the ones who settled here were the renegades, who simply refused to go farther. But mainly it was known for the place Walter White first cooked meth in an RV in *Breaking Bad.* We'd be in Grants in an hour, in Gallup in three.

Sitting in the passenger seat, Grace practiced songs for her music school application.

"Mom, will you help me decide which song I should submit for my cover?"

She sang through "Someday You Will Be Loved" by Death Cab for Cutie, then "A Girl, A Boy and a Graveyard," followed by a song about lovers who run through the desert plains all night. This last song hung in the high blue sky, as though the three of us had unleashed parts of ourselves to race through rock and sand and piñon, each our own direction, searching even as our other selves traveled together as a unit on the straight line of road toward the western horizon. The lived life, tethered to the unlived life, let loose under the open sky.

Each time we stopped, I felt the fragility of these dusty places. The desert was harsh, ever harsher as we entered the reservation. We were insulated from it as we drove, but when we emerged in Gallup, I was reminded how nowhere we were. That Gallup has one of the grandest convenience stores I had ever seen was defiant to this severe landscape. Paul opted to stay in the car while Grace and I explored. Inside, we found dream catchers, Kachina dolls and Zuni fetishes. I lifted a dreamcatcher to examine it, tan suede wrapped around a ring, brown-and-white-striped feathers gracefully curling from a string of rotund turquoise beads. Inside the ring, plastic webbing created a pattern of petals that spiraled to a center. One glass bead represented the caught dream. Did a caught dream mean you had gotten it in your grasp and you were on your way? Or did a caught dream mean a captured dream, that you could hold it but never live it? My glass ceiling question again. Kachina dolls stared out at us with minus-sign eyes and pyramid noses, adorned with squash-blossom headdresses. One doll wearing aqua boots back kicked, frozen in a story dance. After a quarter century in New Mexico, I tried to train fresh eyes on them. Really, I was trying.

Grace, our movie whisperer, pointed to a Ryan Gosling DVD. "We should buy it," she said. "It's *The Ides of March*."

That is what tomorrow will be. Today is Pi Day, the day MIT tells you whether you are in or whether you are out. They have picked the world's most famous mathematical constant, numerically expressed as a day, to determine the destiny of my son, who really has his hopes up. I won't ask him, I vowed, as we returned to the car. I'll let him tell me.

"We bought a movie," Grace announced. "The Airbnb has a DVD player and a s'mores maker."

"Hunh." Paul barely looked up.

We crossed into Arizona, moving like a blaze of lightning across the Hopi reservation, heading to the Petrified Forest. Between Holbrook and Payson, Paul announced he'd received a text from MIT announcing that the decision was being announced in his email. We were skipping along a two-lane highway through the Petrified Forest where roadside stores were stacked with red-rimmed logs that had become sleek stone with ochre-and-ash-gray centers. The Painted Desert faded behind us in the rearview mirror as we entered the Coconino Forest. We were out of cell-tower range.

"It's loading," Paul said.

Miles later, we stopped to change drivers at Overgaard. A pond sat on the north side of the road, the first spot of water we'd seen since we left the Rio Grande. Slate-green water reflected the high sun.

"I didn't get in." Paul tossed his phone on the back seat beside him. He turned his face to the window and trained his gaze on the pond, looking like he would rather jump in and drown.

"It's OK, Paul," Grace said in her merriest voice. It was the perfect pitch for a preschool teacher, the one all the little ones love, the one who makes even the most reluctant child feel enthusiastic about gluing colored macaroni to a piece of construction paper. "You'll get in somewhere else. And you already got into BC and Cal Poly."

"You were competing against every other brilliant seventeen-year-old in the world," I said.

"Meh," he said with a shrug and plugged back into his headphones.

ON MY FIRST APPROACH TO PHOENIX, years ago, I took the Mogollón Rim from another angle, out of Oak Creek Canyon and the red rocks of Sedona. The year was 1989 when I moved to

Arizona from Kentucky. I had taken a job at *The Arizona Republic*, then the sixth largest newspaper in the country, one of the biggest leaps of my career. What this approach to Phoenix felt like_ and still did twenty-eight years later_was the preparation for a great opportunity. Driving into the heart of the ponderosa forest, knowing that what's ahead for my family was a desert splayed out before our eyes, it felt like a ticket of admission, arriving at the gates of potential. The thrill of making something from nothing. The road grew quiet as we descended, and silence washed into me like a flooding arroyo, a fierce torrent that quieted me with its force. *You must prepare yourself to enter a city.* This was the way of the desert, to honor its terrible, fragile beauty, to honor the city mirage as the same. I remembered what the city of fountains and rose-pink flowers promised me, how it lied. I knew how the city had stung me. I also knew how it had loved me, how bittersweet that was.

So many things I wanted to say to the twins, one last download of mom advice as they chart their course for livelihood and love, but I was choked silent as we dropped into the valley. We headed on the downside slope of the Mogollón Rim. "Who can spot the first saguaro?" I said instead, though I imagined I was the only taker for this game. I think of these thick-armed sentinels as the first greeters, the water storers, the survivors.

We'd come to Phoenix for an official college visit last October. For me, it had been a convenient excuse to see Maureen and Dennis, but the truth was ASU had gotten on our radar after Grace had declared she wanted to major in music therapy, and ASU was ranked No. 1 in the nation for that. We had toured both campuses, the main one in Tempe and the sleek new Polytechnic campus. We'd marveled at the conversion from the military dorms of Williams Air Force Base to a college campus with a fierce statement of desert sustainability—corrugated steel, etched copper sheaths, open-sky passageways misted from above, and elegant rows of palo verde trees and buttercup-dotted potentillas.

This time we arrived sinking with the sun as it set, descending into the city lights between Camelback Mountain and Piestewa Peak. Night had fallen, and we crawled across the rim of the bowl of the city. On reflex, I looked south to spot the silver planes gliding behind the downtown office towers, a marker for me to remember something I had vowed never to forget. Decades ago, on the eve of a job interview with *The Arizona Republic*, I had sat looking south from my hotel tower in awe as I watched the lights, dipping and sailing like ruby fireflies. Those lights soothed the sore spots in me, enthralled me with new vision, something way outside the bounds of what had been expected of me had I stayed in Kentucky, had I stayed home.

ON THE BACK PORCH, Dennis sipped Writer's Block Irish whiskey, I'm not kidding, and Maureen and I drank a decent chardonnay as the twins talked about their futures and we watched, the good witnesses. The promise of the future was the subject Maureen and I had been talking about since I was nineteen and I first met her in the newsroom at *The Lexington Leader*, a newspaper that long ago was twinned into the *Lexington Herald-Leader*, which had once been one thing but had survived as another thing. Maureen and I knew each other again in a second newspaper life at *The Arizona Republic* as women trying to figure out how to balance career, money, and family along with the unwieldy nobility of our profession as vanguards of truth and justice and enlightenment, in 2017 more tenuous than ever. On Election Night in 2016, she had texted me when the horrific seemed inevitable, "I am going to bed now. I don't want to see the rest. I know what happens next." I had stomached it, looked into the bald, beady eye of this unthinkable thing that had happened to my country, the unbroken glass ceiling at the Javits Center, at that hour a brittle shell emptying out. I had thought I was living in a world in which women's inferiority wasn't a given. I thought I was living in a world where women could win, but this made it clear what the game really was: Women must always come in second. And that we could not even come together to birth our own new future narrative. In the days and weeks that followed, I learned I had been betrayed by my own kind. A headline in *Quartz* proclaimed, "Women voted overwhelmingly for Clinton, except for white women." White women in Middle America without college degrees had voted with their husbands, while women of color had cast their votes overwhelmingly with Clinton, 94 percent of black women, 68 percent of Latinas. As Jill Filipovic had written in *The New York Times*, every woman in America just got told that no matter how good she is at her work, she's not good enough.

Five months before, on this same patio, Paul had confessed he wanted to try for Stanford but he thought he couldn't get in. One of his classmates was the son of an early Apple developer, a Stanford grad who had worked with Steve Jobs. That Paul's classmate would go to Stanford was practically a birthright. Paul and his classmate had collaborated on a project they'd posted on GitHub. "Who am I to think I can go to Stanford?" he had asked.

Three years ago, on a spring break trip to California, during the dark days of ninth grade when the burden of nine years of school and the demands of AP classes had taken their toll, and Grace had been on the brink of quitting life, we had stood on the oval lawn of Stanford. The whole road trip had been an unvoiced suicide hotline, help offered not in words and not with therapists but in the landscape before us, the wild sea at Big Sur, the Google campus, and the buff sandstone arches of Stanford. It was Easter Sunday, and proud parents were taking photos of students. Grace had turned to me, marveling. "Everyone who is here is someone who has worked hard to get here," she had said. It had been a breakthrough and a balm. We'd seen something there, a payoff. In the bookstore, I bought them sweatshirts with the Block S and the Palo Alto tree. The twins wore them until the sleeves were ragged.

Stanford had come up again that October night when we sat on Dennis and Maureen's patio after touring the sustainability wonder that was ASU Polytechnic. "If there is someplace you're dreaming of going, I would not let doubt hold you back," Dennis had said to my son. Dennis knew whereof he spoke. His son had been seventh in his class at a Phoenix magnet school but had written a killer essay that had gotten him into Stanford on a full ride. Paul had said yes to Dennis's challenge. We'd brainstormed on his essay, and Dennis had edited Paul's first draft.

Now on this spring evening, as the five of us chatted and we were ever so close to the decisions, Grace took up her ukulele to sing. This time she added, "Look What They've Done to My Song, Ma," written by Melanie. Grace's version was tinged with tragedy. As her mother, the person to whom the songwriter was singing, I felt a deeper layer of confession, pure outrage at the violating. A song has been raped, gang-raped, by someone. It's not recognizable to its creator. To hear her sing, "Well it's the only thing I could do half right / And it's turning out all wrong," with self-deprecation, then "Well if the people are buying tears / I'll be rich someday, ma," with resignation—it put a lump in my throat.

"I like your version better!" Maureen said.

We sat with that a moment. Melanie's song was about regrets of selling out to advertisers, who did turn that song into three commercial jingles ("Look what they've done to my Lifebuoy," "Look what they've done to my Ramada," and finally, for Oatmeal Crisp cereal, "Look what they've done to my oatmeal.")

"It's about making your life your own song," Dennis said.

"Then someone else takes it," I said.

"Melanie is going to be here," Maureen said.

Dennis stood, held his phone out like a microphone, and commanded Siri to search it down. In minutes, Siri proved Maureen right. Melanie would be in concert Saturday night when we came back through Phoenix on the way home from California. We started to make a plan.

Melanie had a heartbreakingly innocent voice. She stepped

out onto the Woodstock stage as an eighteen-year-old, near midnight in the pouring rain, because someone else refused to go on, and she sang her heart out. Her appreciative (and probably very stoned) audience lit candles for her. Afterward, she wrote the anthem "(Lay Down) Candles in the Rain," inspired by the flow of community and gratitude that washed over her as she watched the hillside light up like a web of fireflies.

As Maureen and I cleared the dishes and moved to the kitchen, I mentioned that, unexpectedly, I had two companies pursuing me ardently for a J.O.B. I launched my author development/book editing agency in 2015, building on the success of my seven published books and my MFA in Writing from Spalding, and all was going well. I gave up on looking for a job in journalism ages ago, choosing instead to teach journalism at UNM and do news media consulting. It was surprising that these suitors had shown up. One was in Rochester, Minnesota; the other was in Saratoga Springs, New York.

"Would you go?" she asked.

"Both are premium jobs," I said. "Where were they in 2007, I wonder?"

Out beyond the cinder block wall, an urgent river of traffic rushed through the concrete canyons of Phoenix.

Surrounded by friends and in a familiar city from a past life, it was easy to set aside for the moment the questions brimming around us. Tonight, we were branded with our shared hopes and dreams, our stories and songs, through the pure, simple fact that we had voiced them to each other. That makes them indelible already. If you asked me tonight whether we were a family, I would say yes.

THE NEXT MORNING, Paul took the wheel as we dribbled out of the city at the end of Grand Avenue, where it emptied out into dive bars and halfway houses. Freeway canyons opened to a speedway and cotton fields. An outlet mall with a monolithic Easter-Island stone-faced frown appeared, and then we were past this sprawling city-mirage and slipping back into the dazzling light of an ocotillo desert. It would be hundreds of miles to the white windmills of Palm Springs.

Paul hit cruising speed. I nestled in the back of my Prius and played "passenger absorbed in a book as the miles roll away." I was reading *Commonwealth* by Ann Patchett and thinking about other complicated families, curiously undisturbed by Paul's radical passing strategy. As he settled into his lane, it occurred to me that I could have that conversation my son likes to have, the one that activates his nihilistic worldview that discredits and discounts everything. This is the one where he says it is up to us to create meaning from our postmodern nothingness but every time we have this conversation, it leaves us both feeling lonely and absurd. With anxious eyes, I glanced back at the massive truck that had just nearly shaved off our fender.

We could do that...or not. Because while the twins startle me with the magnificence of their inner lives, most of the time they want to quash all inquiries. This is what it means to be seventeen and be a beacon of potential, so infused with it that the whole world is looking at you. It's everything, and it's too much. I can see it because I am three decades distant from it, and I don't have it. (This is the other reason I am not asking—I am aware of what I lack.) The three of us are held speechless before the Promethean fire of youth, agility, and brilliance. It blazes in our midst and goes with us where we go. This, in two lives that once tipped too close to the still, dark point of death. They are now effulgent with light. We utterly don't know what to do with it.

When we saw the first Joshua trees, we stopped to fuel up. "We're in California," I said, though this was obvious to everyone. It was just to break the silence. I took the wheel at Needles, where I could not help but feel grateful to have made it across this unforgiving landscape. For the longest time, as the miles melted away, my eyes searched for the snow-capped peaks of Palomar Mountain.

In Palm Springs at the Trader Joe's, I stocked up for the cabin with blackened salmon, salad makings, eggs. Grace reminded me that the Airbnb had a s'more maker, so we grabbed graham crackers, marshmallows, and dark chocolate. Grace and I inquired about the crystallized ginger, Paul's favorite and only request as he waited in the car. That had been a go-to study snack, fueling many a college essay application. He seemed to have forgotten about not getting into MIT.

"We removed it from our shelves," the store attendant said when we asked about the crystallized ginger, "because it's carcinogenic."

Oh, fantastic, I've been giving my son cancer all these years. Just when you think you're in the clear, you learn you're never in the clear.

SITTING ON THE DECK at the cabin at Palomar, I watched Grace light the sterno. She assembled a graham cracker with dark chocolate and marshmallow on a metal tray and snapped it closed. As she turned the cage, it caught glints of sun. Paul and I sat in Adirondack chairs, playing "vacationers sitting on a mountain-cabin deck, reading a book." He was reading *GEB*. I had finished *Commonwealth* by Ann Patchett and now was reading Viet Hanh Nguyen's Pulitzer-winning *The Sympathizer*. Today, we had been up to the observatory to see the massive telescope. Also today, Paul nearly drove us off the cliff.

The roads on Palomar were hairpin turns with sharp dropoffs. The blacktop was scarred with skid marks, telling the last seconds of those who failed to navigate life properly. When Paul sensed how nervous I was about the steep cliffs, he tweaked me, roaring up the incline, screeching the brakes at the last possible moment.

A white-rimmed green sign announced the name of the teen boy who did die here. Each time we came to it, Paul blasted up the mountain. My eyes fastened on the boy's name. I wondered how long his ghost had been here, haunting this stretch of road.

I gripped the door. "Slow down!"

Paul laughed.

ARRIVING AT ANZA-BORREGO PARK, the twins were suddenly not in the mood for hiking. This was the trek we'd been building up to all morning—*all week!*—and we had arrived, not in the cool early morning but the relentless blaze of noontime. Rangers warned us that the heat was merciless. Also, Palm Canyon was not a respite from the near 100-degree heat—it was your worst nightmare. They eyed our water jugs and deemed them to be less than half of what we'd really need. The station was crowded with dusty hikers who were turning into lobsters just standing there trying to decide if they believed the rangers.

"I would really like to do this," I said. "This is why we came, and I'll be disapp—"

"We don't care about your feelings," Paul announced.

The time at the cabin had been the parade of preferences—digs about kitschy bear-in-the-woods décor, criminal inquiries into perceived housekeeping lapses but also laced with startling insights in late-night conversations about income inequality and climate change along with genuine requests for life advice. One minute they say they don't want to hear what I think, the next they are telling me I'm a good mother and they love me. Their wisdom can sometimes leave me speechless. Their obstinance, when it borders on all-out destruction, leaves me shattered. The illogic of this too-bad-so-sad-no-desert-ghost-flowers-for-you leaves me fulminating senselessly.

We agreed to do a part of the trail. We'd turn back when our water dwindled to half. At this point, the twins decided it would be a fun game to play "ditch Mom" on the trail and put distance between us, laughing as I plodded along in the heat. Grace had less of a heart for the game than Paul and kept circling back to me. I was just about to cave to their barrage of requests to return to the cabin in the cool mountains when Paul said, "Whoa!" and pointed ahead to a rim of white rock. Bighorn sheep. We snapped three photos. "Enough?" he said. "Back to the cabin?" I agreed, and this diffused all the tension. They had won. As we exited the trail, four paramedics rushed in to rescue a heatstroke victim.

We stopped to buy gargantuan icy drinks in Polynesian colors with fat red straws. Grace bought a yellow Squirt and pressed the cool aluminum can to her forehead. Next to the convenience store was a nursery offering desert plants. It was underneath a vine-covered lattice, so we agreed it offered enough shade to be worth exploring. They each bought two cactus plants, and I reminded them of our spring break trip in Tucson when Paul bought a grandfather cactus. They were six then. "We don't remember," Grace said. "I'm sure it happened, I just have no memory whatsoever."

So many of these memories were vivid to me, moments when were a happy family, webbed together in the discovery of life. The twins had made log flutes and floated them on the water. The ranger had lifted a rattlesnake out of the plexiglass and held it up for all the kids. Life throws all these sensations, scenes, and singular tastes your way, and they feel real at the time. We do all these things together, and they make us a family. But then we forget? What is family, really, if we can't remember, can't access the same set of shared memories, if two of the three of us don't even want those memories? I wanted them. I wanted them too much.

IN THE CABIN KITCHEN, I dried the last of the dishes. Our suitcases were gathered at the door with our cooler and bags of food.

"About ready to go, Mom?" Paul asked in a demanding voice.

"First I need to—" I was about to explain that we needed to wait for the first washer load to finish, so I could turn it to the dryer, then we could go. I turned to the living room and looked at his face, red with anger. I stopped in my tracks.

"Get out of my fucking life!" he screamed. "I hate you, I fucking hate you. You can go to fucking hell. I hope you burn in fucking hell forever and then, I hope you fucking die."

I was too shaken to respond. Explaining the logistics of leaving the cabin wouldn't work. Shouting that I didn't deserve that wouldn't work. Asking what was wrong wouldn't work. I was absolutely certain this wasn't the right time to explain how hell even works—first people die, *then* they go to hell.

I'd had enough. I was weary. How much mindfulness did it take to achieve peace and equanimity, the ability to say, compassionately, "I see that you're hurting and you're angry. How can we talk about that?" I was a progressive, but I wasn't that progressive. I'd logged plenty of rounds with the liberal game of Stockholm syndrome, where you identify with your abuser's pain and empathize to the point of relinquishing justice and basic soundness of mind. We were seventeen years into this war, and I knew the battlefield. The thing I had always been trying to save was their childhood.

These outbursts had been Paul's millstone. My otherwise blithe son—the one who, moments after birth, had lain in the bassinet like he was lying on a beach while one foot away his twin sister wailed at the injustice of the bright lights and cold metal probes—sometimes exploded in anger, though these outbursts had diminished as he moved through puberty. When he lost it like this, I didn't know him as my son. I only saw his irrational father, screaming at me, face contorted as he pushed me against the wall, verbally slaughtering me while our toddler son clung to my legs trying to defend me. Those tiny arms encircling my ankles, clinging to the fortress of me, that tiny body shielding me from the hate pressing its forehead to mine—saving my babies was the reason I had left the marriage.

I had barely been able to tell my mother through my sobs that tiny Paul had thrown his body between us. "He was trying to be safe and be brave at the same time. Trying to make it stop," I said. My mother had said, "You have to get those two babies out of the war zone." For the first time in my adult life, she sent me money.

In the morning light of the Palomar cabin, my son wasn't my son anymore. I stopped seeing him. I could only see the root of his confusion. I wanted to get him back to that place before the confusion. And I couldn't. I'd always felt confused about it too.

I felt my jaw quiver. I bored my gaze into his. Who was this young man standing before me? Had I had anything to do with creating him? Right now, I hoped not.

Paul must have caught the tears in my eyes. He stomped out onto the deck.

I held my tongue. I have not always held my tongue. I had logged in plenty of hours screaming back, the usual maternal fare: You need to respect your mother. I don't deserve this. Haven't I given everything to you?

The twins stood out on the deck, whispering. I turned to the sink and blasted warm water over the plates. I lifted a dish towel and began to dry the skillet.

I had failed. Other people have happy vacations. Other people have devoted children. Other people raise fine adults who are ready to contribute to the world. I am sure the world does not want this contribution—more hate, more anger, more selfishness, no emotional regulation, no personal ownership of anger, someone who hates his mother.

I had given everything. This was why I was spent. My son needed more, something I wanted to give him but didn't know if he would accept. "Mom, are you OK?" Grace said when she entered the kitchen. Her voice was tender but petulant. She didn't want to have to be the mediator. She was weary of it too. She caught my gaze. She touched my shoulder. I shook off tears.

"Here, let's just listen to some music while we wait," she said. Grace walked to the living room and turned on Pandora on the Apple TV. A song came on with soaring synths, a flock of birds lifting out over the desert floor, embarking. A bass reverb echoed through the song, holding back the flight. The reverb called me— to my pain, to the scars of their childhoods, to how much it hurts to be a mother, how much it hurts to love someone who is leaving, and leaving this way.

"You see the cage, it called," the song went. "I said, come on in."

"'Song for Zula,'" Grace said when I came out to the living room and stood staring at the screen, "by Phosphorescent. One of my covers."

That song, I thought. Her voice had been in my ears across every mile of the desert and up into this forest. I hadn't known what to name the melody, had never thought to ask who did it before my daughter sang it, only knew it through her voice. "Of course," I said with a lump in my throat. "I like your version better."

AS I ROLLED OUR LUGGAGE to the car, Grace rushed up beside me on the deck to whisper in my ear. "Mom, you raised an asshole." This did not help.

We managed to agree to take one more loop up to Palomar observatory before we headed down the mountain. The possibility of seeing the ocean still dangled before us. There seemed to be enough time left in the day.

"I'm sorry, Mom," Paul said from the back seat as we passed Mother's Kitchen and all the bikers.

Nearing the peak, it came to me. Like that song, I was the

reverb, the beat pulling them back. They were the flock of birds, about to achieve gliding altitude. This *was* the letting go. *This* was what it looked like.

"I want to tell you something," I said, and I remembered that day I prayed for them to come to me, for my two lost babies to come back and inhabit my womb. "You're both so intent on leaving, and you're focused on your future. It seems like you're struggling against me. But the absolute truth is that I have the same goal you do. I have been preparing all of your lives for you to leave me. If it feels like there is a benevolent force helping you go, I want you to know that that is me. That's been my job for the past seventeen years. I'm not fighting you. I've been helping you leave me all along."

A peace settled over the car. When we arrived at the white-domed observatory, both twins hugged me.

WE DIDN'T GO TO THE MELANIE CONCERT. Back in Phoenix, we went with Maureen and Dennis to an all-ages jazz club on Roosevelt Street and we called it an early night. The next day we pressed on to New Mexico as Grace practiced for her music video. She called ahead to her music teacher to make sure she could meet to film the video. Her application would come in just under the wire.

"Some say love . . ." she sang, in the choked voice of a devastated lover. Love is not a fiery ring, as others say. It is a caged thing, a wild animal, disfigured, feral, capable of doing unthinkable destruction because it loves so much. Love has altered the singer into something he can no longer recognize. As we closed out the trip across the Painted Desert of Arizona, we arrived in Gallup. Each time Grace sang the song, she added a stray two lines of verse, leaving the two lovers in their story, racing out on the desert plains all night. The note hung woefully in the air. Her voice soared toward the climax. "My heart is wild / My bones are steam . . ."

"*Steel*," Paul said from the back seat. "Your bones are *steel*. You're singing it wrong."

"Steam," she said. "You don't know what you're talking about."

He produced his phone, extending his arm from the back seat. She'd been singing it this way for 283 miles, up out of Phoenix, through Payson, across the Mogollón Rim, and into New Mexico. She batted him away and searched on her phone for the lyric, found it in seconds.

"Steam," she said, thrusting her phone in his face.

I pulled into a grocery store in Gallup, so we could go to the restroom, maybe grab milk and eggs for home, breakfast for the morning as they returned to school, and I returned to work. We had 138 miles to go. The twins bickered about the lyric until we hit the automatic doors of the Shop N' Save. We entered, and we were the minorities, the only non-Native people in the store. We scattered, me to the eggs, Paul to the restroom, Grace to the milk. It seemed inevitable: This family will break apart.

five

Disfigure Me

THE DOOR SLAMMED. Crashed into the house. Made it rock and reverberate so that the whole adobe box—flagstone fireplace; knotty pine beams; one iron bed frame; two twin mattresses, one king; thousands of books that exposed my insatiable addiction for all things literary; green, Spanish glass dishes; Santa Fe-rustic spice rack; cherrywood piano; my grandmother's Art Deco waterfall vanity with the gigant-O round mirror; and five espresso-bean leather bar stools that perfectly match the house—all of it toppled down the hill. Oh, not really. From my office, I heard the twins rolling their suitcases across the sidewalk. That door latch again.

The only way to properly close our front door was to delicately turn the knob completely to the left, the opposite of what was natural, then press your thumb to the tab and pull the door gently closed. The twins, particularly Paul, never did this. His strategy was to yank it hard into the frame. If the door didn't latch, he would walk away, leaving the house unlocked. If you don't like it, fix the door, he'd tell me. I'd remind him the door worked just fine if you closed it right.

The twins had packed the minivan. Each a suitcase, Grace her ukulele, Paul his guitar. This departure, in one form or another, had happened every other Thursday for fifteen years since their father and I divorced. That it had been fifteen years would suggest it was a routine to which we were all accustomed. But it's a routine we all hate. We hate it for different reasons. The twins hate it because they have had to live in two places for most of their lives. I hate it because they leave.

Should we have the door-latch argument again? I decided no.

I walked out to the white minivan that used to be my "mom" car, back when I believed white minivans were the price of admission to the soccer world, and now was my children's shared car. The minivan was a sight to behold. Along the length of the passenger side was a jagged scratch. The driver-side window was patched with silver duct tape where the glass pane wouldn't close all the way because the motor was tired, buckling under the weight of the window, whirring pointlessly. Randomly, when you take a right turn, the driver-side door flies open, so you have to be sure to slam it shut and lock it. Ironic, all the slamming that was required for twins to leave the house and get on the road. This wasn't lost on me.

Inside, however, the minivan smelled like dust and vanilla, musty in a good way because it's old and it's seen a lot, including a mouse who lived in it all through second grade. Vanilla because we have juiced it with car-scent products. It's been the perfect vehicle to junk up through the twins' early driving adventures. It's the kind that can get "keyed" in the school parking lot—I'm pretty sure that's the real story about that scratch—and it won't matter. The twins bristled at the practicality, but they understood it, and for this I was grateful. Honestly, this minivan had been a fondly thought-of relative always good for laughs, the one so Lucille-Ball-screwball that you want to sit next to her at Thanksgiving because she'll keep you from falling asleep from the tryptophan or the sheer banality of your family. You simply cannot be pretentious when you drive a car like this.

It was dusk, a few weeks after daylight saving time began, so the extended light still felt fresh and new. Grace hopped to the passenger seat wearing a frown at her displeasure of this every-other-week ritual that had been forced upon her life. Paul took the wheel, the curtain of his face closed, gaze trained on the dashboard. I came around to his window. Even before the door slam, he had been back talking me, the usual teenage fare. Many times

I'd agonized about what to say to stamp that out, but at this point, four weeks and counting to college decision day, eight weeks and counting to graduation, I knew the most meaningful gift I could give them was my gaze. I knew this because my mother died.

What I missed the most was her gaze, giving me attention, even attention I didn't want, such as when she thought my high heels too sassy ("Is that the fashion now?") and when she really, really, no, I mean really, did not like that I added blond highlights to my auburn hair one year in my forties. When I let the high-lights fade and my pure auburn hair returned, she made a point each time she saw me for the next ten years to say, "Your hair is beautiful now." I missed her ears, listening from the other room as I plodded through a new piano piece. "That's lovely, honey," she would say when I was six fifteen thirty-one forty-three fifty. When I faltered through a piece with six sharps and a string of sixteenth and thirty-second notes, she would say, "Play as slow as you need to play it until you know it. Then you can bring it up to tempo." I missed her listening presence when I talked when she waited for me to say more even though I'd already talked aplenty. Of all the people, ever, on this planet, whose eyes and ears I wanted on me, she was the one.

Lately, when the twins were hyperreactive, quick to escalate to the usual arguments, what I had been doing was saying nothing. I gave them my gaze.

Standing barefoot in the driveway, I looked into their faces. Inside the dim shadows of the minivan, I saw a genuine smile spread across Grace's face. "This minivan's seen it all, don't you think?" I said as I reached to close the door for Paul. "Remember the day we were on our way to fifth-grade graduation when you climbed on top of it?"

Paul had performed a gymnastics maneuver worthy of an Olympic pommel-horse routine on the roof of the minivan, twirl-ing his legs as he clutched the luggage rack. Our house was the highest point on the hill, overlooking rolling, sandy slopes of sagebrush and chamisa across the high desert mesa. Hawks gathered in our cottonwoods because the view was great for spotting rabbits. Paul was literally on top of his world as he swished like a giant eel across the roof of the minivan, the pure ocean of sky slurping him up. With that flourish, the twins had set off to grab their elementary school diplomas and graduate to middle school.

I saw Paul's face grow tender. Once I'd read that attention is a form of prayer.

"Here's let's slam this shut, and don't forget to lock the door . . ." I said, so it doesn't swing open, be safe, my son, but I could see he had this.

Paul sailed the minivan back for a quick turnaround in the gravel, so he could point it forward onto Saratoga Drive. I waved until they reached the end of the driveway half an acre away and I waved as they headed north, dipping down and up the hill. Half a mile away, they passed the speed trap, crossed an arroyo, and turned east toward the mountains, onto the street where their elementary school is, past the place where they learned the building blocks of language.

So, we'd said goodbye, as we had twenty-six times a year for fifteen years. It never got easier. My life was filled with friends, a calling to write, and much travel. I had plenty of passionate pursuits, plenty of people who loved me. But my favorite people were those two people, who vanished behind the Iron Curtain of divorce every other week.

You could say I was more prepared than most to empty the nest. Another way of looking at this was that I had been practicing letting go for fifteen years. You could say instead that I disappeared behind the Soul Curtain every other week, and that would be true too. Over the years since I'd cowritten a book on mindfulness meditation, I had deepened my practice to the point that I was a skillful and committed meditator who could substantiate the benefits with science and lived experience. The sheer forces of stress in my life as a single parent working in a deadline-driven, high-wire profession demanded a discipline of self-care and a compassionate and resourceful support network. My life was impossible if I didn't protect the relics of awe and beauty in my life and practice rituals that animated my soul. When the twins were gone, I had blocks of time to write and for my meditation practice to grow into the Christian contemplative practice known as centering prayer. I also had time to just go places, when I wanted, like wine bars and hiking trails.

Sometimes I agreed with my married friends, who were most often the ones to advance the theory that I'd been on an early curriculum for empty nesting. They were the quickest to express envy about my every-other-weekend block of complete downtime. "You make divorce look good," they would say. Good, except that I'd only known half of their childhoods. Good, except for the perpetual state of grieving. I'd lived in an extended Holy Saturday. Every other weekend, I had had to relinquish my identity as a mother and reacquaint myself to a lost marriage. I still had to live in the same place and have the same friends. I still had to inhabit that zone in the darkest night where I held vigil for the twins but between us was a blank screen. Where are you, my two angels?

For so many years, I had been the one who gazed, the one who listened, the one who lived in reference to someone else. I was the object of the sentence, not the subject. Not the one who acts.

I was about to become no one. It was time to remember how to be someone.

TO BE CLEAR, I WAS ALREADY A SOMEONE. I had led an award-winning magazine for sixteen years, worked in senior management in the newspaper industry, and coauthored seven books published with Penguin Putnam. If you googled my name, I would be one who filled the first search screen, except for the occasional notorious other same-named me who might make the news for acts that—and I'm here to clear this up now—I did not commit. I'd also won literary prizes and given a TEDx talk that increasingly got views and drew gushing thank-yous for the inspiration. My LinkedIn profile did a nice impression of a someone, to be sure. Clearly, I existed.

But what I really was: Someone who was chafing. The handwriting had been on the wall about the newspaper business since 2008 when ad revenue plummeted from $49 billion to $24 billion in one stomach-thrilling death drop. The internet had already been threatening print newspapers with extinction, and digital news yielded only pennies to the dollar in revenue compared to the bread-and-butter of print. We were making it, just not at profit margins of 30 percent like the good old days. Online revenue was growing, but expanding from zero was still small. We had a fighting chance to move to digital first while we were still healthy.

The Wall Street shenanigans of 2008 landed the killing blow. From that point on, the *Albuquerque Journal* could never recover, still has not, and might not ever. After the Great Recession, the publisher took away all end-of-year bonuses, pensions, and 401(k) matching, then froze all salaries. The immediate impact was a pay cut of 20 percent. For the next eight years, no one in the newsroom got a cost-of-living raise, with a net effect of a 25 percent pay cut by the time the twins were graduating from high school. Even state employees, adjunct professors, and public school teachers got cost-of-living raises. As the twins were college tracking, my real income was plummeting. I was bleeding, and bleeding fast.

Young journalists scrambled to get themselves to the safer shores of law school or grad school in a STEM. They fled in droves so that those of us forty-five and older in the newsroom consoled ourselves that we were "accumulating value" as the wisdom in a nearly empty room. This comforting idea did not take the form of raises, promotions, or bonuses—more like a pat on the back. We were training greener and greener people. It was harder and harder to get people in the door, and as a result, hiring standards hit a new low. Halfway-through-journalism school or absolutely-no-newspaper-experience, but a creative writing degree or history degree were good enough. Those of us who remained became the guardians of journalistic standards that those entering the newsroom had never been schooled in.

Agile, middle-aged journalists who had built up clout after years of expertise covering water issues, education, or state politics got academic or policy-making jobs, instantly doubling their salaries. The socially gifted got jobs as communication directors for UNM Hospital, City of Albuquerque Economic Development, Sandia National Laboratories, museums in Santa Fe, or the governor. Right there that should tell you that New Mexico had a dearth of private-sector jobs. Every one of those was a city, state, or federal taxpayer-funded entity.

The not-so-agile late middle-agers who were close enough to retirement decided to hang on for dear life. No buyouts were in sight, not like at big media companies like *The New York Times* or *The Washington Post*. Not like at Intel, where my friend Roma took the over-55 buyout. In this newsroom, "buyout" was a tacit agreement that they would not lay you off if you kept showing up to work, even if what arrived to the desk was a shell of a person. If you were a body in a chair, you could stay while the room emptied out around you. In this respect, coming to work each day felt like a visit to the nursing home, where too many of my colleagues were just waiting to die.

In 2011, the *Journal* slaughtered all the magazines, dropping mine to quarterly but dangling the carrot to readers of premium printing, a carrot that was lost on most readers because a product that only shows up every three months is not much of a product. It was not unlike showing up for a date unshowered, then ghosting the person for three months. No matter what I advocated for— *no matter what the leading edge technology editors I considered my allies in the newsroom lobbied for*—this company just kept doubling down on print. And management kept doubling down on male-dominated news—crime, business, sports—and told me that women didn't need a magazine or a social network community around it because all the issues of feminism had been settled. Women did not need a place to talk to other women.

"Don't you think that's all over?" our managing editor said. I looked in her face. A woman my age was telling me that women had achieved perfect equality. A white woman. The words "tone deaf" scrolled through my mind. I would not be allowed to argue this. I would only be allowed to nod.

Of course, *she* thinks it's over, battle won. She got the one slot. That past fall, on the eve of the 2016 election, I had been in New York City at BinderCon, the conference for women writers, and Anna Quindlen had keynoted. When she was promoted to assistant city editor at the *New York Times*, she had been warned she should not get pregnant. That would be inconvenient, they told her, if we promote a woman and then she takes a three-month leave. Quindlen had been the beneficiary of an effort to equalize the newsroom after the *Newsweek* lawsuit had exposed discriminatory hiring-and-salary practices toward women. *The New York Times* had been facing a similar lawsuit but headed it off by correcting its policies. Quindlen's promotion had been one of the remedies. At the time, she sharply put into perspective the flaw in their small-minded logic that three months away from a job to take care of a baby was fatal to making everything look right like they were really taking care of women now. She struck at the flaw in their strategy. "As long as you have a one-fer policy, you'll always be bumping into this issue," she had told them at the time and repeated to the audience at Cooper Union to a round of laughter that had a sharp, high-strung note and faded too quickly. The room produced a palpable twinge that perhaps Quindlen had not spoken about the past but had too cleverly spoken to our shared present reality, a room that was nervous about whether we really were on the cusp of electing a woman president. Quindlen's point: Promote more than one woman. Just be nice and try it. If you do, you'll head off the problem. One woman's three-month leave won't even hurt you if you have a cadre of brilliant women. Promise.

Sitting across from the managing editor, I was bearing witness to the colossal failure of a one-fer policy. The One who had been promoted had dropped her babies and moved up the ladder. All the other women had had to maneuver their way through pretending like they didn't have families. All the other women had had to make it by working twice as hard. Just to stay in the same place.

This "there is no such thing as sexism" talk was the opposite of what readers had been consistently telling me since 1999. The issues that drew people to my magazine weren't just gender pay equity, sexual harassment in the workplace, or intimate partner violence. The core issue was the day-to-day not even listening to you when you talked, dismissing your small, not-booming voice. Being trained to be the shuttle diplomats of the corporate family but not being compensated for negotiating agreements on the level of peace in the Gaza Strip. The double shift of working at the office and maintaining the Grand Central train schedule of home life. The accumulated cost of "going along to get along." The price of the disease to please. The pressure to stay silent and not see what we see and be told we didn't see it. The storm clouds of #metoo were brewing, but my female boss could not see them. No more could we dim the gaslights and pretend they were still as bright—and not have a place to talk about it. The No. 1 thing readers loved about the magazine was that it gave them a place—a refuge and a forum—where they could tend, befriend, sound it out, strengthen their networks, celebrate their wins. And call things by their real names. Calling things by their real names was better than a massage at a day spa, the ultimate in self-care.

Sage magazine won best national magazine in the National Federation of Press Women for its twenty-fifth anniversary edition in fall 2014. The *Journal* killed it in February 2015. By September

2015, I had left to start my book-coaching business and teach journalism at the University of New Mexico as an adjunct, subject to the whims of low class enrollments and dwindling revenue as the state's oil and gas industry dipped with the recession. The journalism department had been mandated to hire four professors of practice—a job that could have my name on it—but due to budget cuts, only one of those positions had materialized and been filled, even though accreditation was imperiled if they did not. These effects on every avenue I pursued to better myself were permanent. Anyone else would have left New Mexico, but I was co-parenting with someone in New Mexico.

So I waited. I chafed and tried not to chafe. I was single parenting on a salary that had been frozen since 2008. I strained at a yoke I had not chosen. Every day. But I loved my children. So I calmed myself, and I waited for a miracle.

For ten years, I looked for a better job. I had always landed on my feet, but I already had had one of the top jobs for women in media in New Mexico, even in a good economy. I had hit the glass ceiling a long time ago. I lived in a media desert, and lest I had doubted that, in the spring of 2017, I was right in the middle of a project for the Democracy Fund, doing interviews that proved to me exactly what my search for a better job the past ten years had already told me. In interview after interview, journalism leaders and entrepreneurs in the state reiterated, story after story after story, that there was no place for me to go… in New Mexico. Anyone who was talented in media in New Mexico had already drained off to somewhere else. Except for all the co-parents. I liked to think we were a secret galactic force. The Jedi journalists.

MY FRIEND AND COLLEAGUE LIAM INSISTED I should interview with the Saratoga magazine for the editor-in-chief position. He said the consultant who was acting as interim publisher would be calling me to book an interview. On the phone, Liam and I tried to figure out flights that would coincide with his visit there, where he would present the first round of design prototypes. All of this made sense, in his mind.

To humor him, we looked at the map.

"Would I fly into New York?" I said. It looked like it was three hours away.

"Could be Albany. Montpelier or Boston," he said. "If you flew into Boston or Providence, we could travel over there together."

He continued describing this scenario, but I was not listening. Three hours north of New York, three hours south of Montreal. Five hours from Boston. Montpelier and Albany were small airports. This place seems even harder to get to than Albuquerque.

"It seems like it's far away," I said. "From everything."

"Albany, Albuquerque, they're both hard to get to," he said, as he liked to remind me. It's our running joke, I suppose: Albuquerque is nowhere, New Mexico has an upper-limit problem, and I hit that upper limit long ago, probably 1998, the year before the twins were born. Sometimes his opinion irritated me. Sometimes I admitted I agreed with him.

Liam travels across the country for his media consulting business, which sells software for digital production, leads newsroom training, develops print and digital design, and consults on strategic business vision. His company will redesign the Saratoga print and web products and has been integral to the business strategy for the new owner of the magazine. The whole time I've known him, he has racked up a trove of airport horror stories: heart-pounding dashes to the jetway, lost luggage, sleepless nights on a cot in Terminal K in O'Hare. Almost every place he goes to requires two hops on a plane, plus an hour to three hours of driving. Rock Springs, Wyoming. Rochester, Minnesota. St. Augustine, Florida. LaSalle, Illinois. No place is convenient. This is his normal. This is his America.

But I am not thinking about this as a two-airport hop for a job interview. I am thinking about where I would live and where the twins would live. I am thinking about how I would get to where they are when they need me. I am thinking about that leap from the bed where I sleep to the crib where they lie, still breathing. I am thinking like a mother.

APRIL ARRIVED, GRACE CHOSE CU Denver, and Paul announced, "I'll just go to UNM," but the resignation in his voice hooked my heart. I remembered the day we walked into the UNM campus to fix his honors program admittance and I had gushed about the John Gaw Meem architecture in Pueblo Revival style. Paul looked around and scorched it all with, "I'll never go here, Mom."

We got the call that the senior photos were ready. The three of us gathered in the photographer's studio, viewing the signature photo, now mounted on a borderless frame, light shining on its glossy finish. Behind the twins shimmered a curtain of champagne-and-bronze brambles that disappeared into a lemon-white sky. I smiled to remember the twins standing in the golden leaves, remembering Grace scaling the fallen cottonwood in her maroon Keds. I had called that one "Get Behind Me Satan" like they were the White Stripes. Another photo captured them emerging from a winter-bronzed forest under a canopy of ancient cottonwoods. Grace was wearing my lace-up, cut-out toe, platform shoes, pouting a little. I called this one "liner notes" or "how we wrote these songs." In another frame, Grace sprawled on the green grass before a row of cottonwoods, yellow-gold leaves, and paper-white trunks with her ukulele. I called this one "Cottonwood Tour 2017." Still others showed her in a Navajo-patterned dress and denim jacket against a weathered barn. This one said "lonesome songwriter." Paul's solo photos showed him sitting on a cottonwood, his sienna-tinged goatee and pencil-thin soul patch assimilating him into the sunlit trees. His hair swooped up in a rolling, hair-gelled wave from his forehead. He looked like he could run an AI company. Tomorrow. We'd call this one "CEO, bitch."

The photographer asked that usual question. "Where are you going to college?" Her son was pre-med at UNM and her daughter, one of Grace's best friends, also will go to UNM.

Paul shrugged.

"You were so excited about UNM," she said, "that day we took the photos."

I hadn't remembered this, any excitement about UNM. But that winter day at the bosque with the snow geese arriving, this had been the choice and it had seemed a done deal. UNM, where he already had worked a summer in the quantum computing department at Sandia National Laboratories and where he would intern again this summer, would put him in good stead with his career path. The labs hired a lot of UNM grads and worked with the university on tech transfer. This seemed like a prime choice for him.

The Saratoga interview was two weeks away. All weekend I thought about calling them to say, "My son has decided to go to UNM, and I'm not in a position to relocate." That would make all of this so simple.

Something stopped me, and I was grateful, because the next day, Paul was crunching numbers on British Columbia, growing hopeful about Carnegie-Mellon, and holding out for Stanford. The dry-erase board on the refrigerator held only those three names.

I ARRIVED HOME to see my ex-husband's car parked in my space. Paul and his father stood in the shade on my porch, and his father paced angrily back and forth. He turned to Paul, throwing his palms open in a gesture of "I give up," known to me as the martyr position or the end to any argument I had ever hoped would be logical. He turned on his heel and stalked out of the shadows.

His face sagged, and his eyes were glossed with a beleaguered disgust. I wanted to say, "What are you doing on my porch?" which really meant, "Why are you on my porch stirring things up?" He was about to pass me as though he didn't see me and he hadn't been on my property. Nearly past me, he turned back, touching his tongue to the crack of his lip. He wagged his head, eyes darting to me. "*You* talk to him."

My mind worked to process the logic of Paul's father stirring things up at my house, leaving destruction in his wake, and asking me to fix it. Instead, I asked, "What's this about?"

"I guess he just wants to go out of state," he said. "I guess that is just what will happen."

THAT EVENING, THE TWINS AND I gathered to eat pizza on the front porch. A fiery-orange sun was setting on the horizon.

"Dad wants me to go to UNM," Paul announced. "He pressured me to go. It will be free. That makes sense to me. But I want to go out of state. I told him that."

Grace and I took bites of our pizza as we absorbed this. It occurred to me I need do nothing here. Paul knew what he wanted, and he had told his dad. I could stop protecting him.

"So I mentioned ASU," Paul continued. "That would give me the out-of-state college experience, and it's got the academics."

ASU was ranked No. 1 in the country for innovation, ahead of Stanford and MIT. Its Barrett Honors program was considered one of the best honors programs in the country. ASU also had a pipeline to the labs, Intel, Silicon Valley, and more.

"I'd forgotten about ASU," I said. "But you may be right about that. It's a little taste of what you were hoping for with a Stanford or an MIT without the price tag. They offered you a decent amount of money. And it would give you the out-of-state experience."

The truth is, I'd crossed it off the list entirely. I hadn't thought it was so unbelievably better than UNM that it was worth the extra cost. But Maureen taught there. Roma, as worldwide workforce director for Intel, had worked with the president of ASU to cultivate a network of talent when Intel opened its plant in Vietnam, and she had been advocating ASU as a good fit for Paul. ASU had been out there in the background of our search all along. It could be the middle ground we had been seeking.

Paul articulated his case for ASU, and Grace validated it. I listened to his reasons, thinking about how he'd stood up to his father and told him what he wanted. I thought about the strange way in which his father had produced a viable solution by pressuring Paul to do something he didn't want to do. Mostly I thought, I want to keep this young man. He's good.

THEY LEFT AGAIN. The scene unfolded with its usual undercurrent of turmoil, but this time and every other time as we headed into decision day, I sensed an emerging glide of grace. Waiting for Grace to be ready, Paul had been playing "Canon in D" on his acoustic guitar. The chords walked from D major to A to B minor in a processional. Grace appeared with her smoky, dramatic green eyes, announcing it was time. He wordlessly snapped his guitar into the case and they went. The house was still again. I called my sister April.

"I know, right?" she said, because her divorce was about to become final, and she knew the split life. She had left her husband of twenty years in January and now she was trading weekends with him. She and her two children, my niece, Rosaria, and my nephew, Tomas, stood at the threshold of this.

"What is it, then? Why do we pine for them?" I asked. "Are we just wired that way?"

"It's an evolutionary necessity," April said. "The species needed us. To care this much."

"It still feels like I'm cutting a vital organ out of my body when they leave."

"You're going to pull this off gloriously," she said. Our pact is that we are saving so much on therapy bills by having these conversations. "It will be a fantastic party. Quiche, strawberries and melon, French pastries, mimosas . . ."

"Promise me you've got this," I whispered. We were referring to high school graduation, the brunch I am hosting for the twins and all their friends, my sisters and all of their children—a total of eight cousins, all of my mother's grandchildren assembled. I needed a party planner, a co-hostess, and April volunteered to take the lead.

"And no one will have to know you're really back in the master bath curled up in the fetal position in the spa tub, sobbing to the point of slobbering," she continued.

"I feel calm," I insisted. I would always insist on my self-sufficiency, the myth that I could keep all the plates spinning. If they all spun fast enough all the time, no plates would fall. My life depended on this gyroscopic effect. Otherwise, it would shatter.

"You *need* that. The drama is part of it," April said. "If you *don't* collapse in a sobbing mess, we'll be worried about you. That's why we're coming. So you can."

April was living on a horse farm in the rolling hills outside Lexington, Kentucky, an Airbnb that will tide her over until the divorce settlement. We'd each gotten married within a year after our father died, thinking we needed a refuge. We can see we rushed it, and we can also see that marriage would have been much easier if another person with all his messiness hadn't been involved.

"It's so much easier to love a child," I said. "They have the hope of growing up."

But I love this—I have loved it all. The entwinement of my heart with theirs; the entrenchment of us being us (because we live in the Be Who You Are house); the crabbiness of immature people seeking autonomy at any cost; the sheer messiness; the crazy enabling that I know I'm not supposed to be doing; the enraptured feeling when I see them; the maddening sense that they sometimes are doing it all wrong; the sinking feeling that no, *I* am the one doing it all wrong; the exhilarating, frustrating, exposing, too-beautiful-for-words love that resides here in my chest every day, bursting.

STANDING IN THE WARM SUN in Civic Plaza at a food truck, I heard a man behind me on the phone registering a complaint about his hotel room. In the sun, the olive and gray fibers of the herringbone pattern in his jacket shimmered a little. To the person on the other end of the line, he was forceful but gracious. I was close enough to him that I caught his smoky leather scent. As he pocketed his phone, he caught my eye.

"What brought you here?" he asked me. We are attending the Trinity Conference, a three-day event featuring Franciscan Catholic priest Father Richard Rohr, whose book *Divine Dance* just released. Rohr leads the Center for Action and Contemplation, and joining him at this conference are Episcopal priest and centering prayer teacher Cynthia Bourgeault and Protestant speaker William Paul Young, author of *The Shack*, a book I perceive to be evangelical fairy dust but turns out not to be. What drew me to the Center for Action and Contemplation was the path of insight meditation, the shock of the near-death of my own children, and the eternal death keen of an unsolvable marriage. Do I tell this handsome man this story? Not yet. I decide I will tell him I'm a skilled meditator and an activist feminist. I decide to start with the name of a man who gave me a new way to think about God.

"Mainly Richard Rohr," I say. "He gave me new pathways through all the problematic ways we try to understand God."

"My life changed after the crash," this man told me, nodding to signal he also had found a life-changing path to redefining God beyond the superficial ways our culture and thin, immature religion put on us. "I was a hedge-fund manager. I realized I was empty." And he told me about his Midtown Manhattan church, where he led diversity and inclusion circles and he did social justice work to end human trafficking.

"The Women's March was here," I said, recognizing I had met a compatriot who believed that contemplation must be paired with making a difference. "Right here in this plaza. I was on the team that organized it. That day, this plaza was filled with nearly ten thousand people."

"I marched. That day was phenomenal," he said. And indeed it was, the largest single-day protest in both the world and the United States. Albuquerque was one of 638 cities in the country that filled with marchers, and I had played a part in filling those streets that flowed into this plaza where I stood now looking up at a man who had seen it from his side of the country. That day Civic Plaza teemed with signs such as "Glass ceilings were meant to be broken," "A feminist is anyone who recognizes the full humanity of women and men," "The future is female," and "We are stronger than fear." Women wearing pussy hats stood resolutely behind huge red posters that proclaimed, "I will not go quietly back to the 1950s." A white-haired lady with a walker proclaimed, "I can't believe I still have to march for this sh*t."

"What are you hoping for?" he asked. This question was so open-ended that it could mean, narrowly, what are you hoping for from this conference, or it could mean what are you hoping for as an educated Western woman who wants to make a difference before she dies, or it could mean what are you hoping for because the two of us have just met and we are two people who have signed up for spiritual enlightenment.

"I'm hoping for a voice," I said. "I'm hoping to contribute."

"I've thought about applying for the Living School," he said, referring to the two-year program that offers the opportunity to participate in contemplative grounding and purpose. Led by Rohr, the intensive study takes participants deep into contemplative solidarity so that they may embody the change they want to see in the world.

The objective of the Trinity Conference was to deepen our contemplative practice, which included meditation, chanting, and yoga. The thrust of it was to shift our understanding of who God even is—a question I've wrestled with since the day the twins nearly died, since 9/11, since divorce, since the 2016 election, since the Iraq war/Muslim ban/mass shootings/black lives don't matter/pussy-grabbing/Russian election interference...the whole 21st century. The accumulation of grief around me—especially for women, because women were silent, women were pleasers, women were conciliatory, women were caregivers, women were relational, women tuned in to the hurt and the violence and the disappearance of care from our world and for our earth, women were crying—it had mounted to a surging lament.

Father Richard says that lamentations are missing from American life, and this is hurting us. He urges us to understand that Christ was not demonstrating on the cross that he was an all-mighty God—he was demonstrating he was an all-suffering God. Christ suffers in solidarity with us. Theologian Dr. Emilie Townes talks about the "communal lament" as necessary and positions lament as a form of protest—not wallowing but activism—a way to address injustice and arrive at healing. Seen that way, lamentations are expressions of hope because they are vows that the way things are cannot remain. It *must* change. Lamentation is grief work, but it's also change work. It's the most honest form of prayer. The voice in between. Perhaps 2017 would be the year we lamented, and it changed.

As the conference unfolded, this man and I pulled more people into our conversation. The Trinitarian shift was this: We're not of independent substance, separate from each other and God; we exist only in relationship. The definition of a holy person is someone who can stay in a relationship at all costs. Whatever it is that is going on with God in a world marked by an infant understanding of Him, is that God is a flow, a radical relatedness, a perfect communion between Three, a circle dance of love. God is not just the dancer; God is the dance itself. God is not the Eternal Threatener, He is the Ultimate Participant. He is not the Omnipotent Monarch; He is Life Itself, the life force of everything. He is the Life Energy between each and every object. We would call this Love.

At the end of the day, he and I joined the same banquet table as two Trump supporters from Louisiana, whereupon we engaged in a civil conversation about how they formed their beliefs. I found myself a participant in a spontaneous, animated conversation that spread through faith (what we share) and fear (one son struggled with drug addiction, and this drove their view toward conservativism). Because I was the commuter conference participant, I left early, vibrating with admiration for my partner in conversation and infused with love for this newfound way of seeing.

COMES A TIME in life when you must see yourself. Comes a time to take inventory. The losses were piling around me. Not just mine: my mother, my father, my marriage, my youthfulness, my ingenuity, my emotional agility, my ability to sustain a faith. My country. But also: the losses my friends seemed to be rapidly accumulating: their parents, their dogs, their horses, their empty-nesting children. In some cases, the declining health of their husbands. Roma had given voice to what it was like to live in the center of much dying. This was forcing us to take stock.

I had created a life. If I didn't make the effort to see it, no one else could. Or would bother. If this "secondness" was what emanated from me, then people would keep thinking they had permission to overlook and underestimate me. In a moment of respite from teenage talk back, Grace had said, "The way you see yourself affects how we all see you." Was this what she was pushing against? She had not been telling me to go away out of willfulness or a striking desire for independence. She had not been renouncing our bond as mother and daughter but rather, demanding I renounce my invisibility. It was a weight that kept her from achieving the velocity she needed to fly. I had wanted to be ballast, not a burden. If I wanted my twins to not "Try Dying" but "Die Trying"—or better yet, "Try Living," living wholeheartedly, fully authentic, wondrously vital—I would have to do that for myself.

SO THIS IS WHO I AM, a woman bearing scars. A pale pink line forms a perfect straight rung across my lower abdomen. It stretches like a high wire from thigh to thigh, thin but taut, sure and unwavering. I am neatly cut in two, exactly at my midpoint, thirty inches from the ground, thirty inches from the crown of my head. For seventeen years, I have been walking around as a bisected creature, my life halved into "before motherhood" and "the forever," the afterlife of having given birth.

I am transfigured by this love. A transfiguration is defined as a complete change of form into a beautiful or more spiritual state. Picture rapturous blinding light. The twins' life-light emerged from inside of me, and it changed me at every layer. I will never be the same. And, I don't want to be.

I am a woman who has allowed the calcium to be leached from her bones because the two babies in her womb needed it more than she did, and now my bones are porous and need a magical injection called Prolia twice a year to fix the problem. I am a woman whose metabolism completely ground to a halt because every nutrient went to making milk to feed two babies. My personal best in the Breast Milk Pumping Olympics was thirty-six ounces in twenty minutes. For some reason that will never be explained by medical science, my daily breast milk pumping ses-sions transformed me permanently from a B cup to a D cup, a feat that will never be explained to my A-cup sister, who also pumped. But at least there is that.

I am content to be this person with the track marks all over her body that say, "I was a mother." I have chosen to be this bro-ken, scarred person who loves two people anyway, no matter how they scorn me.

This love is immense. It slays me. I fall onto the love seat next to my writing desk and extend my arms to the heavens, defense-less. I open my heart center, not one ounce of my body shielded from suffering, from attack. This moment feels like heaven, a per-fection of peace and the full flow of love. It feels like heaven because I tingle with the joy of having allowed it, letting myself feel the ever-replenishing flow, the water in the mill. From here, I have a sight line to the Sandia Mountains out my living room win-dow, majestic, flush pink with the sun, and solid as cobalt.

I am pierced.

This is going to hurt like hell.

six

The Yawning Grave

THE ENTRANCE TO THE WRITER'S COLONY AT YADDO appeared before me, a black plaque bolted in stone, five simple letters in gold, the tail of the *Y* tipping in a jaunty wave. The advertising director and I have spent a wild misty morning circling Saratoga Springs, rolling past horse farms and lakes, and just like that, there it is: Yaddo.

Last night, the billionaire owner of the magazine told me he served on the Yaddo board. "It means the opposite of shadow," he had said. "The daughter of the Trasks. That was a word she made up. She died as a child."

This morning, instead of more interviews, the advertising director had been instructed to take me on a tour of Saratoga Springs to impress me. The tide at last has come in, nourishing my sand with its salty water. Apparently, the job was mine if I wanted it. Today was to be about making me want it.

This was how job interviews were supposed to go, how I remembered them from before. Before the newspaper industry fell into a death spiral, and job interviews became few and far between. In the current era, if job interviews happened, they were a gauntlet, group interviews characterized by a barrage of senseless, repetitive, and psychological tongue-twisters that analyzed every possible angle of any potential decision I might face in a job that no one on the interview team fully understood. The grilling would be followed by ardent persuasion that the salary might not be the salary advertised, but, nevertheless, my skills were valued, and would I accept a pay cut?

Before I turned fifty and became an unwanted person on the job market, I had been a hard-working optimist and an idealistic feminist. Despite the fact that many feminist writers like myself put forth the idea that men build their careers fast and women build them slowly, this brilliant thought-leading thought had not landed in the reality of the post-2008 labor market. Women accumulate value as they age. Yet I had been treated like a man over fifty. Unwanted. The "mommy track" myth that corporations support women's career development through their childbearing years, the promise of the golden age of women's empowerment, the aspirations of women's magazines like *Working Mother* or like my own, the one I helmed for sixteen years—it was all just a joke. A jerk off. A mirage. Something people wanted to believe in, the same way people wanted to believe in elite colleges and Bitcoin. What I had learned the hard way after the 2008 crash landed splat on my middle-aged career, was that no matter what anyone hyped, corporations were building their human resources strategy on an old model: Thirty years of you, then out you go.

Not women, I wanted to say. Not us. We're different. We build slowly. We take time out for children. We're a second wave of wisdom in the workplace. We're your secret weapon. Women have tons of energy after menopause. For the twenty-fifth anniversary of my magazine, we had profiled twenty-five women who had made a difference in New Mexico, and many of them had really kicked it from fifty to fifty-nine. None of this was noticed by anyone but me, it seemed. I was the Jedi on this, a tiny ardent contingent on a lonely planet, gathering strength and laser swords, hoping one day to fight for good. But here I was on a job interview that wasn't even an interview anymore. It had morphed into showcasing the place they hoped I could imagine as home: Saratoga Springs.

That morning, I had awakened in my hotel room and lifted the blinds to a dreamy early dawn, watching a small town come to life in all of its Americana sincerity. After all, this was the town of horses, health, and history, the site of the decisive battle of the Revolutionary War. I decided to walk the streets, so I could watch the city from the inside. My hotel was nestled against a small arts district with galleries and cafes. These streets reminded me of the Chevy Chase arts district in my hometown of Lexington, Kentucky, bungalows with hand-painted oval signs hanging from eaves and lampposts, artisan studios offering violin lessons, art classes, and yoga. A textile studio with expansive glass windows showcased looms resting silently in the low violet light of morning. At the end of the street sat a rambling white house with a wraparound porch; it had been refurbished into a collective of boutique shops and offices. When I was growing up in Lexington, my mother had taken me to a preschool in a district that looked like this. My mother had been a piano and violin teacher who had put her own music on hold. She would go to the sheet music store while I went to the Tiny Tot Personality School where, the teachers promised, I could acquire a personality.

Here was where I stopped, looking at the long, wood-planked porch curving above a tidy green lawn. Saratoga Springs was full of small spaces to discover, not like Albuquerque where the spaces were wide and vast, flaxen grass and turquoise sky. Albuquerque was expanse, breadth not depth, a city you could view from end to end from my back patio, which looked out at the Sandia Mountains, the balloon fiesta field, downtown, and beyond to the Air Force base and the East Mountains. But Saratoga Springs wasn't so "out there." Saratoga Springs ran placidly on the surface, but a certain aesthetic trickled into every crook and cranny like a secret elixir.

THE DAY BEFORE, the interview hadn't gone well, or so I had thought. Standing in the diamond plaster-finish walls of the exclusive dining room at Salt & Char, I was introduced to the billionaire owner of the magazine, who gave me a perfunctory nod. He turned to the consultants and instructed them to do whatever it took to buy the media property that was third in the market—essentially, to eliminate a competitor. "Buy it at any price," he said. "I don't care what you have to do." Five minutes later, the socialite who had started the online magazine walked in, and acquiring her was the focus, except for one brief moment when I mentioned once I had lived near New Orleans, and the owner said, "I hate New Orleans." Interview over, now my assignment was to make pleasant conversation as impressive dish after impressive dish arrived, compliments of Salt & Char, clearly very aware of the magazine owner's billionaire status. Raw oysters arrived on crushed ice, adorned with fresh pea shoots.

SO I HAD NOTHING TO LOSE as I approached the gates of Yaddo with the twenty-seven-year-old advertising director being groomed by the billionaire and the consultants seeking to hire me. She crossed her SUV over a causeway that stretched over a glassy green pond. She pushed up the hill to a clearing.

"Would you like to see the garden?" Nerilla said.

She asked me what it was, Yaddo. Would she know any of the writers who came here to work?

Carson McCullers, I said. Katherine Anne Porter. James Baldwin. John Cheever.

I kept trying. Langston Hughes. Flannery O'Connor? A slight nod. Maybe someone more recent. Terry McMillan. Jonathan Franzen. Finally, I landed on Colm Toibin.

"You know, like *Brooklyn*, the movie last year," I said. "The one with Saoirse Ronan."

Nerilla nodded. I realized I'd been holding my breath. I hadn't wanted her to feel bad.

Because it had rained the past two days, the trail leading upward was shingled with sodden leaves. Under a dove-gray sky, we arrived to a formal rose garden hedged off in quadrants. We climbed to a stretch of gravel walkway and stood at a sundial, looking out at four white marble statues below. Because it was still winter here, they were caged in plexiglass.

"Your resume is stellar," Nerilla began. "We've been looking for a long time for someone like you." She tucked her hands in the pockets of her black overcoat and looked out at the dormant garden. She went on to detail the positives: my editorial knowledge, the literary pedigree a plus, my branding and promotion experience, my consulting with news and magazine outlets across the country—everything I have been banking in the storehouse the past decade as I waited for the chance to be seen, to leave New Mexico for something better. For a long time, nose to the grindstone, I could forget why I was building the resume. I had let go of whether anyone would see the pattern, that it added to something. I'd been trying so hard to see the pattern myself. Nerilla turned to me. "I think if we looked the whole world over, we couldn't find a better fit."

I felt my heart beat again. "Thank you, I appreciate that," I said. "I knew I couldn't leave New Mexico for a while, so I focused on building my credentials behind the curtain. So that I would be ready when the day came."

A glorious sensation pulsed through me. I may have been right, all these years, to put my faith in the idea that investing in adding professional value would someday be recognized. But I'd also been investing in my children's future. That was not the complete picture. A spotlight for me alone was not enough.

"I've been building this up because I want to make a better life for my children," I said. "If I change my life, I'm looking for a financial game changer."

So there it was. I'd planted it.

"You have another offer on the table, I understand," she said.

"Yes, and it's a good one." This was Rochester, Minnesota, and a good amount of money.

Nerilla changed the subject to Kenneth, the consultant who had recruited me and who would function as publisher of the magazine. The deal he had pulled off the day before had been brilliant. What was most impressive was not the details of his market research or distribution plan; it was the way he presented the case so that the billionaire owner would make an immediate, informed decision and feel confident about it. "I have a lot to learn from him," she said, and I agreed that I did too. But I wouldn't come here, not unless it was a financial game changer, and then if . . . We swiveled our gaze to the four statues below.

"Who are they?" I asked her.

"Do you want to go down and see?" she said.

I was not going to come here and live. I had come here to be blessed by someone seeing my worth, and then I would go.

I struggled to take it in, this not-yet-spring scene in a rose garden, its lushness curtailed, brown serrated leaves of hybrids and floribundas and heirloom roses drooping in the rain, marble statues, rust-stained and barely breathing beneath the glass, their gleaming smooth skin dulled by gray sky that refused to let in any light. Standing before their cages, I watched them looking at me, afraid of what they might say.

"We should head to the airport now," I said.

Driving down Interstate 87 to Albany, I turned my thoughts to open blue skies and my daughter. Grace had gotten into music school. She had figured out her own plan, music and neuroscience, a fascination with how music affects the brain and how songs might heal us. A song popped up on Nerilla's Spotify: "Song for Zula."

I wasn't coming here. Taking this job. I was leaving this place. I would not be back someday. I said, "This is the song my daughter sang for her music school audition."

Nerilla wanted to listen too. She turned up the volume.

As we headed south, the wings of the flock of white birds fluttered high above. Love had pressed its face to mine, so close I couldn't see all I needed to see. A corridor of air rushed in beneath us.

Weeks after Palomar Mountain, I had watched the video for Grace's song. A feral woman in burlap rags, her skin charred with dirt, clasped a heavy stone. Chains bound her ankles as a winter wind blew brown leaves in a whistling chill. In extreme slow motion, she raised the stone above her head. With each crash of slate to black iron, she knife-cut the chain. The wild-eyed woman slammed her rock against the chain, again, again, again.

seven

Hero

"WHAT ARE YOU DOING?"

It was a text from Liam, but I knew what he meant and how he talked, so read that again and hear his tone like this: Disgust, disbelief, judgment. I've lost my mind.

For two days, Saratoga and I had been negotiating. I was asking a lot of questions. The offer had been nice but not so wonderful it was unmistakably a good decision for me. They had countered with more money and more vacation time.

"You've spooked them," he said on the phone when I called him, so I could hear the tone of his real voice. "Why are you asking all these questions?"

Because I wanted clarification on my career path? Because I wanted to know, if I was going to move across the country and start a new life, what the promotion opportunities were? Would I have a chance at an ownership share? And what about a 401(k)? I was under the impression that these were questions someone asked when considering a job offer.

It crossed my mind that I may have just violated some "woman in a meeting" credo in which I was not supposed to speak simply and directly because someone would think I was scary or angry. Of course, I was thinking of Alexandra Petri's 2015 essay in *The Washington Post* in which she recast famous quotes from history in the way a woman would have to say them in a meeting just to get heard. "We hold these truths to be self-evident, that all men are created equal" would have to become "I'm sorry, it really feels to me like we're all equal, you know? I just feel really strongly on this." I may have stumbled into the higher level of that game, a level I'll call "woman negotiating pay," definitely the level with bright green laser swords and wicked trapdoors. I'll call my version "woman negotiating pay so she doesn't start out 24 cents out of a dollar behind what someone would pay a man, then never catch up."

Do I explain this to Liam? He knows the encyclopedia of feminism that swirls in my mind. Sometimes, he's a feminist too.

Or, because he is my friend, I could explain it to him this way, a story about what was happening in my house the day before.

THE TWINS ARRIVED HOME, their last day of classes as seniors. They burst into the house, exhilarated. Thirteen years of school, dusted and done.

But this quickly settled down. Dinner was shoveled from their plates and a retreat was beaten to their rooms. The loneliness stabbed deep. I am not a person who is afraid to be alone. I love my solitude. I am a writer, and this goes with the territory. I am a person who feels lonely when I think I am in a family but it doesn't feel like I'm in a family. I decided to go out, just out, I don't know where. Being home only reminded me we are a home no more. I drove until I thought of something. Not Walmart, with its plenitude of useless things. Nearly everything in that store was about building a home. I chose Turtle Mountain with its microbrews and wood-fired pizza, where immediately a man came over to flirt. I took note that the first time I emerged out of deep single motherhood into a bar, I had been approached. Really, it can't be this easy.

Two hours later, I snuck back into the house like I was the teenager. Except no one had noticed my departure or my arrival. So, I was not in trouble, per se. I had failed, even, at being a teenager.

As I considered my options for the empty-nest life, I kept forgetting that the only sure thing was that this house would be empty of the twins. This one fact slipped from my mind every time. The only question was whether *I* would be in it. Yet my habit of thought was debating "Albuquerque with twins" versus "Saratoga with not-twins." I had to forcefully stop this thought train. No, it's "Albuquerque-twins away" or "Saratoga-twins away." This house felt so much like our anchor that it was one and the same with who we were as a family. It seemed impossible to imagine our next iteration. For the first time in my life as a mother highly skilled at negative fantasies; a journalist who believes all stories can be hunted down; and a writer who creates worlds, I was experiencing a failure of the imagination.

Truly, the only question was what *my* iteration would be. Would it be "Here when you need me," preserving their rooms? Or would it be "You know where to find me" as we all three closed this chapter and each chose an adventure?

"I am not the kind of mom who builds shrines to childhood," I told April on the phone.

That was ironic because I am a memory collector. That's the river that runs through my life as a journalist, first recorder of history, as well as a novelist and memoirist. I write to taste life twice, as Anais Nin once said. Just to prove this, let me show you my garage. No, I cannot show you that, let you see that about myself. You would not like me anymore. You would stop hanging out here in these pages. Let's just say my garage is a bit . . . full. Tote bins full of the twins' artwork, my mother's dining room set that we're saving for Grace, an original Mac SE from 1985, and boxes of newspaper clips. A lot of "saving of things" has happened. Mistakes were made. Notice how I'm leaving the subject out of these sentences? My feat of syntax is an attempt to disguise who is responsible for all this "saving of things."

When I tried to imagine the empty-nest life, I didn't see shrine-building in it. The very idea of enshrining their childhoods felt like I was giving them baggage. I'm not ready to be a museum curator.

"That's gloomy," said April, astonished that I could not lift myself out of this.

"It's the sheer constant force of their pushing me away," I said. "You're just not there yet." April's two children were fourteen and eleven. She was on the cusp.

This colossal failure of the imagination filled me with dismay. I hardly recognized myself. I could not imagine doing the same stuck life I'd been doing, only without them. They were the reason I got through this same stuck life for all these stuck years. The stuckness had a point. At some point, it would no longer have a point. We were reaching that point.

"You've been wanting a change," my lawyer friend Deborah told me on the phone when I sought her advice about the terms of the Saratoga deal. "But ask about the 401(k). And key man clause. Start-ups have them. It's a reasonable question."

Her questions were the ones I asked Friday morning, the ones that spooked Kenneth.

"SO, DID I BLOW IT?" I asked Liam.

He didn't answer that question. "This is a good job." His voice rumbled with emotion. Fear, a tinge of anger. He really was afraid I might lose the opportunity. "Jobs like this don't come along in media anymore."

Don't I know it.

"Just tell him you'll take the job," he said. "Today. Don't wait through the weekend."

Right now, I could not imagine having this undecided through the weekend. I would either take the job today or I would decline it today. Monday would not make any difference. Monday, May 1, the very last day for college selection. Paul still had not officially accepted ASU. He'd told me he'd do it before noon today. More time to think about my job or his college will not make it easier or clearer.

We may have decision fatigue.

I told myself not to overthink this. It's a net gain, and same old, same old is not an option. I composed the email and accepted the job. I shut my laptop.

I walked over to the olive-green suede sofa and lay there, looking up at the knotty pine beams. I stared at the patterns in the wood, two sad, sable-eyed cats, their tails dripping like sap. What have I just done?

It will be OK, I hear. You do not have to stay forever. It is just a four-year adventure. That is the voice in my head pretending to be the wiser me. I skipped past this imposter to God. I prayed. *If I have just messed up, please carry me.* I don't understand why this has happened. Enormous changes at the last minute, I think, like the Grace Paley story collection. "Everyone, real or imagined, deserves the open destiny of life," she wrote in that collection, which was populated with characters who didn't seem to have many choices left, pregnant social workers and her own dying father, who pleads with her to tell a simple story about simple people. We are not simple people.

I heard Paul enter the hallway, heading toward the living room, and my wet tears dried up like a desert rain cloud before any moisture could fall. I lizarded myself up off the couch.

"I took the job." I tried to look happier.

"Congratulations, Mom," he said.

"So you don't need to have any doubt," I said. "This puts us over the top. You can accept ASU with confidence." We were OK before, but this does give us breathing room. We now have a margin of error.

"What about British Columbia?" he said.

"Look, Paul," I said, composing my words carefully, "if that one is still the one, then choose it. We're good." We never visited Vancouver, but Paul had never been able to stop thinking about British Columbia. I trembled a little on the inside that he, too, could make enormous changes at the last minute. I kicked myself for not insisting that we visit UBC or cross it off the list.

He returned to his room down the hall.

I lay back down on the couch, uncannily detached from Paul's decision. I just wanted it to be done. I looked up at the sable cat eyes and hoped for them to assemble into a form on the oracle level, a Cheshire cat of sorts, cheery and advice-dispensing about careers and college and destiny. I soothed myself that the Saratoga magazine would pay for movers, and people would pack this house. I envisioned a smooth transition, clean corrugated cardboard boxes labeled with black Sharpies, living room, master bedroom, kitchen . . . I had moved before. I would move again. Still, I shuddered.

I decided I was not doing much good lying on the couch pondering the enormity of the decision I had just made. I returned to my laptop at the dining room table. Kenneth was pleased I had accepted the job. He promised an instantaneous wire transfer of the signing bonus. He wished me a good weekend and signed off by asking me to send him an email next week about my start date. Start date? Another decision to make?

Minutes later, Paul strolled into the kitchen. "Mom, I think I'll just go to UNM."

I must have sent the "mom might freak out signal," the one where I brace my temples with a thumb and ring finger, swipe my fingers across my eyelids, and pinch the bridge of my nose. The one where I try to hold my tongue. Instead what happened next resembled an electric transformer shorting out, sparks sizzling to parched earth. I did not hold my tongue. "Paul, I just accepted a job to move 2,200 miles across the country, and to be perfectly clear, I did that for you and Grace. I did that so you wouldn't have to feel like your only choice was UNM."

He stormed out of the room.

A better mom would have said, "Whatever you think is best, honey. I just want you to be happy," or "Hey, let's go for a walk along the bosque and just chill. I know this decision is hard." But

I was not that mom. It took every ounce of love in me not to say, "Just fucking go to ASU."

Within the hour, he signed up for ASU.

The next announcement came. "I couldn't get my major of choice. I had to go with ASU West."

"What?" At this point, I was supremely challenged at disguising my alarm. "ASU West? We didn't even visit that camp—"

The door slammed.

"—us," I said to an empty room.

I hope it tells you a lot to say that I was used to speaking in broken sentences. I had developed the habit of speaking the last syllable even if no one was still in the room, just for the record.

One minute later, I was on that couch on my back, looking up to that wood-beamed ceiling with a thousand woeful eyes.

THE FOLLOWING WEEK I hurtled due west under an endless radiant sky straight for Arizona, this time alone. I was driving to Phoenix to the International Women's Summit, a networking opportunity and another chance to see Maureen and Dennis. Earlier that week, I had shipped Grace off for her senior experience, a whitewater-rafting trip through Glen Canyon, which was a sort of eastern suburb of the Grand Canyon. Paul immersed himself in his senior experience, a project for Los Alamos National Laboratory comparing the computing strength of LANL's quantum computers with IBM's.

This was me, retracing our steps from spring break. Now it had been decided. Grace to Colorado, Paul to Arizona, me to New York. "It's a financial game changer," I told my sister Samantha on the phone. I'd doubled my income. For years, I'd sacrificed salary and career growth so the twins could live in the same state with both parents, just a hop away from each other. Whether their co-parented childhood had been pretty or not, I'd done the right thing. "It's beautiful," Samantha told me.

Every day I woke up resisting all of it. Every day the Resistance flooded in, threatened to overtake me, and every day I entered into meditation and prayer to remove the Resistance. Resistance had become my wingman, positioned behind and outside the leading aircraft that was me living my life, part of the formation. Resistance flew just off my right wing because Resistance wanted to protect me. Resistance was vigilant.

The day after I said yes to Saratoga, I burned the right side of my body, ribs to knees. A tray carrying my super-hot latte flew out of my hands. The pain took my breath away. I fell to the outdoor chair on the patio of Flying Star Café as fiery pain seethed through me. A woman rushed over, thinking I had suffered a heart attack. For a moment, I thought my heart *had* stopped. The cafe manager brought cold compresses for the burn, but my skin shined lobster pink, and I told her I thought I was having a shock response. "We will send you to urgent care," she said. "We will pay for it. You need to be seen."

No one can quibble with what I have done. There simply is no argument against it. I was prepared for a job like this, it just didn't exist in New Mexico. When I say, "I've left no stone unturned in New Mexico," no one disagreed. As hot air balloons rose on the horizon against the blue mountains, urgently pressing on my mind the uniqueness of Albuquerque, New Mexico, I told my therapist, who had supported me through the divorce and single motherhood. She was not worried. Roma, not worried. Deborah, not worried. Plus, I trusted Liam with my soul. When he told me, "This is the best job you could ever imagine," I believed him. But still . . . I didn't think he knew all of me. It was true, the words the woman manager at Flying Star Cafe had spoken. I needed to be seen.

WHEN I DESCENDED INTO PHOENIX at sunset, I was the sparking line severing the dry, red crackling heat. The sky was a sheet of fire. By the time I drove to the door of Maureen and Dennis' house, night had fallen, the desert's grace.

"There is just one thing," I said to them as we assembled on the patio. "At the last minute, Paul got switched to ASU West."

Maureen made a face like she had just eaten a fermented peach.

"I thought you'd react that way," I said.

"We'll visit the campus," she said. "You'll see."

To get to west Phoenix, we traveled block after block after block. Central Phoenix is one thing, mission-style houses and mid-century homes, blue neon jazz clubs, and brushed-steel coffeehouses serving up nitro lattes. But west Phoenix is a part of Phoenix I never visited during the whole three years I lived in Phoenix. There was no need. Kind of like Alamogordo. You could ignore it for a quarter of a century and not care for another quarter of a century.

Arriving at the driveway that funneled us into campus, I could see clearly that ASU West was a lonely outpost. Master design landscaping and refreshed architecture could not dress up the fact that it was strictly a commuter campus, a community college for those not quite ready for college. Not my son. My son had done everything he knew how to do to be ready for MIT. He had taken MIT's MOOC on artificial intelligence. In his free time.

"How do I say this right?" I turned to Maureen. I was thinking of Paul's near-perfect ACT score, his interviews with Princeton, MIT, and Stanford and the aspirations those stirred in him. I was thinking about how, in his spare time, he also took MOOCs from Stanford and Yale and, just for good measure, watched lectures on physics, computer science, and applied math from the University of South Wales and the University of British Columbia. Who does this? Someone who wants it.

My challenge from the get-go—for both of them—was to steer them into educational opportunities that would be stimulating enough for them, so they would stay alive, alert, and curious, so they wouldn't get bored with learning and think it wasn't worth it. For Paul in particular, if he wasn't in something that elevated him, he would have no reason to be, think, or live.

Maureen shook her head woefully. She didn't want to come right out and say it would be a mistake of disastrous proportions. That was my line to say.

"My son would be depressed here," I said. "Depressed. I have not been raising a boy who goes here." I heard the giant sucking sound of seventeen years slurping down a thirsty drain. "I know him. I know his mind. He has always needed more than anyone could give him. I've been on a seventeen-year sprint to stay one or two steps ahead of him."

"He's cerebral," was what people said about him. He didn't "read" as a nerd because he was not socially disabled. His emotional intelligence was high. He has a twin sister, after all. They have been "reading" each other from womb time.

ASU Polytechnic might not even be cerebral enough for Paul, but this was the best we could do for now, just switch back to where we were from the start.

AT THE INTERNATIONAL WOMEN'S SUMMIT, I was suddenly struck by the realization that for women, the 2016 election was not over. Especially women in red Arizona. They had come here to find solace with like-minded souls. This roomful of women ached. They did not feel heard. They felt silenced. I was not alone. The Women's March wasn't the end point. It was the beginning.

No way was this over.

If women in Republican states felt it even more deeply than I did, there were more of us than I thought.

When Marianne Williamson stepped onstage for the keynote, she was on fire. In every culture, women who have completed their childbearing years have been valued for their wisdom and served a vital role in society. They became the elders, the wise women, like the members of the Grand Council of the Iroquois Confederacy, which had given us the foundational ideas of America. Among all species that thrive, there was one common phenomenon—the fierce wisdom of an adult female when she sees a threat to her cubs. The lioness. The primary assignment of the divine feminine is to take care of the children, each other, and the planet. The first sacred container of life is the womb; the next sacred container is the wisdom of the feminine elders.

Yet though we are the most educated and most powerful group of women in the history of the world, we're not speaking. "Why are we, especially American women, so quiet on this?" she asked the room. We do not have a rite of passage for a woman to step into her natural wisdom voice. Not in this time of life when the invisibility threatens to sweep us away, rendering us voiceless. We need to provide a red carpet for that rite of passage. "We need the young to produce the babies," she said. "[Yet] our species will not survive unless someone is producing the wisdom. We have it within us like a mother has milk."

I broke out to make a fervent call to the University of British Columbia, to see if Paul could still get in, should he decide to change at the last minute. Yes, they said, send us an email real quick. That night, hope came in the form of a friend of Maureen and Dennis, who headed the ASU Alumni Association. She immediately understood what kind of student Paul was and the campus-major mix-up was just a crossing of wires. "ASU wants him, and I'll fix it," she assured me.

OH, THE HORROR! I turned from this crisis to the tasks ahead over an English muffin with raspberry jam that Maureen set before me. Maureen wisely saw I could not face them alone and helped me organize a to-do list. This is a list of plates, which I must set spinning at enough velocity that not a single one of them will fall and shatter. We brainstormed categories of spinning plates: graduation brunch, graduation trip, renting the house, clearing out stuff (she's thinking garage sale; I would rather die), moving.

The house, the dog, the cars. Which car goes to New York, and how does it get there? We had three people and two cars, one of them on its last breath.

I would have to make one or twelve major decisions each day because if I didn't, the next day I would have twelve or twenty-four major decisions.

By the time I left Phoenix, I had assurances that Paul was set. My heart brimmed with gratitude to these two people who are my friends and the twins' "godparents." They were lifesavers, generous and wise, and I felt lucky to know them. How do I explain this to the twins? This kind of gift doesn't just happen. It happens when you invest in people. As I headed due east on the 202, looking for the turn north to Beeline Highway, I decided I could cross off a task from the to-do list on the seven-hour drive back. I can buy Paul a car. I call him to say I'm willing to put in half on a used car, no loan. "Get on cars.com and make a list of good candidates," I said. "Text them to me. When I stop for lunch, I'll look at them." I point the car northeast, peeling off from the outer rim of Phoenix, and climb out of the cauldron of the city.

One hundred and forty-eight miles later at Overgaard, I stopped at Al & Diane's Red Onion Lounge for a green-chile cheeseburger and onion rings. My lunch was juicy and wild and I liked it. I had a text-lunch with Paul about the cars he'd chosen. Soon I was back on the road, hopping along the Petrified Forest. I had watched all their disappointments and all their mistakes, in swimming and soccer and dating and driving. For seventeen years, I had stored these two souls in me. I had chased them down with high hopes and sensible plans, juice boxes and sunscreen. Now, I was not sure they ever wanted the high hopes—or the juice boxes. The boundless blue sky of the Arizona desert took from me this thing so deeply rooted in me that it felt like it had always been me. That tossed-up thing soared through a sea of azure sky, riding a color saturated with love and creation. I could trust it to take my children. I could be generous.

They were ready. I could let go.

I could get the fuck out of their lives.

By the time I reached Gallup, Paul had his father on board to pay for half of the car, and Paul had three picked out. "Can you go look at cars with me tomorrow?" he texted.

eight

The Giving Tree

JUST MAKE A DECISION. Even if it's a bad one. My father's perennial advice. Just make a decision and keep moving. I gave Saratoga a start date well after graduation and our graduation road trip to Grand Canyon and Zion but before the summer track issue, the biggest of the year, about which they were already getting frantic. As a concession for the delayed start date, I agreed to participate in a conference call that included the outgoing editor; Nerilla; and the socialite Regan, who just sold her magazine to us and will be blended into our brand as a social scene columnist. Thanks to Liam, I knew this new development was not poised for smoothness. A firestorm was brewing on the other side of the country, but I had my own chaos and many decisions to make before I slept. The only thought I could give to this was, "Maybe these people are adults and can figure out how to get along."

I turned to my Albuquerque list of spinning plates. I hired a property management company to rent the house, and the man I will come to call The Pedantic One came to evaluate the property. "Picture it without the painting disasters or the clutter," I cajoled him, and he didn't crack a smile. I arranged for a carpet cleaner who would erase what the dog had done and a handyman who would erase what the twins had done (read: Paul)—doors that have been kicked in (early teen years), the smashed doorbell that was a karate demonstration (age ten). I would not concern myself about the pet door spray-painted orange (circa age eight, Nerf Gun Club years). I called an auction company that would accomplish faster what a garage sale would do. Grace returned from her

Glen Canyon trip and dove into her Senior Experience project on mindfulness meditation and nature immersion as therapy for anxiety and depression. Paul and I bought a blue Toyota Yaris from a man who met us in a parking lot to sign papers, and I was too busy to give a single thought to the sketchiness of this. I bent to hood of the car and signed away. I bought the twins gelato and asked Grace if she would drive across the country with me. This was asking a lot. Thus, the gelato. I called a tree trimmer, and three dudes showed up with chain saws on Mother's Day weekend.

This decision was my first mistake.

IT TURNED OUT THAT I had been living with a family. Quite an active and fertile family. A family had been living in our garage, which now I must mention to you. I am willing to come clean. For a while now, it had been impossible to walk from one end of the garage to the other. To access the other side of the garage, where the garden tools were, for instance, where the breaker box was, for instance, I must push the garage-door button on the wall, go back into the house and out the front door, and pierce the elephant hide of this garage from its opposite flank. In between were a largely unused ping-pong table, stacks of boxes, and two huge crates containing my mother's dining room furniture and china, which she willed to me upon her death.

Also living here was a family of mice. While we had had our noses to the grindstone (me: working and raising kids; the twins: earning college-track grades while hormonally flooded), our mice had been having a little jamboree. They seemed to like the south wall the best because I had invitingly stacked boxes, which made for a fun run through all of my collected and uncurated memories. Apparently, we had created a nice nest for them.

The one we will come to call Sad Auction Lady pulled up into the driveway, positioning her car around the painter's neat little cream-puff Mini Cooper and the industrial-green dumpster. Inside the house, Grace and Paul wrote their Senior Experience papers or watched *Pretty Little Liars* (Grace)/played video games (Paul). All went smoothly as Sad Auction Lady inventoried the house, but when she saw the garage, struck by horror, she called her boss.

All of this must be way more interesting than Senior Experience papers/binge TV-binge video gaming: It drew the twins out of their rooms. We clustered on the porch, watching Sad Auction Lady on the phone, standing in our driveway as she explained the dire situation to her boss. The main issue was that all of my mother's dining room furniture remained crated.

"We'll uncrate it for you," I hopped over to tell her. This needed to happen today. Tomorrow brought another barrage of decisions. I turned to the twins, who weren't scattering.

WE GATHERED THERE. My mother, seated in the cherrywood captain's chair, a cheese souffle, and lightly salted green beans on her plate, lifting a glass stein of skim milk to her lips, her lunch on schedule, no matter the swirl of seventeen different routines around her, my sisters, our husbands, all of our children. As our family grew, we ate in shifts, kids first, or we spilled out into the kitchen and the sunporch. But always, no matter the meal, no matter the number of us, she was our point of orientation. Every time I visited, I liked to sit nearest her, tucked in alongside the wall of portraits, ten grandchildren in 8 by 10s with gilded frames, where I could look at her and see over her shoulder into the front room where her Steinway music-room grand piano sat. The full view of her, family, faith, and music.

In the mornings, when it was just me and the twins in her house, my sisters and their children returned to their own homes, we shared breakfast of salted cantaloupe and oaty cereal. I would make coffee in her percolator, watching until the dark teak liquid popped through the glass bubble in the tin lid, then set the oven timer for seven minutes. I spooned white sugar from a copper cone into a coffee mug and waited. Then I'd join her and the twins at the table, sitting this time on the opposite side, my back to the kitchen at the end next to my dad's place, where the holly tree brushed its pin needles against the windowpane. The twins held their jiggly selves across from me, taking uncertain bites. The food was different at Bon-Bon's house, simple and bland, but for the twins, she also always bought a gigantic Walmart-sized box of Cheez-Its and often stocked the pantry with Dr Pepper.

At this table, after dinner was cleared and someone was assigned to watch all the grandchildren in the basement to make sure no one bled or died, is where the grown-ups would gather for euchre, a trick-taking card game that is simple enough to start up easily but subtle enough that a family could play it for generations, which is what we have done. This game brought out the ferocity in my mother, a genteel sort of ferocity but fierce mama lioness pouncing, nonetheless. Diamonds were her suit. She could win a hand on a left bower and a nine of diamonds. Sometimes on just one diamond, when dealt the right one. "Diamonds are a girl's best friend," she would coo, and this was her code for "take it up," or make diamonds trumps. You wanted to be her partner when she said this, and never her opponent. Her moxie was on display, a bit of luck and an ounce of guile. This is when she trash-talked.

If you have never seen a steel magnolia trash-talk, it's a fine sight to see. As a young woman, my mother was a Southern belle in the sense that she was pure, beautiful, and demure to a point of mystery. In those days of my childhood, trucks still delivered milk to the front porch, placing two cartons in a galvanized steel box. A Southern lady in a frilled hoop skirt and arm-length gloves appeared to curtsy on the front of it. A swirl of red above her head indicated a fascinator. A spooled curl dangled over her left shoulder. It hardly seemed like she was milking cows or drinking milk, more like she was drinking a coquettish bourbon in a prismed glass. Each time I lifted a milk carton out of the box, I thought of that delicate red lady with a skirt so billowing it could contain the upright, vaguely Hollywood-esque script of the Southern Belle dairy logo.

As a gray-haired widow, our mother was a lioness, fierce-hearted for her grandchildren, yet fragile-boned, collapsing right before our eyes, vanishing from the inside out.

To this table we came for Easter, for Christmas, for Mother's Day, for summer vacations when the twins and I made up for being 1,400 miles away. On fancy days, we broke out the Franciscan dinnerware, a faux hand-painted pattern called "desert rose" that reminded her that her oldest daughter lived across the country in the wild terrain where the rain didn't fall, the colors were delicate, and the flowers were rare and beautiful.

Days after my mother died, I arrived at the house to be gathered by the hand and guided by Samantha to our mother's room. "I want you to see," she said in a whisper, knowing that the first time I entered our mother's house without our mother in it would be heartbreaking. I felt the firm, delicate tracery of my sister's fingers, now wearing our mother's Tiffany diamond. She bolstered me as we circled the room like we were executing the precise steps of a square dance. "Here," she said, stopping to hold us in place in the center of the room, "is where we found her." Our mother had awoken on Christmas morning and gone to her piano to play, "I Heard the Bells on Christmas Day," the words from a poem by Henry Wadsworth Longfellow. She'd returned to her room, feeling faint, and collapsed on the floor with a massive cerebellum stroke. My sister and I stood on the spot together, our hands intertwined.

The dining room table was where the officiant sat when he came to the house, minutes after my sister had acclimated me to the space and our mother's disappearance from it. Samantha had tried to soften the blow, but still, I couldn't breathe. In my mother's place, he sat. He guided us gently through what would be her service. I agreed to speak the eulogy.

WE HAD MET CHAINSAW GUY four years ago on our way back from my mother's funeral when everything had arrived back to Albuquerque but our luggage. He had been the one to deliver our bags from the airline a day later when they arrived from the dark tunnels of O'Hare. "Your trees, they need trimming," he said. "I do that on the side." I had saved his card all this time.

As Chain Saw Guy and his crew roared to action in my front yard, I was deep in the garage, diligently sorting through boxes. In one box, I found *The Giving Tree* by Shel Silverstein. The tree was an apple tree, and the boy loved playing on her, shimmying up the trunk and hanging from her branches. As a teenager, he brought his girl to the tree, and they carved their initials into the bark, cutting into her woody flesh. The tree gave him apples, which he sold for money. The tree gave him her branches, which he built into a house. The tree gave him her trunk, which he built into a boat. Finally, the tree was a stump. She apologized that she could not give the boy shade. He replied that he was an old man and he did not need shade, just a place to sit and be at peace.

After the deed was done, the crew drove away, leaving the dismembered tree sticking awkwardly out of the green dumpster bin, a lovely bones sort of thing. It felt like a coffin that didn't quite fit, giving me the sense that the tree had been buried alive. I bought a festive-looking hanging basket of annuals, purple lobelias and red geraniums, and plunked it on the stump that remained, already knowing it was helpless beneath the unshade we had created. The sun would blaze upon it, unforgiving. The tree was having its last word.

Sinking into near despair, I realized my mother was *in* that tree. It was the tree in which the hawks perched on the highest branches for miles and miles. From there, they could keep vigil over the desert floor that surrounded us, guarding our moat of sand. My mother was that sturdy wood and that net of branches shielding our front door from the battering wind. She had been our sentinel.

The next morning, on Mother's Day, I awakened to look out the window at a gaping view to the blue sky. She's gone, and the twins will be gone, then I'll be gone. Yet what I remember is that I looked. My yearning eyes needed a place to rest, and now the view had opened up to something that was beyond us, something that before we could only make out through the lace of heart-shaped leaves. It was not true that after the twins left, I would only occupy a sliver of their hearts. I knew this because my mother was not just a sliver. Every year, she occupied more and more space.

Some days I grew excited about the financial game changer. I felt lucky about the timing. Other days I was dragged kicking and screaming into the day because I would be far away from where the twins were going. I wasn't ready to say goodbye in quite this way. When I tried to hold in my mind the good, the bad, and the ugly of the disfigured skyline and the uncanny magnificence of what was emerging, the only thing I could do was trust. I carried my mother in my heart, and the twins would carry me. It was possible that my mother had gone on out ahead of me, just beyond, to Saratoga Springs. She wouldn't perch here for me. She would perch herself in Saratoga, a gentler landscape, and she would wait for me.

AT MY REQUEST, PAUL DISMANTLED the swing set in the backyard. Even if I wasn't preparing the house for renters, we needed to do this. We had needed to do it for years. The dried-out lumber was rickety, to understate the matter. The red awning was frayed from the brutal New Mexico wind, faded pink from the relentless sun. Years ago, we had moved the yellow scallop of slide to the hill where we dug out a cliff ledge worthy of the ancient settlement at Bandelier National Monument. We had transferred the twins' toddler-size table set with the bright, lush rainforest chairs to this ledge of bare sand in a sort of ironic patio.

Dismantling wasn't exactly the right word for the way Paul approached the project. He hacked it to bits with a maniacal glee. The lumber was so brittle he could stomp on a post and break it in two. Within seconds, the swing set was in splinters and the sand wiped clean.

The signals that the end of childhood was nigh had been accumulating for a long time. "Brick by brick, the house of innocence falls to ruins," the poet John O'Donohue writes. The twins and I had very different views on this. I had been trying to slow the high-speed abandonment of play, and they had been trying to catapult out of here to find the place where they belonged. "Adult belonging is never as natural, innocent, or playful," O'Donohue writes. "Adult belonging has to be chosen, received, or renewed. It is a lifetime's work."

I know this, and they don't, and it doesn't change one damn thing.

WE'VE UNCRATED MY MOTHER'S DINING ROOM FURNITURE, slashed through the eggy strips of plastic that bound it together. It's a pleasure to see the hutch again. Grace and I set out the Franciscan dishes and stacked them like we were serving brunch in the driveway. As we unwrapped milk vases and green glassware, Paul circled out occasionally to check on the status of things. I was still undecided. This whole set was not mine but Grace's. She had been fourteen when Bon-Bon died, and I had told her that the dining room table and china were hers. She had been elated, enthralled with the idea that it had been bestowed on her to be the "keeper of the table," the one who would hold us together. Samantha often says that Grace and her daughter Tabitha will be the ones who keep us together through the changes ahead.

They are the ones most undaunted by the task of assembling us all when we are intent on scattering. They will hound us to "be there or be square," and Grace will own the table we all remember.

Yet it was hard to imagine where this table would be. After college in Colorado, she would face many years of school before she could even know. Do I keep it for her, carting it across the country, or store it here? When it is just a table. I had asked Roma, owner of a vintage Etsy store and a collector of mid-century modern, whether this furniture and this desert rose china were worth something. The answer was: only to us. If it looked like *Mad Men*, mid-century is worth something; if it looked like Paul Revere, forget it; if it looked like the desert and a mirage of someone else's memory, forget it.

Now the hutch and dining room table sat in a configuration on our driveway under the blazing-hot sun and a crystal blue sky. Sad Auction Lady took notes on her clipboard, occasionally snapping photos.

"I'm OK with auctioning it, Mom," Grace said, understanding the years ahead when one or both of us would be storing it and hauling it around. "It's the memory that matters, not the furniture. I remember."

With this, I felt confident. She had sealed her memory as I had sealed mine. She will carry on the memory, with or without furniture.

So it went on the list. I held back the Native American-patterned tablecloth with its green and gold and coral arrows and zigzags. "We'll keep this," I told Sad Auction Lady. "But you can log in everything else." To the southwest, the sky grew dark. A wind picked up in the high branches of the two surviving trees.

"It might rain," Sad Auction Lady said. "We should hurry."

I looked to the blank space in the yard between the catalpa tree and the two surviving cottonwoods. A storm was coming, but it was still far away. We still had to unwrap all the dishes and set them out so Sad Auction Lady could take photos. Grace said she could keep helping us. Each new unwrapping was a discovery and a decision, delight in it, then decide if it will go or stay. We just finished stacking the dishes on the shining cherrywood when a gust blew the hutch top off. It twisted in the wind and landed on the concrete, splitting the footer on the right side. I read Sad Auction Lady's face: This was bad.

nine

Everyone Deserves a Chance To ...

THE FIRST BIG WAVE OF FAMILY set out on the train from Chicago. The twins and I had made this twenty-five-hour trek heading west to east for many years to maximize our travel budget and be sure we saw family twice a year. Now the journey was flipped. At first, it had been lots of fun for the twins. You had plenty of space and could bring blankets, pillows, books, and all forms of addicting electronic entertainment. You could walk down to the observation car to stretch your legs and watch the view. You could play cards and board games.

All of these factors compensated for the obvious disadvantage: lengthy travel. When we compared it to the amount of time to travel to one airport, take a shuttle to a different terminal, board another plane, then drive to Lexington, it didn't add up to that many more hours. When we compared the quality of the hours, the train won. We weren't being herded around and packed in like the ultrathin, brined fish creatures that we were not. We weren't barraged with announcements, expensive airport food, extra charges, and marketing to get us to spend even more than we were already spending. We could build little forts in our train space and have all the comforts and pleasures that we chose at the moment we wanted to choose them. Nor did we have weather delays, mechanical failures, and germ-ridden, fuel-toxic air. Never did we have the threat of a canceled flight with the extra expense of a hotel (or a miserable night sleeping on a cot in Terminal K) and useless apologies from airline attendants handing us pitiful plastic tooth-brushes with sour, rigid bristles. It was one load-up, plenty of time to think and write and be a family, then arrival. When I totaled up the weariness factor, it was even. When I totaled up weariness plus expense, the train won.

For years, this was how we had sold my family on this trek, complete with Chicago deep dish pizza and astonishing views of the mighty Mississippi River at dawn or sunset (depending on the direction of travel). Somehow, we had managed to make it sound like fun. All of the cousins were excited—cousin party on the train! The adults knew full well what they were getting into but appreciated the sheer economics of it.

I MET DEBORAH AT COSTCO TO STOCK UP for the graduation brunch. I disliked Costco because I saw it as a monstrous box full of temptations to impulse-buy in bulk. It was kind of like a casino: once you were inside you could not track the light of day and you lost sight of how much was spilling out of your wallet. But shopping with Deborah was another experience entirely. We were focused and fast, zigging and zagging through frenzied shoppers, loading up carts with slot-machine zeal. We ducked into the refrigerated area for produce, and she held up a humongous package of baby carrots like an orange flag. "Some carrots, maybe?" she said. "How about some strawberries?" I nodded and she loaded a crate of Valentine's chocolate-worthy red gems into the cart. We were quite the team, me with a list and her with an inner radar of the lay of the land. Imagine this at the speed of winged warrior hand-maidens sweeping into the battlefield, collecting slain soldiers to a Valhalla afterlife. Set it to the soundtrack of the soaring violins of "Flight of the Valkyries." We were brisk, we were flying, and we were purposeful. We were the choosers of the fallen. We weren't shopping; we were scooping up heroes. As we exited, I flashed my ribboned receipt at the clerk, who hashed it with a yellow high-lighter. With that, our purchasing mission was done.

LATE INTO THE HOT, SUNNY AFTERNOON, Grace and I trekked downtown in our two cars, the Prius and the minivan, thinking we'd need both for all the luggage and people. True to form, the minivan gave us a bit of grief as we set out. One of the removable seats refused to go in, so we just left its forty- pound self out in the driveway, baking in the sun. Picture a *Breaking Bad* scene, from a strange, broken angle, quintessential Vince Gilligan.

So this was it. Everyone was arriving, and in two days the twins would graduate. For some of the cousins, it would be their first time in Albuquerque or even out west. For our part, we had been a dutiful tourism bureau, extending the invitation early and often. We had talked it up for years, stoking any smoke trail of interest. The youngest cousin gravitated to story after story about Indians and Roswell space aliens. Yet when we had talked about the stunning open-sky vistas and the 330 days of sunshine, we'd gotten only the slightest stir of interest. The idea of New Mexico was so exotic no one could hold it in their minds. We'd attended their soccer games and ballet recitals, but they had never seen Grace sing or Paul demonstrate karate. We'd slept in their rooms and eaten at their tables, but they could not tell you whether Grace's room was painted lavender, ocean blue or peach ice cream. (The answer is: All three.) The twins had always played the role of foreigner, not the familiar. For years, the twins and I had been reentering their lives as though we were the exiles, while our true lives had unfurled in this desert wilderness.

When we were young, my longtime childhood friend Portia and I had shared sleepovers in a room where we snuggled beneath the covers and vowed we would raise our families together and live in side-by-side houses. In our living fantasy, it would be just like the street where we grew up, where everyone knew everyone else, moms were home all day, and we were in and out of each other's houses. Her kids and mine would play fairies and elves under my magic weeping willow, and my kids and hers would play with Barbies and Breyer horses in her treehouse. I'd been in the delivery room with Portia as she gave birth to her first daughter. I'd been in the labor room with my sister Samantha as she labored with Clarissa, and I'd waited in the hall as they put her under and delivered Clarissa by C-section. I'd been the first to lay eyes on my niece. I'd wallpapered the nursery for her, though that house was now gone, ravaged by Hurricane Katrina. I'd etched pencil lines on the wall and smoothed the strips of wallpaper by hand. The twins and I had watched Rosaria when my sister April rushed baby Tomas to the emergency room for an EpiPen injection on New Year's Eve. Somehow, we'd managed to keep them all alive.

In this arrival, we will demonstrate who we are, a family that will cross prairies and mountains to be together.

But mainly they would be bedraggled, stumbling out of the train station, clutching pillows like zombies, blinking in the relentless sun. As Grace and I shared sweaty hugs with them, the only one who had any energy left was cheerleader Tabitha. The window was closing for collecting their rental cars, and "there is a little complication," Samantha whispered.

A preview, please? Apparently, my train-traveling sisters had left their driver's licenses in Kentucky. There was a sheepish giggle and a promise of a story about this that may or may not conclude with a speed-run to the train bar car, but it would have to wait. We decided that my nineteen-year-old niece Clarissa would be the driver of the rental, and I would be her navigator as she took on a city that she last saw when she was nine months old. This was how about half of us ended up as passengers heading up Interstate 25 with The Lumineers cranked up on the sound system, the whole car chanting, "O-o-phelia, you've been on my mind, girl, like a drug!" In between chorus and verse, I gave directions to my house.

Meanwhile, Grace had spirited my brother-in-law to the airport to get his rental car. There are other details in this picture that I have not captured. A Snapchat map of all our locations would have shown our cartoon avatars popping up in every pocket of Albuquerque. Somehow, not everyone could fit in the first wave of cars going to get cars, a certain unspecified number of people are perhaps at the train station, and once all of us get distributed to a total of four cars at three different locations, we would get ourselves to my house, where April awaited and where Paul may or may not be.

With the arrival of ten people today and three more to come, the logistics of all of this have just become monumental, and you may wonder if I just thrive on this or if as a single mother, I am too desensitized to think, "Oh this is stressful! I should take a deep breath." It's nothing compared to the daily jottings in my planner, which have included mapping out moving scenarios like this, all of which must be perfectly executed like clockwork. The list hopped from here to Denver to Kansas City, through Louisville to see Portia, through Pittsburgh to see author client Peg, all in the Prius. Furniture would arrive. Five days to unpack. Flights back and forth to Albuquerque to get the house ready to show. Each day ticked off with high activity, a million transactions, and thousands of miles. Somehow, the whole echocardiogram would arrive with me living in a fully furnished and unpacked house and a fully functional job that would give me financial freedom.

Myriad variables could throw any of this off, such as when does the dog go to New York? In the car with Grace and me? This schedule didn't account for flight delays or furniture delays or any messiness at a new job or any complications with vendors repairing my house. None of those things can happen. But it was all planned now, flights booked, details arranged. It was a neat little package waiting for me after graduation and the family trip to the Grand Canyon and Zion. It was time to just enjoy this moment.

"You're forgetting something," April reminded me.

Forgetting something, just the kind of language that could jolt any single mother to attention. "You have a role to play," she said with mock solemnity.

She explained my lines, my staging, led me to the spa tub. "The role you are supposed to play while your sisters are here to support you is: Grieving Empty-Nester Curled Up in Fetal Position in Spa Tub, Sobbing Uncontrollably."

This, now, is the time to cry.

"This is why we have come," April said. "You can completely abandon yourself to grief while we serve quiche and mimosas. No one at the brunch even has to know. They'll all be saying, 'I can't believe how well she's handling this. She's so calm. . . . where is she?" April waved her hand like she was a real estate agent showcasing amenities. Such as places to cry.

THE NIGHT BEFORE THE TWINS GRADUATE, just a little crisis. We had one more cousin to reel in, Stella. Stella was only three months younger, and together, they made a set of triplets, holding the center of our spilling-out-all-over extended family. Collecting Stella at the airport went off without a hitch. It was the part about the minivan, which insisted on running true to its obstinate self. It wouldn't start.

A series of texts from Samantha announced the trouble. From home, I started dispensing advice about calling "Triple A." Samantha was in communication, but the twins were not because they . . . were teenagers. "Not the battery" was one text from Samantha. "Engine locked up" was another. "Needs to be towed" came another about an hour later.

This of course raised a whole other round of questions. How were they all going to get back from the airport? I sat poised for a retrieval mission. But then a phone call came from Paul. They would have the minivan towed to the mechanic, where Paul's car was still parked, awaiting repairs. They would swap the cars, a nice little mechanic subterfuge that is kind of like when the Irish fairies replace your child with a changeling. They would leave the minivan and take the Yaris, sort of a way to strengthen the fairy stock. And that was how everyone got home: in the car we just happened to buy two weeks ago.

When I thanked Samantha, she told me, "I didn't do anything. The twins figured it out." She described how they already had called Grace's boyfriend and his dad, so they didn't need Triple A. Her boyfriend and his dad tried to jump-start the minivan but to no avail. They also added oil, but the engine had seized up, and that was that. They worked out the plan to get the minivan towed to the mechanic and take the Yaris. "They want you to know they had been taking care of oil changes," Samantha added. "I watched them. They totally had this."

PORTIA SAVES ME A SEAT at the end of the center aisle. The Sandia Prep gym fills with a quickening 6/8 time. We are two rows. I am deeply cloaked in family. April and her children choose a higher seat near the right side of the stage for a better photo angle. As more and more familiar faces gather to take seats around and above me, I hear beneath the murmur a small sprouting of higher tones, the flowering of happy voices. My own internal rhythm pulses, ascends, holds, a one-two-three-four-and tempo. I sit in the center of a colossal room. To my right and behind me, my nieces tweedle and chirp as they set and reset their camera phones to be ready for the pictures. They flip through the program to spot the twins' photos and lean to each other, whisper the names of my children. A hush falls over the room. Graduates enter, boys in black suits, girls in white dresses, coming right up the center aisle toward me at marching pace. I see their faces together, Grace walking two steps ahead of her brother, holding a long-stemmed red rose, shimmering with a sweet smile of delight, Paul behind her with a closed-lip smile of pride. For one instant, our eyes lock in a trine, each of us an arc completing a full circle. I snap off three frames, and then they are past me, heading to the stage. Just like that, they have become adults.

IN THOSE LONG MINUTES BETWEEN MOTION AND IMPACT, there is the illusion of self-motion. Yet I am still. I am not moving. The roar of a truck erupting from Utah canyonlands. A force thrusting me backward on the road. A crimson sky slamming me back, a screaming hand. Glass shatters, limbs tumble through the sky. It is I who am moving, and it is Time who has stopped. It is the twins who are moving, who look to us, desperate grimaces, taut with death fear. What happens in the space between are words about dreams and ambitions. They come in showers. They come on cards with black mortarboards and silver tassels. Congratulations, congratulations. Once a dream becomes real, a thousand dreams become possible. Let us be travelers, let us be brave. Let us seek our fortunes together. The words come as lauds, daybreak prayers, songs of praise. The words come as the faint chants of the matins, the most vigilant ones, the hardest to say. Commence, commence. Commence the questions. Let us be lovers of fortunes and the ones who live the questions. Map your world with love and lemons. A graduation trip, then, to the Grand Canyon, red sandstone cliffs of Zion, and brilliant coral sand dunes. Two cars, laughter and cousins, and the secret song of the Narrows. The Glen Canyon badlands. "They're passing us," my sister is saying. A bell ringing out. A landscape of ash. A truck barreling out of the canyonlands at meteoric speed. My sister brakes hard. The twins whip through the slot, veer to our lane. Look for the mile markers, the beat beat beat of a shining wind as the truck passes.

A few things happen after the twins graduate and before I leave for Saratoga. I will tell the story in snapshots:

I.

My son tosses the key fob in the coral sands. To be cool, to watch me grovel, to laugh, to oppose all the hard questions being asked of his future. I don't know, only that the $500 object exists as our only way home, otherwise we will languish in the wilderness hungering for a Triple-A call. Is my son ready for adulthood? Moments later, the twelve of us—two of my sisters, my twins, their children—stand at the lookout point, where two young sons of two perfectly great parents skateboard across the coral sands, swishing balletic paths across pristine hummocks. Their mom turns to me and explains the precise brand of skateboards, narrating how the older son instructs the younger one. We watch them grand jeté across the dunes. Why is my son not that?

II.

My son nearly kills himself, his twin sister, and three cousins in a head-on collision on the highway near Escalante, the landscape of ashen staircases.

III.

My daughter takes the wheel.

IV.

Saratoga still has not paid my signing bonus. It's been forty-five days. Portia says, "If they aren't keeping their promises, you don't have to change your life for them." Seconds before I dial, they call. So sorry for the oversight, they say. It's being wired right now.

V.

Moments after watching the twins and their cousins nearly be crushed to death, my heart is still pounding. They fishtail through the arroyo in the Glen Canyon badlands as they pass us again. "Stop the car," I tell my sister. I stomp out into the gravelly sand and stalk the twins' car, waving my arms like a crazed Black Friday Walmart shopper. "What the fuck?" I am saying this to slag canyons and a green metal contraption that sways on the sand as it speeds away. At last, it stops. They can't hear me. I can't catch them. I scream until my throat is raw. Glen Canyon is huge enough and bleak enough and sad enough that it can hold my screams. Mercifully, the car stops. My sister is walking out ahead, stalking toward our reckless teenagers.

VI.

After the "talks" are had, all parents are briefed. From deep in the minivan, Rosaria cuts through the heated debate of adults who just almost saw their children die with this: "I don't feel comfortable with my brother in that car." My ballerina niece, the quiet and graceful almost sister to Grace, has spoken. It is decided that her brother will be rescued from the "party car" as we will call it later in moments of greater levity. And that Paul will never drive again for the rest of his life. My nephew, successfully won back to safety in the negotiations, walks across the vast and bleak sand in the prisoner exchange, grateful to reach safe terrain.

Immediately after this, we get word that after a long and courageous fight, death has come to the minivan.

VII.

Back in Albuquerque, all family gone, the minivan truly dead, the movers come and load two-thirds of the house. The other pieces are going to college. The house is nearly empty, the cupboards bare. The twins and I gather in the kitchen, where they used to climb on step stools to roll out cookie dough. Cookie cutters and muffin tins and coffee pots lay deep in brown boxes on a van traveling across the prairie. "Remember the pumpkin and spider cookies, Halloween?" Paul wears a look that is astonished and content. "Remember the train tracks we looped through the kitchen?" They nod. Maybe they're thinking about this. "I'm not selling it, not our memories. We'll be back someday."

"Mom, after this day, we're not living here anymore," Paul says. "We'll live at college. Then we'll live somewhere else."

Right, right. We won't gather here, in this kitchen. I'll carry their toys to New York. They will take a four-year adventure to Colorado and Arizona. And I'll take one to New York. After that, we'll figure out where we'll meet up, but it won't be here.

VIII.

Paul tells me, "I don't think I'll go to ASU. I'll just go to UNM."

IX.

Grace and I drive to Colorado Springs anyway because we just have to keep going.

Some parts of the house do not die. They do not dim, even when we leave it, remove all of our objects, turn off the lights, and go. The creamy walls and honey pine beams gather light. The small creatures come more alive. The windows open their arms and hold more sky.

part two

-

Songs of Experience

ten

Little House on the Prairie

COME WITH ME ACROSS THIS AMERICA I am not sure I recognize anymore. I want you to be its mother, the one hoping to nurture it and protect it and hold us together. I want you to wonder how family stays family, how we choose the lived life and steer clear of choosing the uninhabited lifeless life—how my son is wrestling with this now even as I leave him behind. I want you to hop in the Prius with me and his twin sister as we leave our home, touch down in the state where she will go to college and pursue the destiny she has chosen. Zoom with us across the prairie and accompany us as we reverse-migrate across the mighty Mississippi. Pull up the on-ramp and roar out of Denver across Interstate 70, slipping from majestic mountain to tawny gold front range. Keep your eyes on a pale blue horizon that doesn't say "beyond" so much as it says "return."

For the longest time, as Grace and I crossed the front range, I believed the Colorado-Kansas line would appear soon on our horizon. I was wrong. I was wrong as we bobbed along amid semitrailers. I was wrong as we plodded past feed silos. I was wrong wrong wrong. Because I was a mother, not a father. Fathers leave their families to find gold, send money back, set up stakes and build a homestead, provide for their families even if it means the sacrifice of disappearing themselves from their children's lives. (And hope they can show up for the end—or if delayed, the next generation, arriving with noble myths of their battles and tins of sugary confections!) But mothers choose to stay poor because they choose to stay near at all costs. As a single parent, I had had to be both of these people.

We stopped at the Fast-N-Friendly in Limon, Colorado, for gas. Inside the tiny store, Grace explored to see if she could discover something cool, and she emerged with peach-flavored licorice stems that only seem cool for forty-five seconds. Soon, we were in Kansas.

Each of these prairie outposts was an unruly child of sorts, like my son now was, reneging on being part of the whole. Disobeying, diverging in each its own way, prairie grass standing to the sweep of a brave wind. It confounded me that Paul would commit to ASU, then say, "I'll just go to UNM," which was the way he said it every time, with the "just" that knocked it to the basement of all colleges. It confounded me that I'd marshaled all the resources I could muster to set it aright for him, even been willing to pivot to British Columbia, only to hear on the eve of our road trip —"I'll just go to UNM." It confounded me that we could never have a conversation about it—he cut me off with "you're so fucking stupid" at every pass. I'd had to leave at the crack of dawn with nothing settled at all about one of my children. I felt like Miriam setting a small basket to be placed in the bullrushes to float on the Nile River, hoping some other kind soul would find my Moses and take care of him. Like Miriam, I watched.

Like those prairie families, we were pioneers, only we were going back. Pioneers divided the labor and bootstrapped to survive. Older children fed and clothed younger children, and breadwinners migrated to where work could be found. Whether our migration was chosen like a manifest destiny or forced like the Cherokee Nation, this was the raucous debate in my head, as a descendent of both the Irish-Scottish and the matrilineal Cherokee. Yes, this moment presented a financial game changer for my family. Yes, given that the nest was empty, this made sense. And yes, Resistance was still hanging out at the tip of my wing, flying through a fluid blue sky. We passed beneath white clouds, which swirled in elegant braids high above our heads. I didn't understand what made us a family, then, if we were going to have all these majestic skies between us.

Ah, but sink into the rhythm of the highway and see now the trucks and tractors and silos that store seeds and wheat and corn. See now the work, the day-to-day toil this land asks of its inhabitants. Hear how it called out to the willing, people in towns like St. Louis and Pittsburgh and Buffalo, promising soil that could be prepared to receive them. Read the posters, hear their proclamations, stapled to posts in those river towns, promising our ancestors that the soil here was rich, something to envy, something that would make you want to cut into it with a blade and render wheat, one small grain that could be baked into life-giving bread and fill a belly. See the seeds that drop into the furrows, seeds that hope to become something, to join a chorus of other seeds, standing in a network of roots. See the wheat stalks grow high, reaching into the blue summer sky, speaking to the clouds, to say here I am and here I always will be. And see the toil that goes into protecting the seeds to hold life and call rain and catch light. See the vigilance to guard against locusts that chomp wheat and to temper volatile markets, so the gold reaped from the fields has somewhere to go. Notice now, stopping at the McDonald's in Hays, how the toil depends on Right Equipment—the thrasher that harvests, the truck that hauls—and Right Thinking, as the Bible study group gathers fervently in the silver-tiled corner where walls and floors are of the same material.

As we crossed the prairie, Grace played Kendrick Lamar's "Damn," which will win the 2017 Pulitzer Prize for music, the first rapper to win the award. For miles, we had listened to Louise Erdrich's National Book Award-winning *The Round House*, a Native American story about brutal rape. This was how we traversed the heart of America—listening to a rapper's stories about blackness, street life, police brutality, perseverance, survival, and self-worth; listening to an Ojibwe woman's story in a justice trilogy about a young man seeking to avenge the violation of his mother's body. We were listening to the stories of the conquered and colonized.

I have lost my country.

I have lost my family.

We won't see a city for 252 miles.

I feel sad about leaving Albuquerque. I feel sad because I loved it for twenty-five years and I love it still. I feel sad because some terrible things happened to me there. I feel sad because not everything worked out. I feel sad because I'm giving up before everything worked out because it still could. I feel sad because I waited so long for everything to work out and it didn't. I feel sad because I love the place and I don't want to give up on it. This is the cage I'm in.

We have the whole day to contemplate Kansas, where the topsoil is rich because a diverse array of native grasses—western wheatgrass, buffalo, grama, little bluestem—shade it and enrich it. A network of dense, fibrous roots hosts a wealth of microorganisms that are the unseen sustenance for an astonishing ecosystem. When the first homesteaders came to the Great Plains in the 1870s, they tore away at the protective grasses, harming roots and exposing bare soil to fierce dry winds and hot sun. The riches of Kansas topsoil blew away or evaporated.

Had I disturbed the topsoil of my family? In reaching for a better economic future, had I disturbed our ecosystem? I had to remind myself that like the homesteaders who took a stab at it in the 1870s, only for their descendants to be starved and disrupted in the Dust Bowl years, my ecosystem already had been disturbed. Since the economic crash of September 2008, it had been fragile, and before that, it had been fragile because of divorce. In the perseverance I presented to the world—some would say it was admirable—I'd accumulated many points of fragility, a million tiny fractures still tender to the touch. In her last months of life, my mother had told me what she most desired for me was stability, an unshakeable fortress, an established settlement. She had not lived to see this happen.

ALSO WHAT HAD NOT COME: A passage for someone like me. In the typical empty-nest narrative, the woman returned to her marriage wholeheartedly, if she had one, or put all of her material possessions in storage and trek to a romantic place like Paris or Tuscany, where she fell in love. (Was this where all the good men were and not in New Mexico? Was there a secret code that sent all the good men to Paris or Tuscany, so they could be in a movie plot?) In those narratives, the reward for hard years of mothering was: a man.

At the risk of riling my fellow feminists, who loved to say, "A man is not a plan,"—I'll say here that that solution would have been quite nice. It was always the ones who were still wives who were quick to dispense such not-needing-a-man wisdom. In the same breath, they would tell me I was the lucky one and launch into how difficult it was to live with the old men their husbands had become. Yet a good man might have distracted me for a good ten, fifteen years until I became a grandmother, a sage woman, a storehouse of wisdom, worthy of the Grand Council of the Iroquois. I could have easily just ridden along in a second-half-of-life romance until it was time to neatly tuck myself into the next developmental phase and done it without a hiccup.

I found myself at the full completion of a life, post-death and no eulogy. And with no anthropological precedent, really, for the space in between. I was not retiring. I was still becoming. I was still on the road to somewhere, even if it felt like a road to nowhere.

GRACE AND I ARRIVED AT THE OUTDOOR AMPHI-THEATER in Bonner Springs, Kansas, for the concert I'd offered to sweeten the deal. As we made our way to a spot on the lawn, it hit me: It was full-on summer. A season had passed, and now I was in a new season. For the moment, I was homeless. A man named Lloyd had all my worldly possessions on a Northwestern moving van he may or may not have shuttle-loaded in the parking lot of the shuttered Kmart in Rio Rancho, New Mexico, and he may or may not show up at a loft apartment in upstate New York that I have never seen. It was requiring a lot of trust to be season-less. Suddenly, I realized I'd lost spring, and now it was another season entirely. Young women wore bikini tops and gauzy skirts that billowed around their ankle tattoos. All around us, people who weren't doing stressful things like move across the country and totally relocate their lives were settling in to watch the Glass Animals, the headliners, who were kind of an edgy Coldplay.

I can't take this place/I just want to go/where I can get some space

Millennials all around me roused to their feet, cheering as they took up this chant and, in some cases, their boomer mothers and fathers who brought them here were just as adamant. Together we chanted in unison: We want our place, the place where we can get some space. This was "Gooey," a song that felt like being inside the color bubbles in a lava lamp. Listening to the music roll out and up the slope of the grassy hill, it felt like we were slurping it.

Outside the gates, the Westboro Baptist Church protested the concert. No one around us understood what the objection was. "It might be because one of them is gay, but I don't know," Grace said, shrugging and turning her eyes back to the gigantic *G* and *A* on the stage bathed in champagne-gold light. It will turn out that it's because the band is British, and the sins of the brutish Brits are many, as the church announced in a press release in hysterical, bold all caps. I noted the irony that the Glass Animals' new release was "How to Be a Human Being."

The bright, wide disc of the full moon slipped above feathery pines in the inky sky, and suddenly it struck me that I had no worries about Paul. No matter how much I wanted to solve this problem of whether Paul went to UNM or ASU or British Columbia, no matter how much I wanted his path to be certain, he was the one who would have to figure it out. I knew my son. He would be happy and successful on any path. All I was required to do was bear witness to him as he worked his way there, wherever there would be.

The Glass Animals ushered in a melodic cascade that washed over us as we lay in the summer grass. "Agnes," the song that apparently had most infuriated the Westboro folks, was about losing a friend to death at her own hand. The song built to banshee lament, "You see the sad in everything." Through a white-doves-in-flight kaleidoscope over the whirs and purrs of synths came the final chant, "You're gone but you're on my mind/I'm lost but I don't know why." The notes broke like shattering glass, scattering us to three winds like the tiny glass animals we were.

SOON INTO THE NEXT DAY, WE CROSSED THE MISSISSIPPI RIVER to the eastern side of the country. Through Illinois and Indiana, the dense woodlands hugging the Ohio River promised familiar territory ahead as we approached my home country, Kentucky. We stopped in Indiana to refuel, and it became clear we'd left the West long behind. I looked west to farmland marked off in neat green and bronze squares. In the distance, a tractor was stilled in the field. Once, this had been the outer frontier of my childhood. A shaft of sunlight fell from high, gray clouds on the horizon from which I just traveled. I was reentering the place that birthed me, but on this trip, we would barely touch home. Late that night, we entered the city of Derby hats, blankets of red roses, and sleek horses. We crashed at Portia's.

We struck out early, reaching the Ohio River at Cincinnati

before the sun could burn off the morning clouds. For four days, I'd lived in a car bubble with my daughter, my son outside it, my worldly goods outside it, stripped to the essence of us. In my Prayer of the Hours, I wanted to tell the twins about how rare and beautiful it is to forge through. But there were no words, no listening audience, only the territory we crossed. Fur trappers and fort builders had arrived to these deep forests and staked a claim along the river where I had spent my childhood, a landscape of outdoor summer concerts, the brilliant sheen of stadium lights, and the longing to leave. So many old whispers, this place, tugging at me with the felt sense of a past life, my mother short of breath, explaining the infinite, how she would always be near. But she was gone now and we wouldn't stop here. I struggled for the words I could offer Grace but I kept silent as the land dropped out from beneath us and we spanned the river.

SOON WE REALIZED THE SHORTEST ROUTE to Saratoga would take us through Buffalo, where Grace's ninety-six-year-old Ukrainian grandmother lived. She was my ex-mother-in-law, so I was not expecting she would want to see me, but I was happy with hanging out at a Starbucks while Grace shared lunch with her grandmother. To my surprise, Oksana insisted I join them for a light lunch of boiled bratwurst and potato salad. This tiny bungalow in Amherst, New York, was still an enclave of immigrants like herself who had fled the Nazis or the Soviets or both, so tightly connected that, during lunch, somehow, Oksana's friend Jutta knew of Grace's arrival and popped over to give Grace a graduation card. Grace had spent nearly every summer of her childhood here, so she knew the rhythms of the home and the way Oksana commanded over it as the empress who watched the dance of sparrows and hummingbirds through the trees, the climber roses along the wooden fence. For years, from this house, Oksana had made sweet rose-petal jam and shipped it to her children and grandchildren. My children were her only grandchildren.

Eighteen years ago, I'd come to these rooms where my husband once had been a rambunctious boy strafing the rooms with laughter and play. I had held my palm to my belly and told Oksana she was going to be a grandmother. She had cupped my cheeks and beamed her joy to me. Then she clasped her hands to her heart and uttered, "Ach! But I am so old," worried she might not live to see them grow up.

As before, we stood heart to heart, our hands interlocked. Our promises as mother to mother joined one to another, birdsong and river and prairie. One promise I had broken, to take good care of her son. At the wedding reception, my husband's parents had presented us with Ukrainian brown bread, and we had dipped it in salt. Good luck and good health. His father had led the toast, which when translated from Ukrainian came across in plain terms: You must stay married! Until . . . you are dead! To this, surrounded by family and friends, we had raised glasses of champagne and promised.

The other promise I had fulfilled. "Look at her," I said as we swiveled to Grace. "Isn't she beautiful?"

We sat down to Oksana's table, and Grace carried the conversation, speaking to her grandmother in Ukrainian, turning to me after each exchange, translating to English. Oksana marveled that we had traveled by car, so many miles that our car had been in New Mexico and Colorado and all the places in between. As we went to leave, Oksana followed us out to the driveway to see our New Mexico license plate, a bright yellow Zia on a turquoise background. She insisted that Jutta take photos of the three of us. She gathered her arms around us. "You have come so far!"

eleven

The Fiery Ring

IF I COULD DRAPE MY DAUGHTER IN ROSES every day, that is what I would do on this day and in the hereafter. That would protect her from people who die, men you want to leave, coworkers with fragile egos. We made our first foray into Saratoga Springs, where at a boutique on Broadway, I bought Grace a white silk sundress that spilled over with majestic red roses. My daughter was the kind of beautiful that didn't know it was beautiful, the kind that radiated eternal grace from every pore. On someone else, this dress would be pretentious. It would seem like she was angling for an equestrian estate or cultured pearls. After all, we had found it in a boutique for women who wanted to see and be seen (but mostly seen) at the track. As she twirled before the triangle of mirrors, the dress achieved a more perfect union, an unfolding of innocent beauty of what simply is. The dress was my thank-you for driving with me across the country, but beneath my words I wanted to whisper. "You are the Grail, a vessel of pure kindness. You are precious to me. For you, my wish is play. That is my promise." For too many years in our fractured family, she'd taken on emotional weight as the water bearer, more than a child should carry.

We parted on the street, Grace to shop further, me to attend my first meeting as editor of the magazine.

"I'M JUST HERE TO MAKE SURE MY BRAND DOESN'T GET MURDERED," said Regan as she yanked out a chair in

Anton Leir's office. *Murdered.* Strange words for someone who just sold her brand for half a million dollars. When I scanned the faces at the table, all the men stared down at their leather portfolios. I looked straight at the square set of Regan's jaw to see if she knew she was breaking every glass animal in the room. The contract she'd signed had amounted to "what will it take to make your brand go away?" If someone had given me half a million dollars for what I had accomplished, I would not be here. I would be on Andy Dufresne's glittering white sand beach in Mexico, having slogged through prison shit to escape, never giving another thought to "my brand." I'd have a new brand, and it would be defined by unending days of simple pleasures, looking out to the teeming blue waves of Balboa's unconquerable sea, never giving another thought to landed cities of gold. I am, of course, referring to *The Shawshank Redemption*, a movie April urged me to watch during my years of captivity—the dying newspaper industry years and the confining co-parenting years. She had been trying to help me see I was in a prison, much of it my own making. She'd been trying to make me see that beyond the stone walls was a glittering white sand beach.

Regan's bitter words sounded the warning shot. I would not start the new job officially until five days later, but it had been in my best interest to be at this meeting, which had not been expected to go well. An apology. Let me be clear. In point of fact, savage cries had gone up throughout the land for Liam's severed head to be placed on a spike. The purpose of the meeting was for Liam to present the new design of the magazine, which is what his consulting firm had been commissioned to do and which had inspired internecine warfare the past three weeks. "Death to consultants!" had been the battle cry—not an exaggeration—because neither "I'm-so-sexy-in-this-shirt" Nerilla nor "my-father-in-law-is-rich" Regan could bring themselves to imagine why publishing a magazine required expertise. Behind the scenes, Kenneth had assured Liam this would all blow over once designs were presented. Anton

Leir would choose one design, and the new editor, me, would herald a new era.

By the end of the meeting, reservations had been made at Salt & Char, and Grace was invited to join us. I strategically slid in next to Anton Leir, meeting a nod of approval from Liam. Nerilla swiftly looped around the table to place herself at Anton Leir's left. To Liam and Kenneth's relief, Regan could not join us, but to their displeasure, a new threat had emerged, the arrival of The Prognosticator, who was not a billionaire like Anton Leir but the millionaire head of the consulting firm hired to produce the magazine (and, therefore, Kenneth's boss and, therefore, mine). He saw himself as just the right sort of visionary because he was a futurist and frequent cable news pundit on global financial markets. He had commissioned his own artist for the cover of the magazine, something Liam had tried to head off with a scathing email the night before. Before I could signal to Grace what seat to choose, all other chairs were claimed and she was drawing out the one next to The Prognosticator.

After the plates were cleared away and dessert wine poured, The Prognosticator asked Grace to compare his preferred design versus the prevailing preference, though she did not know which was which. She offered a cogent, thorough, and respectful critique of the pluses and minuses. Observing my daughter from across the table, I noticed she had focused on the merits of the design and spoken with no guile. Anton Leir, having witnessed the posturing in our three-hour meeting earlier that day that resolved nothing, must have found this refreshing because he said, "We should hire her," whipping his finger like a fishhook.

So, my daughter became a magazine intern. For a whole summer if she wanted. She did not want. What she wanted was a summer in Albuquerque with her boyfriend, one last summer before college. She wanted a different, imaginary job. A job that was not here in some northern, forested clime with small strips of pale blue sky. As much as this solved two problems for me—she had a summer job now and I had someone I deeply trusted at my side to launch the magazine—I was not sure I wanted this. This brought her into the midst of warring factions. But it was the bird in the hand, better than the bird in the bush. We texted her brother and her dad, who was incredulous but had had it scribed into his DNA to always hear money when it talked. Grace agreed to stay for a few weeks to help get out my first issue, which debuted in thirty-seven days.

SUMMER HAD ARRIVED HERE AHEAD OF ME. Furniture had not, and the moving company was incommunicado. My worldly goods were last tracked to Rochester, maybe Baltimore, possibly Boston, lost in the silence of unreturned calls. Grace convinced me that we could make the best of it. She and everyone else had noticed summer, and I kept looking back at a vanished spring. It pierced me that summer was a season distinct from spring. That was new, after twenty-eight years in the Southwest, though my youth in Kentucky's horse country had scribed into my DNA the memory of delicate spring, dogwoods, and blankets of Derby roses. For this reason, summer's arrival felt urgent, though it was a week away. Its departure felt just as imminent, thirteen weeks away.

At Saratoga Spa State Park, Grace and I heard the joyous waters before we saw them. We crossed a bridge over a stream abundant with fresh minerals. Here in the woods, we came upon a geyser from which water constantly bubbled, sincere, generous, and carbonated.

LATER, I MADE MY FIRST EDITORIAL DECISION, in an event I will come to call The Great Car Wash, from beneath the splattered bodies of 2,200 miles of insects as wide-waled brushes smeared suds over the windshield of my car. Kenneth informed me that I would be receiving a text with the cover art. "Let us know which one you prefer," he said as water swished across my glass, though I knew which one I was supposed to choose. Two nostalgic scenes of elegant people at the Saratoga Race Course were vying to be the symbolic image of the 2017 track season. It would be hard to distinguish the differences between the two—one was by the artist friend of the socialite who just sold her media property but won't let go of it; the other was the more impressionistic, reaching for virtuosity. (Think: Monet and his next-best painting of water lilies as if this New York artist had sojourned to his Giverny, only this was the red-and-white awning of Saratoga Race Course captured in the dim and dazzle of light on sleek chestnut colts, pink peonies, and the ephemeral beauty of women who had once lived, looking upon the best and the fastest thoroughbreds.) As my car rocked and water rattled across the icy-green steel of my Prius, calls from Kenneth and Liam arrived in rapid succession, seeking to claim the battlespace. Their mission today was to decide this—and establish my authority as editor. Anton Leir had decided on the cover, the fonts, the colors, the artist who had captured the right measure of nostalgia for the Saratoga that defined him. The word from Liam was that Anton Leir was an Albany lawyer who made a fortune but also was a Sicilian immigrant whom no one saw as elite or monied. Since he'd moved to Saratoga, he'd been buying his way onto the arts board, the ballet board, Yaddo, the chamber. He'd bought a vineyard. He'd bought the restaurant on Broadway that everyone saw as the place to be elegant. He drove a Ferrari.

In this oil painting, there can be one woman presenting her tender, admiring cheeks beneath the brim of her hat, one silver-haired horse owner, one honored jockey, one iconic awning. There can only be one majestic horse, one garland, one teeming tier of onlookers in the grandstand where the faces fade like flowers in the hot sun. But there can be every kind of story, the old one of belonging here already or the new one of trying desperately to be here.

I am told to choose the words, fonts, colors, and painting that Anton Leir has chosen, and I do. I will present it to Nerilla and Regan on Monday, my first day on the job.

TO FORGET I WAS WALKING INTO THE MOUTH OF THE DRAGON, I took Grace to hear a Canadian folk singer at Caffe Lena, a coffeehouse that boasted it still had a Bob Dylan vibe because he'd played there before anyone knew anything about hard rain or rolling stones or the complete unknown. We headed toward the space of rebels and revolutionaries, leaving behind a tree-lined street with elegant Victorians and generous verandas. Signs, signs, everywhere signs, invited guests for track rentals while still holding their traditions turreted out of reach. Grace and I quickened our steps as the rays of the sun lengthened, lingering at the edge of the day that way it does in northern latitudes. How far I was from New Mexico, where sun and dark spun at an even keel. The pressing sun signaled winters here, the sense that I was borrowing light and I would owe a debt later, with interest, when the snows came. Strangely, this felt electric.

Inside Caffe Lena, Grace and I claimed seats at a small-top bistro table one layer back from the stage. The blue-eyed singer Séan McCann had attracted a coterie of devoted fans who knew him from his days in a better-known band, the Great Big Sea, songs with bodhrans, mandolins, and tin whistles that called to a far shore. From here to the cod banks of Newfoundland lay 1,600 miles, and from the fields of potatoes and partridge berries to the sea cliffs of Ireland lay another 1,900 miles.

Seventy minutes into his first set, the singer bent to the microphone and said, "You'll recognize this tribute," and eased his guitar into a cantering rhythm of a dusty Tex-Mex border town. The song began with a heraldic opening. He strummed his guitar with a spritely rhythm that could have summoned forth a mariachi band before us, so his cheery intro deceived the crowd into believing he had launched into a celebratory song. But his solemn voice pounded a warning. This would be about falling irretrievably into the dark center of love's bracing hold. "Love is a burning thing," he announced in a gravelly voice. "And it makes a fiery ring."

At once, Grace and I swiveled to each other as the singer fell down, down, down into a burning ring of fire. Our eyes locked, and I nearly trembled. In my mind, I heard my daughter's voice, singing one season ago as she strummed and our car charged across a boundless desert. "Some say love," and her voice always broke right there, "is a burning thing, that it makes a fiery ring." Above our heads, the Canadian singer's voice billowed, "and the flames went higher." Beneath, deep near my heartbeat, I heard the bewail of my daughter's voice, insisting on protest, "Oh, but I know love as a caging thing…" A few feet away on the stage, the Canadian singer added a Johnny Cash quaver to his voice, but inside I cracked across new and familiar fault lines. Now I lived across the country. In two months, one twin would live looking to ruby mountains west of Denver, the other looking east to the Superstition Mountains in Arizona. By the next season, we may have lives that are not recognizable to each other.

Out in the street after the show, it was still light, though it was half past ten. In the twilight, a red Ferrari approached from a side street, glowing like gold teeth. In this town, it could only be one person: Anton Leir.

twelve

Where, and Nowhere

NO ONE HAS PRAYED AS HARD as I have to be some-where. But nowhere is the place I am. Now that my furniture has arrived—inconveniently on the first day of my new job, inconveniently on the one day I overlapped with the outgoing editor—I cannot find one useful thing. Not even my daughter, whom I've had to send back to Albuquerque temporarily to see her father for Father's Day (or her boyfriend, the one actually meeting her at the airport). Where are the implements that make my life function? Where is the key to the office where I will work? Where will my son go to college? While I had waited all day for a bed and a cof-feemaker, my son had told me he wasn't sure he would actually go to ASU orientation Friday and that I was "toxic" for asking why.

After the moving van emptied its contents into my now-tiny loft apartment, I zoomed up the Northway to downtown Saratoga, where the outgoing editor gave me a reluctant tour. The outgoing editor was a real person named Maria, who guided me through a wild ride through the messy office stacked with maga-zines, walls lined with pen-and-ink etchings of jockeys and horses at the Saratoga track. "Horses, health, and history," Maria chirped, "that's what this town is about." She mentioned the original springs were just steps away from the office, then she stood there and dithered about whether it was best for me to take her office, which was filled to the brim, or her husband's, which was nearly empty except for a '90s-era desk phone. They had sold the magazine to Anton Leir in December, so it was unclear to me why this was a debate. This felt like the same drag I got from Regan, who had sold her brand to someone else and called it an act of "murder." By my count, at least four people thought they owned the place: Maria and her husband; Regan; Anton Leir, who'd actually paid for it; and the consultants who had hired me.

Even as that afternoon Maria was ushering me in as the new editor, Regan was furiously promoting all over her social media a July pre-track gala at Gaffney's. Regan neglected to announce the most central fact—the splash for which I had been hired and for which we were gearing up, the new magazine, our brand with a whole new look. She never mentioned the Gaffney gala was a goodbye party for a brand no reader would find on a newsstand anywhere. After getting his first look at the books, Kenneth would notify me the next day, that for weeks now, Regan had been ordering old-brand swag by shiploads and billing it to her new benefactor, Anton Leir, who had announced to all of us in no uncertain terms he wanted to wipe her brand off the face of the map. I asked Kenneth to clarify: Didn't Anton Leir just buy her out? Shouldn't this be a time to announce the merger, rather than hand out T-shirts and champagne flutes with the old logos of a dying brand? His response: This is just silliness. Let her have her little party.

I thought he was being a man: I had already seen this woman in action, and she was draped in that gossipy mean-girl power that men dismiss. Kenneth, apparently, had never been to middle school. At forty, Regan had been practicing mean-girl power all of her life, stuffing the ballot boxes for prom queen and choosing the band's setlist so as to program the evening for her own personal romance.

Maria escorted me down the hill from Broadway to a restaurant where they frantically macheted lettuce and chopped radishes in preparation for track season. Wearing a sly smile, Maria walked me into the kitchen to meet the chef-owner and introduced me as the new editor of the magazine. This act was the kind of community building a media leader did, yet this would come back to haunt me as I was unprepared for how gossip gets twisted in a small town. What I didn't know yet was that the chef-owner's estranged husband was in a spot of financial/legal trouble, so my wandering into her kitchen by the escort of the outgoing editor, who somehow was a threat to Nerilla, had upset every advertiser in town within hours of my setting foot in the kitchen. It launched an instant whispering campaign, and Nerilla had fired off a scalding text to Anton Leir before I even returned to the office.

Again, Maria flashed her fox smile as we walked to High Rock Park, where spring-water fountains stood, ornate in their bone-white cisterns. So much she was telling me and at once not telling me. Back at the office, she leaned to the magazine rack and untwisted a rubber band from the metal caging. Then Maria sloshed a trail of gasoline around the perimeter of the cabin, lit a match, and ran into the cover of the forest. No, not really. She pressed a fat key into my palm. "I guess you need this," she said like a key to the office was optional. Before I could ask where the bathrooms were, she ran off down the hall. "There's an intern, by the way," she mentioned. "She might help."

REGAN AND NERILLA WERE DISPLEASED. To be precise, Regan and Nerilla were having a fit. Nerilla held her phone in that precious me-and-my-phone stance that millennials have perfected—part amulet bewitched with superpowers that could overwhelm onlookers into the spell of you, part locked-and-loaded semi-automatic weapon. Wearing a pout she believed she'd perfected as sexy, she smacked her thumbs at the keyboard, tapping out a tirade of protest about the magazine design. Never mind that I had just presented the fact that Anton Leir signed off on it—

that had happened during the Great Car Wash last week. I looked across at Nerilla in her bubble, seeming unaware that someone who was her supervisor and had the ear of people who paid her was witnessing her naked aggression. This was my first day as editor of the magazine.

Nerilla's texting had roused Anton Leir and now a meeting was afoot for Tuesday. They were not inviting me.

I, the new editor-in-chief, stood. "Where are we meeting?"

Salt & Char, naturally.

NOWHERE WAS THE PLACE that the outgoing editor had parked incoming stories and photos. Nowhere was the place she put the contact list of writers before she tossed me the key. Nowhere also is the place Regan had put the stories her closing-down brand would contribute to our track issue. Actual photos and captions and stories were nowhere to be found.

The first night alone in my loft apartment, empty of Grace and full of boxes, the same disorientation and displacement pervaded. Boxes of things I had not needed for twenty-five years were in the most accessible places, and boxes of things I actually needed every day, such as a coffeemaker or a fork, were nowhere. Not one box presented itself as a recognizable candidate for these useful things. I had a total of seven utensils—three forks, two knives, three spoons—and only because these stray utensils did not get packed with the official utensil drawer. They had been stowaways who hopped on this ship by hiding out in the dishwasher and tagging along to a last-minute box. The coffeemaker also was absent without leave. I was reminded of a joke Deborah had told me early and often: The worst part about being cast out of the Garden of Eden was not that Adam had to work and Eve had to endure the pain of childbirth. It was that they had to move.

COME 7 A.M. SATURDAY MORNING, I will meet my friend Ella at the Sandia foothills. I will glide down the Northway to the Albany airport, and I will land in Albuquerque, where my trail is calling me. The pragmatic purpose was to complete preparations to get the house rented. The sublime purpose was the sky—I needed to see it. Fifteen days ago, I had left Albuquerque, and already I was forgetting. As I hurtled down the Northway, I felt the promise of flight. I could imagine I had velocity, the air rushing beneath me. I could convince myself that this pale blue slit of sky would open up for me. I would split the cumuli. As cloud-mists rolled over the wings of plane, the land beneath would trundle westward, first green and dense, forested and dotted with silver ponds; then golden, windswept and fearless; until finally, it would rise, blue, rugged and majestic. I would retrace my steps. Somewhere out there, beyond this, was that place.

Here was the plan: I'd land in Albuquerque about 11 p.m. I'd rent a car and drive to my almost-emptied house and sleep there. In the morning, I'd get my Sandia foothills hike, and after that I could face the rest of the weekend, when Sad Auction Lady would arrive for part two. I would prepare the twins' rooms to be painted. Grace would meet me Saturday afternoon, and we'd pack the rest of her belongings, which would go to her father's house until she headed to college.

A week ago, back in Saratoga Springs, we'd worked out the plan. "It's very important," I had told Grace as we sat on the sofa in The Lofts, crowded by boxes that were coming.

"Will you help me pack my room?" she said in a plaintive voice. So many not-yet-packed boxes awaited in Albuquerque, the boxes that were going.

"Of course, honey," I had said.

But when I called Grace from my layover, she didn't answer. I left a message, suggesting 1 p.m., when Sad Auction Lady surely will have wrapped up, late enough that Grace could sleep in.

Arriving to the Albuquerque airport, I did what I usually did. I clacked my heels over the red tiles, headed to the escalators, grabbed my luggage and walked out to the shuttle to airport parking, grateful to see the yellow bus approaching the curb, materializing behind the fizzing white-yellow headlights. I lurched toward it, and then I realized...my Prius is in New York. It was not in the Airport Parking shuttle lot, uncovered, Row F. I don't live here anymore. I needed to head to the rental car lot, a place I'd never been.

MY HOUSE SMELLED DIFFERENT WITH NO PEOPLE. It smelled like fresh paint and dead lizard, which was what I discovered in the shower. I smiled sadly at this friendly lizard with the bright turquoise-flecked, diamond-patterned back, eighteen inches short of the drain, what surely had promised the redemption of one life-saving droplet of water.

Arriving at the trailhead for Pino Canyon, I turned back to the city as I waited for Ella. 7:24 a.m., and already 81 degrees. One hundred miles to the west, Mount Taylor stood majestically, a lighthouse holding space at the edge of what used to be a seabed. The peak appeared clean and blue, no snow. It was the hottest week of the year. The high desert morning, the air tender still, promised something that wouldn't hurt. Albuquerque's three volcanoes rose from the brown-green high desert at the edge of the lava fields. A garland of green ran through the city, hugging the Rio Grande.

Ella and I forged upward into Pino Canyon, our boots crunching in the pink sand. Ella had founded Money Tree Academy. I had met her sitting in the green grass in a circle at Camp Good Life Project in upstate New York, where, ironically, I now lived. She lived in Texas then, and now she lived in Albuquerque.

"It's an adjustment, I won't lie," I told her as we followed the torquing trail deeper into Pino Canyon. Above us loomed maroon ridges of high pines. We wouldn't get that far today.

"They're testing you," she said. "It's an East Coast thing, ritual aggression. We don't do that in the West."

"I see that," I said. "I am odd to them. I'm not used to posturing for position. I had attained position. I am authentic, and that is weird to them, especially the younger women."

"This is a financial game changer for your family," she said.

Yes. That was the why. It would be hard in the short term, but it would pay off in the long run. My retirement would be secure, and the twins would go to college with ease. I would do this. As my boots skitzed through the gravel and sand as we climbed higher, I thought about how I loved the dry air, the open blue sky. I thought about how I loved the gentle feel of a high desert morning, how it felt precious because I knew it was fugitive. Fierce summer sun would dominate the day.

SAD AUCTION LADY DIDN'T COME AND DIDN'T COME. Four hours later, Paul texted with the news I'd awaited through three weeks of silence. He had decided to travel to Arizona State University and register for classes. Whether he'd screamed in rage at his father as he'd announced his choice or whether he'd persuaded his father in a quiet voice that he needed to be someone who went to college out of state, I don't know. The only thing I am told is that registration happened, and they were driving back today. As for the other twin, Grace didn't answer and didn't answer and didn't answer.

When at last I reached her, I was standing in her room looking at everything that needed to be packed. I didn't get "annoyed voice," for which I was grateful. With teenagers, there was an algorithm that only they knew that could reliably predict correlation between the number of times a parent had to leave a message, the number of times the teen stonewalled the message—and the level of condescension and irritation that can be applied when the teen at last gave up the fight and answered the phone. But when Grace answered, she sounded groggy and sweet and a little plaintive. "I'm in Angel Fire," she finally replied. "Can't it wait?"

No, it cannot wait was the obvious answer. Only I didn't say it. I'd said it so many times and clearly that she couldn't have forgotten or misunderstood. She'd traveled the 2,200 miles there with me, every mile, so I didn't need to explain the logistics of distance that made this challenging. She'd traveled the 2,200 miles back by plane with one layover and the attendant baggage reliability issues and threat of spending the night in Terminal K at O'Hare, so she well knew that I couldn't just beam myself from New York when she found she was in the mood to pack her room. What she was saying was that she wanted me to give her a pass. To let her check out. I would. I loved her and I would. I would dismantle her room myself, alone.

So, I entered. First I noticed the Tibetan prayer flags strung above the door frame. I turned to set my gaze on the clothesline photo displays, snapshots of blond Grace with fine wispy curls; fishing Grace, right fist raised in triumph, left hand a dangling wire with an open-mouthed trout; Grace in a yellow tutu; Grace in a green soccer uniform; teenage Grace holding up a collage that showed her ukulele, Bon-Bon's violin and hot air balloons drifting over the horizon. Strings of miniature Christmas lights dipped from the ceiling. Her room had always had the feel of enchantment, a kingdom of great delight and magical ideas. I spun in the room, my hands pinned in my pockets. What remained were the things that mattered most to her. They spoke of her history, the poster of Margot and the Nuclear So-and-Sos, the white wire peacock with ticket stubs from movies and concerts. I closed my eyes and took a deep breath.

After the furious pace of May, packing beds and bookcases

and dishes—yes, a coffeemaker that was "somewhere," silverware too—this was too meaningful to go at high speed. The clock was ticking, I had twenty-seven hours, but this would have to be done slowly. I was packing away the most precious memories of her childhood. This wasn't the way I had wanted to empty the nest. I had always envisioned that it would be something we would do someday, and together. The dismantling was the process of remembering, of preserving the memories, and it seemed wrong that I was the only one here, remembering.

As I swept from east wall to north wall to west wall, I came to the nails where Grace once wrapped green yarn to spell "Try Dying." These nail holes were bigger, standing out from the pins and thumbtacks, reminding me she'd wanted to stop trying to do any of this. Reminding me that I still needed to buoy her up. Once, she'd wanted to stop having to stay alive.

Though I didn't want to, I had to see this. I had to see the story of her whole childhood, writ on these walls, and me, erasing it. I had to see the whole story, the struggle to become, to decide who she was, to decide, even, whether to still be here. What it meant to be here if she stayed.

The last time we painted this room, for her high school years, she wanted to mirror the color blocks and vertical stripes Paul used for his room. Her color blocks were peach, French vanilla, and grape, with dark blueberry stripes. I had thought it felt light and refreshing, but Paul had called it "ice cream parlor," nearly damning it beyond redemption. Beneath these colors, the vibrant colors of middle school could be seen, teal blue, grape, turquoise, and Ella green that got her room featured in an *ABQ the Magazine* spread on cool kids' rooms. And beneath that, the elementary school years, lavender. Three layers of paint, three layers of personas. All were my daughter, and now none of them were her.

I said it out loud. "I am the only one here in a city I forgot I don't live in anymore. Grace is in Angel Fire. Paul is in Arizona." Except for Ella, my friends didn't even know I was here. Twenty-five years, and in fifteen days, there was nearly not one trace of us.

Out the window, I saw the first tinge of pink on the mountains, the heralding of the sunset. I looked up at the place I had been this morning. The city and the mountains were closing down the day with or without us. And then I realized: I had no bed to sleep on. I had taken the love seat to Goodwill , and not one of the air mattresses worked. I had an air mattress in Albuquerque but a pump in New York in a box somewhere. I called my friend Whitney. Yes, I could stay at her house. The sun set.

I ASKED PAUL IF HE WOULD HELP ME get Grace's boxes to their dad's house. He'd returned from Arizona, and so I asked about ASU orientation. He told me none of this was convenient for him, not dropping off boxes, not conversing about ASU. These businesslike words were not the words he used. The actual words were, "You're so fucking stupid, Mom."

"I'm only here for fourteen more hours," I said, hoping the practicalities could now be obvious. He reluctantly agreed.

When Paul sauntered up to the house, he was a sight for sore eyes. I resisted the urge to rush out and hug him like he was a war refugee. We played it cool.

Eyeing the boxes, Paul said, "Mom, you should make her do it. It's her responsibility. You're just enabling her." But we loaded his car and my rental car, a smoke-filled nondescript non-smoking sedan.

"You could choose to view it that way," I said. "But I'm choosing to view it through the eyes of love. I don't know why, but Grace can't do it. So I'm going to help her. I'm not going to be angry. I'm just going to do it as an act of kindness. And with everything I touch, I will touch it with love."

We unloaded Grace's boxes at their dad's. Night fell. I got on a plane.

thirteen

Please, Let Me Die in My Sleep

EVERY MORNING A SWARM OF BANSHEES was unleashed, a wailing demand for magazine world to be put in order, accompanied by a keening mean-girl lament about the presence of the consultants and the showing up of myself, all the decisions we were contracted to make. Armed with a week of data sets, I had pinpointed the unleashing of the death-to-consultants angels occurred at approximately 8:45 a.m. I calculated that this allowed me to arise at 7 a.m., shower, dress and pick up a caramel latte from Panera before I headed up the Northway to Saratoga Springs, a ten-minute drive during which the man who hired me and the man who lured me strategized on the phone about how they would calm down Regan and Nerilla so that we could get a magazine out like proper professionals.

Yet I had hope. I knew I would arrive at the High Rock office to find the intern waiting, wearing a long mane of damp, curly granola hair. Wholesome Intern was just one of the reinforcements I had called in because the first week I had been the only actual inhabitant of the magazine office. No one entering the office could have been persuaded that the magazine's biggest issue of the year was imminent. Also I had called in Actual Real Journalist, recently laid off from an Actual Real Newspaper. Kenneth offered the consultant firm's copy editor, who could work remotely from Kingston. Grace would return to Saratoga Springs tomorrow. With that, I would have a team of four.

This is better.

However.

Last week, the siege was waged against all consultants; this week, the siege was targeting me. "I imagine we'll all get a turn," Liam said on the phone. "Welcome to Saratoga." The cannons turned to me because I'd been the messenger about the cover art. The real reason: I am the editor of the magazine, and Regan is not.

Regan had signed away her magazine on the dotted line. She wanted to be editor AND she wanted to have received a half million dollars for letting Anton Leir buy her magazine. Have the cake, eat the cake, have more cake. She had been going around this small town—and believe me, I was finding out, it was small—telling everyone how much Anton Leir paid her, a bit of gossip that isn't going over well with Anton Leir. He was trying to buy the other magazine, the one that was second in the market because after having bought the No. 3 media property—Regan's—if he bought No. 2, he'd have a monopoly. To state the obvious, her blabbing about getting half a million dollars to everyone was undermining his negotiating power with No. 2. Whether she sensed she'd committed a fatal error or whether attacking the new editor had been her battle plan all along, the shell game of where's-the-story-oops-it's-nowhere continued and the attacks escalated. The lies and obfuscations mounted to a level Kenneth and Liam described, even to their battle-hardened eyes, as "shock and awe." Kenneth told me he saw it as a case of fragile egos (Regan and Nerilla) and lack of leadership (Anton Leir), but they would manage it. He'd scheduled an emergency meeting with Anton Leir.

"This is not productive," I said as I inserted the key in the lock, smiling at Wholesome Intern as I let her in. I made a beeline for my office as I told Kenneth, "It's not professional, and it's not sustainable." The magazine must go to the printer in ten days.

Kenneth promised that shortly, his boss, The Prognosticator, would come on the line, the purpose of which was to reassure me they had a sound strategy for this transition.

Shortly after I decamped, The Prognosticator called. "We understand you've made a great sacrifice to be here."

From my state of "where, and nowhere," my belongings and my family strewn across the country like the debris of a slow-moving plane crash, this seemed apt. At this moment, my toothbrush was somewhere between Chicago and Albany, perhaps flying over a coal mine in Pennsylvania. I was pleased with The Prognosticator's grasp of all facts.

"You must be in a state of shock," he continued. "I promise you, we've got your back. We will deal with this. We have a perfect understanding of it."

This will blow over. That was what all the men were saying. The consultants had presented their case against Regan, which included inferior or missing content, a parade of drama, and a host of lies, the chief of which was the monetary value of her media outlet. Based on Kenneth's market analysis, the best she had was twenty-five thousand followers, which by the standard 1:1 industry marker, translated to a media property worth $25,000. Not $500,000. Anton Leir intended to fire Regan, The Prognosticator told me. Kenneth followed up to reiterate this, detailing the case he'd made. "What Anton Leir has to do is what Anton Leir says he's going to do. This is not an absorption of Regan's brand. Her only job is to write a column and sell ads." Which she wasn't selling, Liam reported later in the day. No ads were in, just like no stories were in. It was all just a fairy tale.

And, it seemed, a parade of integrity lapses. The freelance photographer who covered the social scene called me to introduce herself, frantic that with the folding of Regan's brand into our magazine, she may be out the door. She had covered the party scene for both magazines. The first thing she dropped was that Regan told her she did not have to get names for captions. I explained to her that it was a journalistic imperative to get names for captions. The reason readers were interested in society photos was because they were interested in who's who. Later, I told this to

Liam, and though we were on the phone, I swore I could hear his eyes clacking as they rolled. That I even had to say it showed we were dealing with amateur stuff. But just to stand on solid ground, before I nailed down with the photographer that this was the editorial policy, I checked previous issues of our magazine to see what the standard had been, sent an email to double-check that with the outgoing editor, confirmed it all with Liam and Kenneth. All verifications backed this up. I told the photographer our policy was names had to be with captions or photos didn't get published. She understood what this meant: Unpublished photos were photos she didn't get paid for.

Not long after this conversation, the photographer called me back. "Regan said I didn't have to get captions."

"Regan is not the editor." I could not understand why this was not obvious to the photographer, who then went on to confess to me something I had already learned the week before. I just couldn't believe she was actually telling me. Apparently, Regan bought her a Nikon camera and lighting equipment totaling about $2,000. But, the photographer added, our agreement was that I give her childcare and drive her kids around. So, it's cool, she said.

It's definitely not cool. Another round of phone calls to Kenneth and Liam: Any knowledge of this? Did anyone from our magazine authorize this? Was Regan billing Anton Leir for this as part of his buying her magazine and absorbing her assets? Does Anton Leir know that he's paying for this but Regan's getting childcare? (And his magazine isn't owning the equipment?) Would this ever in a million years be ethical? No, no, no, no (no), and NO.

"I just keep uncovering these integrity lapses," I said to Liam on the phone as I drove to Salt & Char for another command dinner meeting with Anton Leir.

I felt Liam lean in closer to the phone, and when he spoke, his voice lowered to a confidential tone. "You have only just begun, my dear," he said. "There will be more. And more after that. From this point forward, just assume every one of these players is running some kind of game."

Before taking on the consulting work, Liam and Kenneth had performed deep market research, including a full vetting of Anton Leir's business holdings (making sure he wasn't Mafia, white-collar crime, or China white-collar crime) and romantic dealings (making sure he did not have a compromising affair or was sleeping with Nerilla). But as I stepped into the bar of Salt & Char, I was about to find out what they had not.

NERILLA ARRIVED FIRST, and at the end of the bar sat a sixty-ish man nursing a whiskey like he'd worked all his life to live that cliché. He would be joining us tonight. Nerilla already knew him as Anton Leir's business associate. He and Anton Leir had bought several Chinese companies together. But what made his wealth, and he rolled this out right away, was that he ran pharma junkets. "We would take doctors and their wives," he said, conveniently forgetting that sometimes doctors are women and have husbands, "on trips to lush resorts, and we would sell them on pharmaceuticals and medical devices." He tipped his head knowingly to Nerilla in that mansplaining way typical of his generation and his whiteness. "It was good work until the FDA shut us down." He delivered this unabashedly. After all, it wasn't illegal when he did it. Only later. To boost his pharma junket business, he founded a magazine. "It's not lobbying; it's continuing education." Nerilla nodded, believing.

Regan arrived, her phone on fire. Not literally. Just another feud. I was in Week 2, but I was already tuning this out and much more successfully than I was tuning out our president's fulminations on Twitter. So, I had to count this as a step forward in life. It became clear a coup was in the making. Regan had brought Nerilla a sheaf of papers in a crisp brown bag. She slid the pages out, and they glanced through conspiratorially even though I was standing three feet away from them. The pages were a whole new round of prototypes for the design Anton Leir signed off on last week, shortly after the Great Car Wash. From their rogue freelance designer, someone whom Nerilla met at the gym a month ago. Many thanks to an assist from Mr. Pharma Junket, I headed this off at dinner, but I had to burn some valuable capital.

Anton Leir reiterated he'd already made his decision. "Why are you bothering me with this?" he asked, then proceeded to call up a photo on his phone. The next thing I knew I was looking at a photo of a dominatrix, a sexy woman crisscrossed in black leather strips. "This is my girlfriend," he said. "What do you think? I gave her a condo in Miami."

"She's … lovely," I said.

Anton Leir passed his phone around to show her and described how she's trouble. "She's...demanding," he said with a huh-huh.

After dinner, Mr. Pharma Junket took me by the hand and announced he'd walk me to my car to make sure I got home safely. To return the favor, I drove him to the curb of his condo, the new development behind Salt & Char. I turned my face to thank him, and he planted a kiss on my mouth. I pushed him away and waited until he understood he should exit my car.

LATE THAT NIGHT, I briefed Liam on the dominatrix girlfriend in Miami. "Ah, we didn't uncover that one," he said. They had looked for a mistress, he said, because Anton Leir was married. "Married?" I said. Nothing about Anton Leir said married. He was out at Salt & Char or Max London's (which he also owned) every night with young women, often Nerilla. In this small town, this seemed like a hard thing to hide from a wife if everyone was seeing you do it.

"Where did you look for this mistress?" I asked Liam as I noted to myself that Anton Leir's business associate also was a married guy, who just happened to make a move on me.

"Apparently, we didn't look in Miami," Liam said.

A STRANGE MIX OF AGITATION and sleeplessness started to take hold. At home, I felt obligated to empty boxes and get settled. A manic surge of energy propelled me to stay up past midnight, nearly to 2 a.m., unloading boxes. Each one I emptied got tossed down the stairwell to the garage. Exhausted, I fell into bed. It occurred to me that I could pray to die in my sleep. That would be an easy way to slip away. My heart would just stop, and I wouldn't wake up. It wouldn't be my fault.

WITH GRACE'S RETURN I now had a team of Wholesome Intern and Actual Real Journalist. We were humming along. Ten hours later, I looked out into the magazine office and noticed I had a hungry daughter. Grace asked if we could go to the drive-in movie because she'd never been to one. *Wonder Woman* was playing. We positioned the car on the hump between rows, and instead of those vintage speakers hung over a cranked-open window, we listened to the movie through our iPhones. Before she became Wonder Woman, the heroine was known as Diana, princess of the Amazons, growing up on an island paradise. When she learned about the wars men had waged in the world, she decided to fight the war to end all wars. While she loomed large on the screen, becoming an unconquerable warrior, I fell asleep. On the drive back to the loft apartment, I asked Grace to just tell me the ending. "She kills the war god with his own lightning," she said.

A moonless sky appeared beyond the trees. I lay atop my mattress, my back stiff, unyielding to the comfort. Grace slept in the other room. A deep mauve light filled the apartment, holding the two of us and our dog in this loft as if in a castle tower, already split off from my son and her brother, who was so far away I could not remember his face. Though just three days ago, he was storming out of my house, calling me "fucking stupid"—because why?

Because deciding on a college and a future was hard? Because both parents had made it harder for him than it needed to be? Because I'd forgotten something or failed to do something? Like keep lettuce from going bad in the refrigerator or mice from invading a garage? I wanted to wrap my arms around my son and give him hope. But my son rather suspected any hope from me now was a lie, and I cannot hide that I'm flailing. It would be impossible now for me to kindle in his heart what was burning to ash in my own. All I could think about was that I had forgotten his complete vividness and all I wanted to remember was the way the red sandy hair of his beard was growing in, the way it looked in the desert sun.

A now-familiar thought returned in the form of a prayer: *Please, let me die in my sleep.* I lullabied myself into slumber with this wish, waves of forgetfulness lilting at the cradle of sleep. It was bliss to think that I would not have to wake up. This time, I got more explicit with God, who apparently had not heard me. "I want this. No one would question it. No one would investigate it. Please, just let this happen. Please, let me die in my sleep."

I knew my daughter was sleeping in the other room, yet I whispered these words.

NOW THE MEN ARE WORRIED. *Now* they're worried. Was I the only one among us who understood Mean Girl Power? The men wanted to take an aggressive stance on the dramatic power plays, but they had had to walk the razor's edge because Anton Leir hadn't signed the new consulting contract.

What contract? I said.

Oh, the contract that's supposed to be renewed July 1, three days from now, Kenneth was telling me. That was why negotiations with Anton Leir were delicate this morning. Before I could capture my spinning head, Kenneth reported, "Good news!" They had made a full report to Anton Leir presenting their case against Regan—the overselling of the value of her media property; the no-stories, no-ads game, which further devalued the brand she sold to Anton Leir for half a million dollars; the liability issues that her self-dealing presented for Anton Leir; the million little subterfuges that shouted her refusal to honor the foundational agreement that her brand would be eliminated from the market. "It's my brand, and I bought it to kill it," the billionaire said, but he might as well be a king named Lear proclaiming this to the wild winds of the heath.

What do you mean there's no contract? I asked. The reality I had been told was my reality—Kenneth was acting publisher, I was his new hire—was the contract. The contract that was not signed now. But must be signed in three days.

Kenneth continued with his case against Regan, the task that had consumed us. He reported victoriously—and I quote—that Anton Leir's decision was to "Fire her ass!" And, "Do it today," he had said.

OK, the troublemaker was gone. But.

I've moved across the country for people who have not even inked the deal that includes my hiring?

But no, the men weren't worried. They had *a* contract, just needed the *expanded* contract that made Kenneth acting publisher and gave him decision-making power on the financials, which was the way he viewed the distinctions. I, however, viewed it as the contract that preserved everything we agreed upon, everything for which I upended my family and for which I uprooted myself. These were the words I would use. Why hadn't Anton Leir signed off on this? If it was so obvious that he needed consultants—a team that knew how to produce media products on time, knew how to outfox the competition, knew how to build a media empire—then why hadn't he put his signature to it?

All is well, Kenneth assured me, but it was clear he was grateful to have wrested this decision from Anton Leir to fire Regan.

He had told Anton Leir, who had never owned a media property before, "We're performing many miracles here."

MIRACLES, YES. The news that we were standing at the cliff's edge of contractlessness landed as all the normal producing-a-magazine and relocating-my-life events unfolded. The horse racing writer called, frantic that as the new editor, I wouldn't quite understand how esteemed he is. But he was another Actual Real Journalist, and that was evident two seconds into the conversation. His pitch involved an interview with the owner of the Preakness winner, which was trained here. As was the norm among journalists, we had extended family in common. The longtime horse racing writer for my hometown paper was someone we both knew. He was late pitching, his copy would be late, but it would be locked and loaded, ready to roll. I was not worried. Meanwhile, the reports from my handyman and painter in Albuquerque were that the faucets didn't work, the shower leaked, front-door latch was bad, and there was a "bad spot on the roof." Normal, normal, all will pass.

What was not normal was that out of the blue, Nerilla called to say she was bringing the architect to the magazine office. I paused. Seven official business days into this job, I'd already gotten used to the normal that Nerilla, though she was advertising director, never showed up to the office. I had had to insist that meetings take place at our offices, not Regan's old, brand-being-bought-out offices on Broadway. We were now being graced with Nerilla's appearance because the architect wanted to talk about the new offices to which we would move in the fall. The distant, long-time-after-the-track-issue fall when the leaves turn bronze and the days grow shorter and I would try to recall this summer I'm not having.

And yet Nerilla had arrived, in unsweated-on fashion work-out wear, I noted. We met to talk about office dimensions, which included big offices for Nerilla and Regan, who did not yet know she was fired. Nerilla flirted with said architect, suggesting he would be just the right kind of manly to build a brick patio at her personal apartment. Discussions about supple slope and hard stone happened suggestively in front of me, and then Nerilla convinced the architect that in addition to the magazine-office remodel, he must come to her personal apartment this very afternoon to prepare the landscaping bid. I was guessing this meant she would not be out selling ads on this lovely Tuesday afternoon. After they left, Grace looked up from her desk and asked me, "Is she going to sleep with him?"

I watched Nerilla and the architect walk the long corridor to the parking lot, and I didn't answer my daughter's question. Instead, I remembered that it was 2:30 in the afternoon and I had barely eaten breakfast, much less the lunch Grace brought back from her restaurant review. Grace reminded me there was a park outside. "You should at least take ten minutes," she said.

GRACE AND I STEPPED TO THE FOUNTAIN in the center of the gazebo, and I held out my paper cup. The spout had oxidized in the sun, the lip rusted, the opening encrusted with minerals. I tipped the cup to my mouth, and in glided the purest water I had ever tasted. I had expected it to taste like sulfur like a rotten egg had slipped down my throat, lining my mouth with yellow dust. But it didn't. The spring water tasted like silver, shiny and refined, something that would protect me. It glided deeper into me, lining me like satin, something that felt striking and definite and bracing, something that saw the world more clearly than I did. As Grace walked the perimeter, checking the other fountains, I filled my cup a second time.

STILL NO MOON, SAME PRAYER. Grace and our little dog slept in the other room. Though we were across the country, in a loft amid the high pines, this was a modicum of how I had slept through the night for seventeen years. One twin was here, and where her heart beats, he is also. I had put young ones and pets to bed. I had put a house to sleep. A dome of light shone over the silver sink, hope placed at the outer frontier of the next day. All these years, I could attune myself to the breath of a living home, and this smooth silence was it. When they were not here, the sound was hollow. A different kind of quiet.

If I died in my sleep, my daughter would have to find me. She would have to call someone. I asked God if I could die in my sleep but not until next week when she returned to Albuquerque. It could happen then. So she wouldn't have to see it. My death would be abstract to her.

THROUGH FOURTH OF JULY WEEKEND we worked, Wholesome Intern, Actual Real Journalist, Stickler Copy Editor in Kingston, Designer in Providence, Real Daughter, and myself. Though Regan had tried to exert final sign-off rights on all copy, photos, and ads, she strangely disappeared for the long weekend, announcing that her husband was on a business trip to China, which meant she had all four kids solo. Nerilla disappeared to Lake George for the weekend, leaving Liam to hunt down her ads. Despite the madness, Grace insisted on being my stress break, making me take her to the National Museum of Dance on Saturday, then Lake George on Sunday. On Monday, Anton Leir came down to the magazine office to sign off on my editor's letter and the cover design. I sang the praises of my assembled team, Wholesome Intern, Actual Real Journalist, and Real Daughter. "Only one hiring decision I've ever made didn't work out," he said. "My own daughter." This Anton Leir was more subdued than the Anton Leir holding court at Salt & Char, hehe-ing about the idiocy of our billionaire president (but he's *our* useful idiot was the good-ole-boy tone) and the untamability of his Miami mistress. This Anton Leir was regretful.

GRACE AND I MADE LIME-BASIL ICE CREAM. While we waited for the ice cream maker to churn, she asked me if I wanted to play Fireboy and Watergirl. A red-clad boy with flame hair must work with a water-droplet girl to navigate a course of pulleys and lasers. Fireboy could walk across hot lava, but Watergirl melted. Watergirl could glide across water, but Fireboy turned to ash. So they had to help each other, turning prisms to direct light beams to open doors for each other. To make Watergirl move around, I used W, A, S, D. Grace used the arrow keys to move Fireboy. We must both avoid the green puddles of phosphorus. "We have to help each other, see?" she said.

fourteen

Don't You Know How to Hit Send?

I AM LOCKED OUT. We planned to work through the Fourth of July because we needed to send the magazine to the printer in two days. Great idea, unless you're locked out of your own office. Wholesome Intern and I decided to adopt Kru Coffee for the day.

A source for a Regan-pitched story called to say she had "only a few changes" to the article. When I opened the document, I saw she had completely rewritten the writer's work to spin it in the best possible light for her husband's equine business. It had become a puff piece, and the writer was completely violated. The source had rewritten the story. I died inside. But Kenneth said we'd entered new territory, and for the time being, we should just placate and send her a proof. When I called the designer in Providence to request she send it to the source, we decided to just roll over and die.

"That would be easier," I said.

"I agree," she said.

The next call came from a "freelance writer," again one we inherited from Regan's play-to-be-paid world because she just happened also to be an advertiser. Perhaps you noticed the quote marks around "freelance writer." That's because she was Not An Actual Real Journalist. She had written a piece that appeared in a sequence of stories packaged as objective recommendations but just happened to mention her business several times without mentioning any competing businesses as options for sourcing the same product. She was not representing the public; she was representing her self-interested self. She demanded to see a page proof, so she could approve the story.

My jaw dropped, which prevented me from allowing my mouth to move and words to form so that I could explain the most fundamental difference between advertising and journalism. Advertisers paid for space, and, therefore, got to approve content. On the other side of the firewall, journalism rose above all the self-dealing and was objective, fair, and independent, and if obligated to anyone, it was the public. To everyone. Not just special someones. Not just the comfortable. Sources didn't approve content. They were contacted to verify accuracy. That's all they got.

Naturally, we got pushed on this all the time at the *Albuquerque Journal* and every other newspaper for which I worked or consulted. People would always push it to see how far they could go. What so few people understood, in the era when a narcissistic demagogue had stolen the White House and called anything that didn't worship him "fake news," was how many times every day in every way we got pushed.

And how many times we resisted. We resisted and we resisted. We were the leading edge of Resistance. We had arrived to the cause centuries before 2016 happened, and we were trench-tested. We weren't the "enemy of the people"—we were the best friend of democracy. Transparency. Trust. We were the reason people knew injustice when they saw it. When we exposed it, throngs gathered at memorials and murals for the unjustly killed, at airports like JFK for the unjustly banned, squares like Independence Square in Kyiv, in Minneapolis and Prague and Hong Kong and Warsaw, and on and on about revolutions orange and velvet and every other color and texture. When you knew you couldn't breathe anymore, we were the ones who showed that to the world. We were the friend of the full light of the truth, whatever it may reveal. Knee to the neck, sniper bullet to the heart. We were the friend of our best chance at a shared, collective truth, something that made democracies thrive, and we were the friend of evolving, enlightened and educated minds, the path to being better. We'd resisted for years, resisted every day—we were good at resistance. If you want to be battle-tested for integrity, become a journalist. Because everyone wanted you to be their mouthpiece and tell their truth and their truth only. I had the shrapnel lodged in my flesh to prove it. I believed in democracy and the First Amendment. I would die for God. I would die for my children. And I would die for the First Amendment.

Before I died on this hill, I would have to make sure it was the same for Kenneth because he was my boss. He told me this was wrong on every level, but the magazine needed to go to print in two days, and we would clean up all the Regan integrity violations in good time because we were firing her. He took the long view that we would win in the end, that we could not storm the square today. Ironically, we were having this conversation with me in Saratoga, where Gen. George Washington won one of the most decisive battles of the Revolutionary War, and Kenneth in Kingston, where the British took out their huge losses in the battle of Saratoga by burning the place. But, alas, for the history of democracy, with the source who had rewritten our freelance writer's story, we decided to just move on, cut our losses. With the advertiser who also was a paid writer, we decided to humor her.

But on the phone to her, when I explained that when we had the proof, we'd send it, but going forward, all policies would be redefined and all freelance contracts renegotiated bec— she broke in with, "Don't you know how to hit send?"

This woman was speaking to me like I was a Luddite or a toddler. Perhaps I was so deficient in technological matters that I didn't know where the send button was on my email. Which was the way millennials treat baby boomers and the elderly as though not one single old person had figured out this newfangled technology and we were all befuddled, even people like me who had led the technological revolution from the front lines.

Or perhaps I was willful, like a toddler, and I didn't want to hit send. You couldn't make me hit send. Send was a big meanie. Send was hiding in the closet, and I was alone in the dark. I wanted Send to go away. I did not like Send, and for that matter, I didn't think Send liked me. You couldn't make me like Send any more than green eggs and ham.

Or perhaps I didn't want to send it to her because it was clear to me she was self-dealing, an advertiser getting paid to write about herself and make herself look good.

Or perhaps I didn't want to send because she was entitled, and I was astonished at the way the rich presumed that the rest of the world was the hired help. Perhaps I needed a minute to absorb the fact that this was the community in which I was living. Perhaps I needed just a minute to understand I had left the country of meritocracy and arrived at plutocracy, where nothing was trickling down, just expectations of obsequience. I was not living in the territory of the equality of ideas. I was living in the territory where if you had money, you didn't have to have an idea or a talent. You asked and expected and demanded.

Perhaps it was not me who was the toddler. Perhaps this "don't you know how to hit send?" woman was the toddler, and I just heard a temper tantrum.

I took a time out.

I listened to the grinding of Kru coffee beans. I listened to the whirring of milk into a frothy Kru foam. I wondered if I should order a nitro latte.

Or perhaps I was here, a foreigner in a foreign land because I didn't know how to hit send. I didn't know how to send off my two children to a college far away. I didn't know how to send them into adulthood where they didn't need me or want me and I didn't know where to send myself.

So, I sent myself here. Oh please, let me die in my sleep.

I TOLD LIAM that I had been wishing for secret release and cursing that it would not come.

"If you die in your sleep, I will kill you," he said.

"That has no effect on me," I said, "because if I have already died, I won't feel it when you kill me."

I went on to say that perhaps I could just stop taking care of myself, hasten things toward a faster end.

"If leaving is what you want," he said, "I'm here to tell that *that* is a very slow plan. I have not been taking care of myself for sixty years, and look where that's gotten me. I'm still here."

I WOULD TRY A WELCOMING PRAYER. I knew this worked for the "afflictive experience," a really nice word for totally fucked. You are to turn to this practice when, as the Buddhists gently name it, "you experience being unseated." Welcoming Prayer may bear resemblance to Buddhist practices but was developed by a protege of Thomas Keating, one of the principal developers of the contemplative Christian practice of centering prayer. I knew all this, yet when I took a contemplative seat in the loft and I tried to embody the physical sensation of the upset, I could not sit. I wanted to spring from the floor. This wasn't about noticing my right hand tingling or a flutter in my stomach and gently saying, "Welcome, fear." This was my heart racing and my feet batting against my crisscross-applesauce calves like I was trapped in a cage. In Welcoming Prayer, you were supposed to let go, reciting, "I let go of my desire for security and survival. I let go of my desire for esteem and—"

I did not want to meditate. I wanted to stalk a hill and plant a flag on it.

It was time for music. Tonight was Irish acoustic jam night at the Inn at Saratoga. I would drown the afflictive experience in the fiddles and bodhrans of other people's sorrowful songs. I gathered my keys and jogged down the steps to my car.

A BAND CALLED DRANK THE GOLD hosted jam night, gathering around a long table. The song leader with the tweed beret called out the tune, not so much with a word but an utterance. The fiddler tipped her instrument lightly to her chin, tucked her head down, and pulled a sweet melody from the strings. Their eyes connected, the guitar hummed beneath her, and they swooped into the song. She arrived at a section of melody that trickled like water from a rock. Her eyes clicked to those of three other fiddlers, and they joined in at the chorus, bringing the accordion and bouzouki with them. The music built to a joyful pitch.

In the distance, not high above the trees, fireworks bloomed. Here, a British general surrendered his entire army to the patriots. Here, a British general did not succeed in dividing the New England colonies from the southern colonies. Here, allies in France and Spain jumped to our aid. I was reminded distantly of the country I once knew, the one where a man became president because he told the truth. He did chop down the cherry tree. Whether that story in and of itself is myth or truth, it was what formed my ideas about the country I loved and am struggling to love still. Out on the porch of the Inn at Saratoga, buntings of red, white, and blue dressed the railings. The lights bursting in the sky seemed more to the scale of the original patriots, more like spark than burst.

fifteen

This Side of the Rainbow

MY SON WAS CALLING. It would be 6 a.m. in Albuquerque. A full picture bloomed in my mind. He would be standing at the door, waiting for the roofers. And his key would not work. The locks.

"House locked," he said. "Can't get in."

My son was locked out of our house. I was 2,200 miles away and I was locked out of my house. I didn't have the key to my own house. I may own a house to which I have no possible way to enter. A handyman I barely knew had changed the locks, hadn't told me he was changing the locks, and hadn't given me the key. My house had been stolen. I was not in Albuquerque and I could not see my house, so in my mind *poof* gone! The place where I raised my children, the real estate that was one of my biggest financial assets, suddenly, no access.

Of course, my house was not stolen. I owned it on paper. I just couldn't enter. My own property. And the crisis of my son standing at the door of his own property, no longer able to enter, cast out of the nest. I stood in my office in Saratoga, and he stood at the door where when he was ten he demonstrated a karate kick and broke the doorbell.

"I've got to get to work," he said. *I can't be bothered with this,* I heard, what I'd been hearing all spring and summer.

"Hold on, let me make some calls," I said.

"This is *your* problem," he said.

I pleaded, "Give me a second." I'd have to call the handyman to find out what the hell happened. And the roofers, who would be arriving any minute. Paul threatened to walk away that second.

"Are the roofers there yet?" I asked, hoping he would let me talk to them.

"Nope. New doorbell, though." Paul chuckled a little.

The roofers called to say they'd be fifteen minutes late. I reported this to Paul, who insisted it was impossible for him to wait, though that was the purpose for his being there.

"I can't let them in anyway," he said. "Key doesn't work."

The handyman didn't answer. I had to leave a voice mail. My blood pressure rocketed. This could be real. I could have just gotten scammed out of my own house. With the extra touch of my teenage son's commentary about how ridiculous I was that I could not manage a key, a handyman, and a roofer from 2,200 miles away by phone.

Two minutes later, the handyman called. "It's in the lockbox," he said and gave me the code. When he heard the alarm—no, borderline outrage—in my voice, he added, "I was going to tell you. I just figured you could get into the house through your garage-door opener."

"I don't have a garage-door opener," I said flatly. "That was my only entry into the house." I hoped he could read between the lines. I kept hoping someone would see how fragile all of this was. Every day, a lockout, first the office, now my house. Every day, the searching for useful things and the finding of many useless things. Every day, someone hysterical about a word change or a photo placement. Every day, a storm of demands that someone be fired.

The handyman offered a vague apology. Terror still thundered through my heart. But I'd be seeing him Friday at the house when I returned to Albuquerque to make sure he'd done all the work. And the roofers were on the way with no way to get in if Paul had turned from the door and driven off. I gave the handyman a terse, "See you at the house 9 a.m. Friday," and called Paul. I explained how he could get the key.

"I'm not there," he said. "I'm driving to work."

"No, Paul," I pleaded, "the roofers say they'll be there any second if you can just wait for a bit longer. And now we know where the key is."

He hung up.

I called him back. He didn't answer.

I called him one more time. He wouldn't answer.

I called again. He answered. "Mom, this is your mess."

"Just—" I pleaded that I need him to do just this one thing, be a pioneer family on the prairie and do his part. I reminded him he had agreed to it and arranged to go in later to work. Waiting a few more minutes wouldn't put him out as much as he thought it would. "I need your help, honey."

THIS WAS THE DAY IT WOULD ALL GET BETTER. I was sending off the final signature of the magazine, and this pounding horror would be over. All the years in the newspaper business, I had held myself calm amid the storm because I knew that once there was a product, it was over. Everything we did, everything we didn't do, all the crazy stuff we said, over. And a real, live magazine in our hands. In the end, all the words and photos and people cooperated. I had always had faith in this. I got Anton Leir's final sign-off on my editor's letter, and I handed off the contributor page to Maria and Actual Real Journalist, giving the instruction that when the last detail was in place, they could hit send (because we know how to hit send!). I dropped Snowflake off at the kennel and headed to Albany, where I would board the bus to JFK.

One small snag: it turned out the bus station lived under a freeway bridge and I needed cash or check *only* to pay for parking. In a cashless economy, I feared I carried neither of those two things, and my final house-prep expedition would all fall apart on the lack of a dime. Who used cash to pay for parking? Who carried a checkbook? Who stuffed money in yellow envelopes? I dug from the bottomlands of my bag and started stuffing change in the slot. I scrambled to catch the bus.

ON SUNDAY, MY EX-HUSBAND DROVE UP. Before he could approach the sidewalk to my door, I met him in front of the garage. As I stood in front of my bald yard and hollow shell of a house, I realized why he had shown up. He was dropping off the last child-support check. The twins would be eighteen by the end of this month, and that would be the end of court-ordered custody. The check was arriving early, personally delivered. This was not a kindness.

I didn't feel relief. I felt alarm. I had asked him to mail it to Saratoga Springs, so no need to show up in person. Yet no more would he take me to court seeking to reduce the amount, something he had done five times and most recently as just six months ago, when the twins were seventeen and a half. What will he do if he doesn't have this axe to grind? How will I feel when that stops happening?

The fact that he was showing up here was an announcement that he wanted to be done too. So, a peace offering. I'd take it. I was ready, I'd been waiting. Peace, brother. Everybody get together, try to love one another right now. Peace, love, and understanding.

I took the check. "I guess this is the last time we'll see each other," I said, thinking, well, come on, let's have closure. Let's try to remember the most sacred thing that happened here. We raised two children. They're beautiful and they're smart and they're kind.

"Oh, I'm sure we'll be seeing each other," he said, dour and gloomy.

No, let me burst that bubble. I'm a gone girl. I'm going to be living 2,200 miles away from you. That job is going to get better. And it's all going to be okay. I'm probably only seeing you at

Grace's wedding, then Paul's wedding. That will be about it. You won't be seeing me. I will be living on the other side of the country. The other fucking side of the country. A place dense of woods and small of sky.

I was perplexed at the imperviousness to understanding, but at the same time, I was neutral. If I saw him, I'd remember we did this beautiful thing together. If I didn't, I wouldn't have to feel the dissonance anymore. But he was not neutral—that was clear from the glassy-eyed look. I took one step back and assessed him. I looked to his eyes, but they were downcast, staring at the concrete driveway. I followed his gaze, where I noticed a tiny red block from a board game, probably Risk, one more thing that has spilled out of the two childhood stories that never quite got on this page. I turned back to the house, once the source of all exuberance. This structure would always hold this, everything they were becoming.

This man had loved our two children in his own way. They loved aspects of him that I once saw and now no longer see. I had held that image of him for the children, even when it was dissonant. I held what I remembered about him and loved about him even as angry reality thunder-clashed right before my eyes, threatening to crush me.

Now he was handing me the last check, early, and he had chosen to do it face-to-face. Apparently, his reason wasn't emotional closure. He whipped out a paper. The paper informed me that, in his opinion, I ought to be paying $3,700 more than half of Paul's college tuition. On the next sheet, in his handwriting, were numbers that showed I ought to pay $4,700 more than half of Grace's tuition. He had calculated that I should be contributing $8,400 more than he would, and that did not count the $6,800 more per year I would continue paying for health insurance, auto insurance, and cell phones. That added up to me paying $15,200 more than he did, every year for four years.

This man was presenting me with a bill for $60,800.

"I don't think those calculations are accurate," I said.

He repeated the whole spiel, pointing a finger to each amount on his handwritten list of figures, one by one. "You see here, this is what I pay," he said. "This is what you pay. Here's the extra. That's what you pay."

"Again, these numbers aren't even accurate," I said. "There's the WUE tuition discount and a scholarship to factor in. It's pointless to have this conversation."

He wound up the spiel again. The finger pointed to the top amount, slid down to the second, landed on the extra amount I should pay, in his mind.

"Did you hear what I just said?" I broke in. "It's pointless to talk about this without accurate numbers. Where did you get these?"

And he began again.

The next time, I broke in to tell him he could get the accurate numbers by logging into the ASU and CU Denver accounts. If the WUE discounts and scholarships hadn't been applied, we needed to call. "I'm happy to have the conversation with you when we can start it with accurate numbers from an official source."

He looked confused.

He turned to the papers again. They were just his scribblings taken to UPS and photocopied so he could propose them to me today. I noted that he'd gone to an awful lot of trouble to be standing here in my driveway.

"You see here, it shows this is the extra amount that you pay," he said.

"We're not communicating, are we?"

But I took the paper from him.

Plenty has been written in the magazines and self-help books that were my stock in trade about what makes a marriage salvageable. What makes a marriage unbearable is when you cannot be heard. "You don't hear me when I speak in an even tone. You don't hear me when I raise my voice," I said once as he held our nine-month-old daughter in his arms. "You don't hear me when I whisper. You. Don't. Hear me." Grace was a baby who couldn't walk yet and had yet to say her first words. But the look on her face was wondrous. She saw fierceness. I heard a little, "You go, girl!" I'd begged to understand what it was, made the case for trying harder. So much had been at stake.

I returned inside my house, back to the mad shedding and shredding. I reminded myself that the best criticism of the bad was the better. The twins would turn eighteen in three weeks, and they were the evidence of living better.

I kept the paper he brought me. It seemed like an artifact.

I SAVED THE BLACKBOARD FOR LAST. I stood before the Eiffel Tower that stretched from floor to ceiling. The year my mother was dying, I had climbed a ladder, so I could draw the intricate scaffolding for her because she had always wanted to go to Paris. Musical notes and lyrics and poems unfurled across the wall. "Life is a splendid torch," a quote from George Bernard Shaw, arced in orange and pink chalk. This had been our Mother's Day card to Bon-Bon on what we knew would be her last. We had brought the espresso-bean leather stools out into the garage and Skyped with her. The three of us had carved out sections of the wall and worked it all of a Saturday, across a 9-foot-by-21-foot space. "We wanted to give you the *biggest Mother's Day card ever!*" we said in a chorus. She was growing tired and short of breath. Just a few weeks before, her weight had dropped to seventy-six pounds. "She cannot lose more than that," April had said, her way of telling me to rush to our mother's side. We had sat with Bon-Bon on her sunporch as dogwoods and redbuds bloomed, and she had narrated the story of her sheet music, 1950s show tunes and Chopin preludes and Beethoven sonatas, annotated with fingering notes, page-turn indicators, and recording dates.

Now I stood before the blackboard, my sponge soaked from the bucket. I pressed water to the chalk, watching dust dissolve from the wall. I wiped the length of it in a fan-shaped pattern. I ran over it six times.

OUT ON THE HILL, I stood with a glass of pinot grigio and saw a monsoon had rolled through the desert and bruised the clouds with purple light. Below me lay a tiny house where a family had once lived. A rainbow materialized like the glass rim of a fractal, its twin reversed, fainter. A rainbow is an experiment in super attenuation. Sunlight always holds all colors but because it moves at the speed of light, we don't see. When it passes through water, it slows enough to bend. Raindrops hold light in a suspended state, forming an arc across the sky. Each hue refracts differently. Only when we slow down can we truly see.

Just as I was about to unfasten my eyes from the horizon, the rainbow shifted to a strange glow, bands of lime green and violet that I could nearly slip my hand through. For too many years, I'd asked Who this God was who would threaten the lives of two innocents and keep us so fragile. Now a luminous truth spilled from the sky.

I understood now I may have made a mistake. That was why it had always felt like a mistake. My mistake was I belonged here. I understood I had a mission to go to New York and work hard and save money and take care of the future of the two people I loved most in this world. I understood I'd chosen this duty. So I would do it.

But I also understood I was taken care of before and would be taken care of again.

I prayed: And so it is. I promise I'll go work for four years. Then I'll be back one day. I whispered words to God. I understand now. I hear you. I belong to this land, this sky, this light.

Love understands this. Love loves me beyond this. Love will keep me here.

I poured a few drops of pinot grigio into the sand as an offering. I walked through the sand and sagebrush to my car, and I drove to the airport.

sixteen

By the Blue Light

KENNETH WAS CALLING ME. I was on a bus four miles from Albany and poised to return to the office and begin the new era, next stories, next issue, no Regan. I'd published a track issue. The second I got settled at the office in Saratoga Springs, I'd set up the story meeting for the fall issue. We were beyond.

"It's great to hear from you, and I'm ready to—" I started, but something in his silence told me to curb it.

"I spoke with Anton Leir," he said, and it flashed through my mind that he was not going to tell me that Regan was fired. He was going to tell me I was. "He's advised me to go ahead with the separation process."

I heard the rest of this and I didn't. Kenneth was still talking, and his voice was coming through the phone, but the voice I actually heard was the voice of a wise and nurturing Holy Angel, who whispered in a soothing and yet firm voice. "You are going to be fine." By the end of what was being said, Kenneth had explained that Anton Leir intended to "make me whole." I caught that part. The billionaire would do the fair and right thing. Kenneth may or may not have explained that Anton Leir had refused to sign the new contract with the consultants, and he may or may not have elaborated on the wide-ranging impact on him, The Prognosticator, and Liam. What Kenneth did make clear was that I no longer needed to report to the magazine offices.

I felt panic and relief. Panic like a wildfire. Relief because this put me out of my agony. I felt alarm. I also felt numb. This could not be happening. Just then, the bus braked to a squealy stop under the bridge where my car was parked.

A FEW FAMILIAR THINGS EXTENDED THEMSELVES TO ME as stepping stones in these first few minutes after being summarily fired. The first was that my Prius was waiting and not towed. I loaded my luggage in the exact same car I had driven all the way to Palomar Mountain to the Grand Canyon to Bonner Springs to this place. The luggage was the same, the trunk was the same, and the motion of lifting and twisting was the same. The second familiar thing was that I retraced my route to the kennel, where I greeted Snowflake, who was overjoyed to see me. As she and I exited the kennel, my Manhattan author client Trish called, responding to my message seeking a referral to a New York employment lawyer, someone who would make sure they "make me whole."

"I'm happy to give you lawyer names," she said, "but the first thing I want you to do is take care of yourself."

Therein lay the true problem.

"You don't need to solve this problem right away," she continued. "You're going to solve it better if you just take time to relax and soothe yourself. This is a time to meditate and reflect, calm your senses. Can you go for a walk? A swim?"

Nonsense. Who gets fired and then just goes for a swim like that didn't just happ—

Snowflake ran out ahead of me with her retractable leash, which was not locked. An SUV was backing up in the tiny gravel parking lot. She was only a foot away from being crushed under the wheels, and I couldn't tug her back with the leash. "Stop! Snowflake, stop!!!" Alarm flooded my body to the tips of my fingers. The SUV stopped, hearing my desperate screams through the tinted window. I locked Snowflake's leash and yanked her away from danger.

I gathered Snowflake in my arms, still on the phone with Trish, who had just heard what happened. My hysteria only confirmed for her that this needed to be a restorative afternoon. Trish was an integrative physician and a gentle soul, but she was firm about this. Trish's book was about using integrative practices to activate the healing power of the present moment, and it was inspired by the first lines of the Rumi poem "At the Guest House." As she spoke to me, I heard the first lines, "This being human is a guest house/ Every morning a new arrival." When we surrender to Life's daily offering of grace, we have the antidote to the stress that's at the root of all disease. Working on her book proposal, that all seemed logical at the time. Now it seemed untethered from reality, no matter that she served on one of the early National Institutes of Health panels on alternative medicine in the 1990s to develop the body-mind component in national treatment protocols, working with, among others, Dr. Larry Dossey, whose research affirmed the medicinal power of prayer. "A joy, a depression, a meanness/ some momentary awareness comes/as an unexpected visitor/ Welcome and entertain them all!" the poem continued. No way, I wanted to say to this unexpected visitor. Out with you! And taking a swim? This was what Trish was advising? Self-care, a true agony. But then I realized I lived in a loft apartment with an indoor swimming pool empty of people during the day, especially a Tuesday afternoon.

"There is wisdom in this, only you won't see it until later," Trish said. "I'll see it for you. We need each other." As she made her case, I recalled the next lines of the Rumi poem: "Even if they're a crowd of sorrows/who violently sweep your house/ empty of its furniture/Still, treat each guest honorably./He may be clearing you out/For some new delight." Crowd of sorrows was right. Violently sweeping my house, yes. Empty of furniture, true of New Mexico. Empty of furniture, not true of The Lofts. I thought of the crowd of boxes that awaited me, and my heart surged, that wildfire panic again. I took a deep breath because Trish asked me to, because I wrote and published books that told people to.

"Yes, I'll take a swim," I promised her. Anything not to be in the same room with those boxes. If immersing myself in a pool of blue water could shut off the unruly guests in my head, then, yes, I would entertain them all.

SURE ENOUGH, SUPERATTENUATED ME was the only human in the pool at two o'clock on a Tuesday afternoon. And sure enough, the murmuring water soothed me. From behind the arched windows, I watched hazy silhouettes of groundskeepers tending lush grass. All shall be well, and all shall be well, and all manner of things shall be well. Julian of Norwich. If she could write through the plagues of the fourteenth century and become the only woman to write a book in English that survived the times, then I could believe her. What she wrote about was that God's compassionate love is always given to us. With this all-gracious God, there could be no element of wrath. Was not wrath my problem? Wrath that God nearly struck two innocents down, despair that he had left us fragile and abandoned and me depleted. And now utterly rejected, laid waste. The wrath, she wrote, is in *us*— and not God. All that is contrary to peace and love stems from our doubt, our sense that we are not worthy, the moment when we want to cover ourselves, say it was the serpent and not our choices—not, in my case, a supreme lack of self-care, badged in the ideal of what mothering is. God doesn't blame us or judge us. She enfolds us in love. Julian of Norwich, the receiver of sixteen visions, framed God in the experience of motherhood. She referred to Jesus as our Mother.

I leaned my head back and closed my eyes. I let the water touch my skin. I noticed every tactile sensation between me and the water like we had entered a fresh molecular conversation. My heart rate decreased. I felt swaddled. Wombed.

At the sound of a ding, my eyes fluttered open. On the lounge chair, I saw my lit-up phone. I emerged dripping from the pool to see who was calling. The Pedantic One, the rental property manager whom I'd unofficially fired. I'm outed. My now-pristine and dream-worthy rooms were posted online for everyone to covet. By the other rental company. I let it ring. I slipped back into the pool. The warm cerulean water gently rocked me, and I closed my eyes until the phone quit ringing like I'd held a pillow to its face. As the waves rippled over my limbs, I steeled myself against the outrage pouring into the long voice mail. I languished in a fortress of water and stone, submerging myself in the healing waters at The Lofts at Saratoga. The outraged one was on the other side. A lot of people were mad at me right now. All of my unexpected guests, ready to sweep me out.

AS THE AFTERNOON OF BEING SUMMARILY FIRED slipped toward dusk, I sat in the loft at my writing desk, one of the spaces I'd "made whole." Lofts neighbor Judy texted me an invite for a glass of wine on her balcony. I felt obligated to tell her what happened. "Come now," she texted. "And bring Snowflake." I looked at the time, and then it hit me. I had missed an appointment with author-client Peg from Pittsburgh, who was writing *Permission to Live*.

"I have no good reason," I said. "I lost the job." I won't say "let go." I won't say "laid off." I will just say what it is: I got fired. I didn't do this. They did. "So, I'm going home" because it was the only thing I could think to do. "But I can't bear it. I can't see another cross-country trip in my future." Too many miles. I couldn't ask Grace again. "I can't do it alone."

"I'll go with you," she said, just like that. The love and ease in her voice were genuine. This friend really would do this. I pictured arriving in Pittsburgh. I could probably get that far by myself if I knew she was waiting.

I MET MARIA, ACTUAL REAL JOURNALIST, and another freelance journalist at Uncommon Grounds on Broadway to tell them the story of what happened and receive tons of sympathy and job leads, including one at the *Albany Times-Union*. Actual Real Journalist and Maria decided out of duty (Actual Real Journalist) and naked curiosity (Maria) to attend Regan's send-off party for her dying brand at Gaffney's. Actual Real Journalist promised to report back to me when we met up for the Selected Shorts literary evening at Skidmore on Saturday night while Maria introduced me to her sister, whom she just happened to run into on the street and who invited to treat me to dinner at Max London's because she thought I was interesting and felt sorry for me. "I'll pay for your dinner," Maria's can-do sister said, "and we can brainstorm this." Tucked under her wing, I followed her up the street to Max London's, where she ordered a full steak dinner, and I ordered a salad and a glass of wine because I had no appetite.

The evening twilight stretched long, and the streets murmured with the sounds of high summer as track season approached. Nine days and counting. Maria's sister turned out to be just the kind of consummate networker I love. She had the names of several lawyers I could call; a real estate property management company that would help me negotiate my way out of my lease; and a daughter who worked in public relations at Global Foundries, where there might be a job. Because this was a small town, it was no surprise when her daughter walked up a few minutes later, having attended Regan's soiree at Gaffney's. (She had no idea what it was about, but the free drinks were great!) She gave me her card and told me to call her about openings.

Shortly after this, Maria and her husband arrived, Maria brimming with gossip about the Gaffney's party. The artist commissioned to do the magazine cover arrived with his business manager, and he was handsome and polished in a Bobby Flay way as in he wouldn't be (objectively) handsome if his handlers didn't make it so. As track season approached, everyone flooding into this city looked like he'd stepped out of Carly Simon's "You're So Vain," here to be seen, see the horses, then fly the Learjet up to Nova Scotia to see a total eclipse of the sun. As Maria introduced me to the artist and I thanked him for his contribution to the debut issue, Anton Leir swept by, Nerilla on his arm, swiftly heading to the back of the bar.

This did not go unnoted by Maria. "When Nerilla saw you, she went pale as a ghost!"

"Amusing," I said, supposing that Maria and I now found ourselves on the same side of history.

"She really thought you would just *poof* back to Albuquerque," Maria said as her husband sat back and stared out into the bustling street, wearing the look of someone who wanted to be anywhere but here amid this gossip.

"What did she expect?" I said. "That she would engineer my ouster, and I would just abandon my dog and my furniture here? I did relocate my entire life to be here."

I cast a glance back into the golden light of the bar as Anton Leir held court with Nerilla on his arm. Everything I'd worked for to build a life for my children had been shattered by the jealous and insecure whims of a twenty-seven-year-old whose life radius moved from growing up on Lake George, twenty-eight miles away, to here, and a seventy-eight-year-old Albany lawyer who tried to buy his way into the glitterati of Saratoga Springs by gaining board seats, acquiring a magazine, and driving a Ferrari.

This place was the only place for them, the only one they could ever imagine. I remembered I had another place. I remembered I had children. I would have to tell them what had happened. But when?

THERE WAS THIS PART ABOUT SLEEPING. I lay on the sheets as the moon gibbous, losing itself by degrees, rose through the butternut trees and high into a cobalt sky. My thoughts rolled out along forested land cutting a path northward into the Adirondacks. My desperate desires pulsed urgently ahead of my new geography, seeking a mountain a lake a river, the St. Lawrence, a pristine and yielding and fluid path into this land, exploring any way in. So that at once I could discover that moment of surrender, when at last you fall into sleep, when you let it be. I cannot let this be. I won't surrender to sleep. For months, even years afterward, I cannot let myself sleep. The habit of vigilance won't leave me. Lying here on the stiff mattress of this bed, I knew I was cutting a new groove. I had prayed for the peace of sleep but tonight I would not surrender. I would not let myself cross over.

THE NEXT DAY, I BEGAN MY NEW JOB: One, to restore my business as a book coach and writing mentor. Two, to make sure these people make me whole, to negotiate the severance package. I worked on this all day, drawing on a triumvirate of advisers: Deborah for lawyer wisdom, Roma for human resources knowledge, and Portia for tax expertise, laced with her compassion and common sense. My triumvirate is three love-powered women. I don't feel alone. Judy had offered me a balcony and a glass of wine. Peg had offered me a cross-country Thelma-and-Louise-worthy road trip. My clients had all welcomed me back joyously.

But then as the sun slanted through the blinds and fell onto the pages of my portfolio, I saw twilight falling fast. Terror overtook me. The light was fading, I couldn't stop it and I could not release this day. If this day came to an end, it would mean I would have to be alone, out of sight of all those eyes who cared about me by day. But who cared for me by night? I would have to engage in this problem of sleeping again.

I knew I was white-knuckling the calendar, holding it hostage to the expectation that something in these second twenty-four hours of being fired would have yielded something clearer about where I should go, what I must do, and whom I can trust. Two days ago, I had been fired. I was stranded on the opposite side of the country, and I didn't know how I'd get back home. I didn't know what home was. I couldn't go home again. It was not here. But it was not there either.

I hadn't told Grace and Paul yet. Their college education hung in the balance. It was July 13, and they left for college on August 8 (Paul) and August 16 (Grace). I've faced high-stakes deadlines before but not like this. I would need to pay for college or I would need to tell them I could not, and they would not go to college. This felt like a referendum on everything about me.

Suddenly, I jolted from the table. I wanted to flee. The sun had stepped back one less degree of brightness and a blue-violet shadow splayed itself across the stacks of paper on the glass tabletop. This was not a gentle arrival, and I knew it. I heard the banshee wail. I looked to the dark walnut cabinets and saw stacks of unshelved dishes, the sheer undecidedness of it.

I walked to the island, the marble counter where the functions of my new life had collected, water bill, cable bill, things that gave me the grace of ordinary. I looked left, saw the oval mirror over the pedestal sink in the bathroom. I looked right. I pressed my face to the balcony doors, where tangerine and berry ribbons of the windsock lifted wildly in the breeze. The parrot kite the twins and I had once sent aloft in gusting March winds had crashed into a rain-soaked box.

With the sky losing light fast, I felt its weight threatening to roll down around the loft like a hard blanket of rain. I considered walking across for dinner at the trattoria, though I had no money and no job. This thought caused me to dash to the bedrooms upstairs, and for a few frantic moments, I paced, working a trail from the second bedroom to the second bathroom to the loft to my bedroom and back again. I entered the room where Grace had slept, the room with my grandmother's furniture and the silver mirror. I could sleep here tonight, remember her, remember my grandmother, try to place myself somewhere in a lineage that seemed familiar and necessary. Downstairs, there were knives in the drawers. I knew where they were. I felt the suppleness of my waiting skin. If I went down there, there existed the possibility of blood. With all these windows surrounding the loft, this sky quickly draining of light was a yawning grave.

If I was alone here tonight, I wouldn't make it through the night.

I rushed downstairs to my phone. I called April, who knew about these things.

"Thank God you answered," I said.

When I explained the panic attack, the thoughts of harming myself, she skipped right on into compassion. She didn't need to question me or judge me. She knew what I was talking about.

"I can't be alone right now," I said. "That's all I know."

"I'm here with you, talking with you," April said.

"I can't face this," I said. "I don't have a reason to face it."

She read between the lines. "You need a new identity. For eighteen years, you've given all of yourself to your children and your career. There are other things. There is more."

I didn't want more. I couldn't hold any more. There were no other things. These things were the only things. I could not imagine. I didn't remember who I was before. There was no one in here.

April, who had stood at the brink of hopelessness many times, knew what to say. She extended a lifeline. "You have many people who love you," she said, words I had given to her before. "Your sisters."

I resisted. If I failed to test these words, then I'd be inviting in platitudes, which wouldn't salve me. I felt raw and agitated on the outside, mortally wounded on the inside. But these tender words were all I had, so I decided I would take the dose offered to me.

"Okay, I think I can sit on the balcony and drink a glass of wine and talk to you," I said and I did. My heart had been strangling my throat. I realized it only now as it slid down into the cavity in my chest where it belonged. My sister had agreed to sit with me, hold this with me, see me through. I settled in on the balcony where, beyond the grounds of The Lofts on the other side of Blacksmith Lane, the blue lights of the loading dock behind Dunkin' Donuts glowed. Over my left shoulder, I heard the rush of the interstate, the hauling of things onward, north to the border with Canada. Before my eyes, I watched the slowing of trucks arriving at last to their destination, gently rolling to the light of the dock after all those fierce miles.

What happened next over two hours was the patient work of my youngest sister restoring the whole of my life to me.

"You are the daughter of . . ." she began. "You are the older sister of . . . You are the aunt of . . ." and she named each niece and nephew. "You are more than your work. And your work already has inspired many people." Including her daughter, and she began to tell me how much it meant to Rosaria when she and her classmate interviewed me about what the First Amendment means to our country. When Rosaria wrote pieces for her creative writing class, she invoked the name of her aunt as muse. All of this seemed too cognitive and too logical to me, but I submitted to my sister's wise ministrations.

"You are the mother of Grace and Paul," she said, "and that will never change. They love you deeply. They are immature right now, but know that they love you. I have witnessed that. And they still need you. This is your moment to be more than their mother. To restore yourself to yourself."

I didn't want to be myself. That woman was a hard person to live with. This person I have lived with for all these many years, she was cruel to me.

April kept a photo on her piano of herself at four years old.

In the photo, she wore a white smocked summer dress, standing between two abundantly blooming rose bushes, lipstick red and bridal white. April tilted her head, smiling. She called it her "Essence of April" photo. When she forgot who she was, or she felt embattled by having to live with the self she'd been living with—she remembered the sweet little girl in this photo, the person she was before she knew . . .

Before she knew what? That sometimes we aren't wanted. We're told to go away. Sometimes it doesn't work out. Sometimes we hope for something and we work hard for it and we don't get it. Sometimes we have been needing to cry for decades. Sometimes life throws us more than we can bear. The Essence of April is innocent of all that.

I caught a breath, surprised I still had lungs to fill. When I spoke, my voice sounded delicate. "I want to remember," I began. I let the air fill my lungs, circulate a bit, do what it knows to do, nourish me. I took another breath to see if this would happen again. "I want to remember something else, something that is not this, not here."

I absolutely knew which photo was my Essence of Carolyn photo. I was five, and our mother had dressed me in the colors of falling leaves. My auburn hair glowed. I wore a pointy white-lace collar and one tiny white barrette. My head was huge and my forehead so high it was the Arctic Ocean of foreheads. Clearly, the prefrontal lobes were well-developed. My brown eyes were sincere, and my smile was sweet, innocent of all those things I didn't know yet. The only thing I knew how to be was my true self, my essence.

Slowly, as the blue neon lights of the loading dock in front of me dissolved in the fizzy sky, April tucked me back into the whole cloth of my life. Not just this fragment of a life I've been living the past seventeen years as a single parent, not those stray notes that can't find a melody right now, but the whole symphony.

"Carolyn, you have freedom now," she said. "You have the

freedom to redefine your life. Complete freedom."

April reminded me that while I'd been up close and personal with the messy details and the "you're-so-fucking-stupid" outbursts, I had done an admirable job parenting my children. "They are remarkable people. They are resilient and they were more than ready for adulthood, or you wouldn't be in New York in the first place. They are smart and accomplished, but more importantly, they are kind and compassionate people who will make a difference in the world. That's credit to you. Your work is done. Now you are free to go."

Tears stung my eyes. Freedom was confusion.

"In fact, my instructions to you are to start having so much fun, you worry them," April said.

I laughed a little.

"I mean, your goal should be that they don't hear from you for days, and they have to call me and ask me if they should be concerned," April said. "And I'll say in the most casual voice, 'I don't know, I think she's just been hanging out with friends.' Try your best to shock them. Be a little daring. Scandalous, even. Make them gasp a little. It's time."

April was trying, trying hard, to help me see beyond myself. She was saying it was time to create an identity beyond mother and journalist. That was not the whole story of me, she was trying to get through. But all that was here was confusion. And a mighty resistance.

She sensed that. So she left me with this: "Remember: Have so much fun you scare them," she said. "Be daring. Be reckless."

After we said our goodbyes, I walked upstairs and looked out at the loading dock, where the lights glowed brighter. On nights when we stayed at my grandmother's, we slept in her room three stories up, looking down at the blue neon lights of the dry cleaner across the street. Inky light flooded the room where we dreamed, falling on the round beveled mirror. It soaked the room in a liquid gentian light. Like a sleeping potion. In this way, I could remember myself back to the shore of sleep. That night I was sleeping at last.

seventeen

Lake Local

I FORGET THAT I AM A MOTHER. I make plans without talking to anyone. At Carson's Woodside Tavern on Saratoga Lake, Judy and I scooted chairs near the stage at water's edge as the sky cast a cold-quasar pink light over rugged hills in the distance. The last light of a summer day plaited through ghostly pines on the far shore. Summer, the season of bright torches. A band was setting up on a square of tiles on the grass. The singer strummed his guitar three times and lifted his expectant face to the mike.

"This whole time, I have been living three miles from a lake!" I marveled as a desert dweller. I considered my luck that I had chosen The Lofts apartment based on location and amenities but hadn't considered where it figured in the geography of this place.

"There's Round Lake too," Judy said. "I'll have to take you there."

Before us, the surface of the lake started to quake with light, and the woodlands behind the lake houses started to vibrate with wide, looping tracings of insects. Arcs of firefly light strafed through the white oaks and birches rising up the slope while in front of us the band began to play.

I didn't go back to Albuquerque. Instead, I lived day by day, waiting for severance and a safe passage home. I would wait for this to be settled. I would wait for Anton Leir to present a fair offer and I would seek out a social life that would seem frightening to my children. As the evening concluded, Judy introduced me to a friend at the tavern as stars took their shapes in a deep blue sky. When I noticed how his eyes registered on me, I said, perhaps adding a hair flip, "Oh, I'm just here for the summer."

There are places here where the sky opens up. They are called lakes. When you drive up the Northway toward the Adirondacks proper, you can sense them in the pale blue sky beyond the deep forest. They seemed to suggest a light arcing from hill to hill to hill.

Over the next few days, I executed my social plan, starting at The Writer's Institute series at Skidmore, which this year featured Pulitzer-winning Paul Harding, Francine Prose, Cristina Garcia, Joyce Carol Oates, and Pulitzer-winning founder William Kennedy. Joining me are Maria, Actual Real Journalist, and the freelance journalist who is the mother of boy-girl twins. With track season opening in less than a week, the social and arts season was heating up. Something was on the calendar every night.

Sometimes in the evenings, when I walked Snowflake, I came past Judy's balcony, and she would call me up. We would open a bottle of wine. Her loft apartment was a mirror of mine. The only difference was she had completely settled, every item in place, even the plants, every box to recycling, and I had not. As my mother used to say, "I don't know whether I'm coming or going." I was still coming, but I might be going. Judy gave me an idea of what it would be like to just be coming.

I have finally broken the news. Grace's response was tender. "It's for the best, Mom. I was worried for you." She had seen it up close. Paul's response was guarded. "Dad's going to be pissed," he said. What I didn't tell either one of them was that college hung in the balance. Because maybe it didn't.

For their eighteenth birthdays, which were in a few weeks, I worked on their cards, writing lauds. Today's laud was inspired by Sleeping at Last's song "Saturn."

In the lives ahead for you, you will sometimes get a glimpse of the infinite. It will scare you. You'll fall short of breath. Because you'll realize how rare and beautiful it truly is that we exist. Never forget—

Snowflake needed relief. I needed coffee. Specifically, caffeine.

These two things fit together, and the two of us traipsed through the grass between the white pines toward the clubhouse at The Lofts at Saratoga. Along the hillock where Snowflake deposited her offerings, we met a handsome bearded man with a handsome husky with amber and blue eyes. His pure handsomeness, a cut figure in the misty morning, was enough to validate my routine, but when Snowflake and I arrived at the clubhouse, there was the Keurig with hazelnut coffee and beachcomber Marty the maintenance man whose presence gladdened me that I was maintenance-free. This very thought inspired feelings of Buddha-level gratitude because as a single mother of twins, I had once started a photo album on Facebook titled, "I Do Not Like Being a Homeowner," displaying the flood-soaked guts of a pink-insulated ceiling for all to view and like and cry while I searched for a reliable contractor to fix the hole in my roof. As it turned out, Marty loved dogs and appeared with a bone-shaped treat for Snowflake. She was adoring, and so was he. I would not refuse this simple generosity, though I would learn later that it turned her poop neon green, and her emergency deposits would occur on my living room rug.

The truly special thing about Marty was that he loved on my dog while I made coffee. It wasn't my intention to free myself of needing to hunt through every box for a coffeemaker; I hunted every night, usually past midnight, for my perfect Mr. Coffee. It's just that something else happened instead. This felt like getting a hit on a drug I didn't know, interdependent living. I was getting high on sharing.

While I got what I needed, caffeine, I was giving. And my dog was receiving a whole lotta love from Marty. My dog got vitamined up for the day.

"My job ended," I told Marty one day.

I'd gotten this far in the media industry without ever getting laid off, something of a miracle. It had happened already to many of my colleagues. And I had never been fired. Others had told me the story of great "take this job and shove it" moments, but those moments were out of the skill set of a straight-A student and earnest people pleaser.

"Has that ever happened to you?" I asked.

"Yep," he said and told a story about a job where they killed his spirit, and it became a chore just to show up. When layoffs came, he was chosen.

"What did you do?" I asked.

The whereabouts of my coffeemaker were the least-disorienting problem I had at the moment.

"I drank a lot…" he said.

"Oh, I don't know if that's helpful," I said, whimpering a little on the inside. That solution had already occurred to me.

"…but then I got the job here," he said. "In the end, it was the best thing that could have happened. Because these are great people."

This exchange was enough to fuel me through a walk in the moisture-tinged morning air, delighting in the distinction between this amorphous thing from which I drew breath and the rigid, dry air of the high desert mesa. It led me and Snowflake to extend our morning to a tour of the rapid construction of other Lofts-at-Saratoga-aspiring places adjacent, racing against the even more rapid construction to expand The Lofts.

Samantha called. "You now have the most freedom you have ever had in your adult life," she said.

"Yes, I comprehend that," I told her in a calm voice I didn't recognize. Inside, I felt a constant trembling. My breath fell short. I didn't know how to understand what had happened. I let my sister explain to me what freedom was.

"You now have freedom to choose your path, who you will be from this point forward," she said.

No one, I thought. Someone who wants to destroy herself. Someone who can't catch a breath. Someone who cannot sleep. Someone who doesn't believe it is rare and beautiful that we truly exist. Someone who couldn't send that "laud" to her children if she didn't believe it for herself.

Marty had suggested the altered state, but the trembling had become my altered state. It felt fertile with confusion. Samantha was trying to tell me this moment was rare and beautiful. When I was seventeen, I had chosen journalism, but I didn't have freedom. I had obligations, the obligation to create a container for my adult life. This was more freedom than that. The container had already been created and could be re-created, from a wiser view.

"You are completely free," she repeated, and I felt her savoring her own freedom, four years out on her life horizon. She closed the call by promising to text me job leads on content marketing from her tech world.

Even from the beginning, the newspaper world I had entered at seventeen had been imperiled, just for different reasons than it was now. It would always be imperiled because powerful people fear it and because of the impermanence of life. My sister was trying to tell me I had the stamina to stay in this territory of the unknown.

For comfort, I walked on to the pickup window at Panera, where an elliptical "you are beautiful" sticker all in lowercase letters gleamed in silver on the chrome ledge where the servers pass Pick Two sandwiches and soup as trucks roll by on the Northway. I walked in and read the names of pastries behind the glass, describing jelly fillings, adorned with confectioner's sugar.

After I composed the emails of the morning, providing documentation of expenses and infractions incurred, I took off to Wired for a bagel and a cup of a specialty coffee unexpectedly found in upstate New York, though this is horse country too: Kentucky bourbon-flavored coffee. Then I drove around the lushly forested campus of Global Foundries, appreciating the build-it-and-they-will-come ambition of running trails with no one on them.

When I stopped the car at one of the trails, I learned Liam

had sent a blazing email to Anton Leir, which he copied to me. He introduced it with, "Below is my resignation letter," adding, "I'm sure you will enjoy it."

I did not.

The email hit hard. The bottom line: The consultants had had a plan to move this company from producing $400,000 a year in revenue to $3 million. But Anton Leir had chosen not to follow that advice. "In the publishing world, if stories are late or poorly written, they get cut or don't run . . ." Liam's email began. It went on to document the incorrect ads, poor-quality ads, and weeks-late ads. "In the magazine business, people get fired for that. And in this case, the wrong person got fired."

I admit, that line made me feel a notch better.

Then he laid it on the line. "To turn (the magazine) into the multi-million-dollar company it could have been, you need publishing experience": leadership, experience, standards, integrity, team players. He told Anton Leir that unless he did this, he wouldn't be able to salvage his investment, and Liam wouldn't be able to help him. "To do so in this environment would be stepping into quicksand."

Quicksand. That's what I'm in as Liam and Kenneth fire off their salvos. It won't change Anton Leir's mind, and it very likely will sink me. Even a month from now, when Anton Leir will learn that Regan has embezzled from him and they will progress to the point where they only speak to each other through lawyers, it won't change his orientation to trust the elites and socialites of this small town and not the logic and expertise of longtime media business strategists who have emerged from the war zone of the Internet years. In Saratoga Springs, we have encountered both elitism and small-town mentality fused strangely together.

The email concluded with a personal note to me: "I hope you are getting some relaxing time in Saratoga. Hang in there."

"Liam, am I going to be okay?" I said on the phone as I eased the car out of the Global Foundries campus. "Please, tell me I am going to be okay."

"You're going to be okay," he said tenderly.

I WANDERED. From the creperie on Phila Street to the copper-and-glass Zankel Arts Center at Skidmore to Judy's balcony at sunset to the rose garden at Yaddo, I wandered. I received a montage of advice: from Roma, who said, "I'm coming soon," for she will be here as her daughter finishes The Writer's Institute at Skidmore; from Portia, who looked over the severance offer and bolstered me with an anthem to fight harder, "I don't see how this makes you whole"; to Deborah who sized up whether it was worth it to get a New York lawyer; to Whitney the breast cancer survivor, who said, "You're not dead, nobody is dead, you can survive this"; to Maureen, who was worried about me if I came home.

"Come to Phoenix," Maureen said. "Your son will be here at college, and you can live with us until Christmas."

But what she was really saying was, "You can't go back to Albuquerque."

I sensed the danger. The nothingness that was Albuquerque. My house was empty, hollow, echoing, perfectly painted, and wiped clean of a life, displayed now on the Internet as a promise to some other person's life. The rental company called. A woman wanted to pay me a year's worth of rent up front. I was free to live anywhere for a year. But where?

I FOUND SOLACE AT LIMONCELLO, where the hostess greeted me, and I felt like I had met the middle school teacher who understood my existential angst. She walked me to a table on the vine-covered patio. *I lost my job,* I wanted to tell her because, like any good teacher, she would give me a book to read, maybe the empty-nest version of *Are You There God? It's Me, Margaret.*

Another night at the Thirsty Owl, I tried a flight of Finger Lakes wines, including a malbec that rivaled Argentinian wines and a dry rosé that was my discovery of the season. The wine educator told me the story of the vintner, then he told me his own story, his merry eyes lighting up. He was the oldest son of four sons, and I am the oldest daughter of four daughters.

"I'm just here for the summer," I told him. *I got fired,* I wanted to tell him. When he talked about the Finger Lakes terroir, I saw strips of vine-laced land, eleven deep cuts of Cistercian water, pointing to Lake Ontario.

I returned to The Lofts, empty of any purpose other than deciding if I was living there or not living there, emptying a box or filling a box. I was experiencing pure solitude like it was the first time I'd known it. I am a writer but I don't know how to be alone. What I know how to do is surround myself with people I love and invest in them and what's left over goes into writing. I know how to be in solitude in the edges of the day but not if I've been fired. I know how to do the dawns and the midnights. I know how to steal moments from the yawning jaw of a day filled with minivan runs and whip-it-up dinners. I know how to write below the radar of family life. I don't know how to just do it when there is enough time.

THE NEXT NIGHT AT THE WRITER'S INSTITUTE, listening to Cuban American writer Cristina Garcia, I felt a sudden tap on my shoulder. Roma's daughter, Willow. Afterward, at the reception, Maria sat at one table while Pulitzer prize-winning fiction writer and event founder William Kennedy sat at the next table with his wife and his adult children, and she whispered, her preferred form of speech, "I think he is a little tipsy tonight."

She leaned away. "Or I would introduce you." There was always some reason. I struck up a conversation with his son, who was the father of twins, and the whole family and Maria and I walked out together into the summer night.

"She's a writer," Maria chirped. I told William Kennedy that my novel was a semifinalist for a first novel prize, but after that, I stopped sending it to agents.

"You must send it out, then," he said. "Keep sending it."

Can it really be that simple? I like to make it hard. Rob Spillman, editor of *Tin House*, once said at AWP that women need to be encouraged to submit and re-submit. Men get a "no," but hear, "Those guys are idiots who don't yet see your brilliance. Keep sending it out." Women hear "no" and think it means no. Maybe it's because when *we* say "no," we mean no.

THAT NIGHT, UP IN THE LOFT, I cracked open the cellophane on a package of sticky notes bordered with a Greek key design, which focused my vision on my novel that's partially set in Greece. The plot had been tangled up for years, not unlike the books and games and toys that piled on my mother's dining room table and crated hutch. That garage was empty now. I mapped the plot of my novel out on the wall, and I remembered that as a single mother, I was good at untangling things.

AN EMAIL CAME FROM LIAM. "I believe your settlement was confirmed and is in good shape," he wrote. The trucks had left for Saratoga, bearing magazines. They should hit the streets in the morning. The first horses go off at 1 p.m.

That night, Judy and I met up with friends for Hats Off Saratoga. We listened to a platinum-haired, earthy guitarist on

Caroline Street, then a sassy band fronted by Sirsy set up in an ell by the Adirondack Trust Company, next to the store where I bought Grace the rose sundress. The magazine was on display in the window with the lush and nostalgic painting of the track. I picked it up and held it in my hands. This may be the most miraculous magazine I've ever produced.

eighteen
noneedtoflatterme

DAYS GO BY WITHOUT WHOLENESS. While I waited for wholeness to arrive, I committed my days to a work ethic around restoring wholeness. Topping the to-do list was delivering receipts from my moving-here expenses to Kenneth because the magazine still hadn't paid those. To do this, I had to scan each receipt, but my printer was in a box I'd never locate. By midday, I realized the only way I was accomplishing my task was to drive to the Staples at Clifton. I took a deep breath. One more thing that had to be so complicated, but the magazine owed me $2,000, and I'd need this money as soon as possible. What was going to become of me? Another deep breath. I soothed myself with the idea that I would pair this task with that of mailing the twins' birthday cards. I gathered my receipts, a book of poetry, and a box of sidewalk chalk. For their eighteenth birthdays, they were getting money, poetry, and colorful chalk— chalk so they can write a message for me on the wall in the garage for when I come home.

Minutes later, I stood at the Malta post office writing out the lyrics to Jackson Browne's "The Only Child" for Paul. I let him know I admired his independence and ambition but I warned him about how the world makes you hard and wild. So, take good care of your mother, and take good care of your sister. We will stand with you through the disappointments. We will fill your glass with laughter. We will hold you through your illusions. We will—

Just then I looked down at my phone to see a screenful of texts from Paul's father. My first fear was that it'd leaked to him that I'm kaput in New York, but, no, he was worked up about Paul's auto insurance.

I texted, "I told you in May," when we bought Paul the car. "This is all taken care of."

I turned back to the card, assured all was well. Twice, I had called my Albuquerque insurance agent to make sure nothing was amiss. I'd sent my ex-husband the documents. On Paul's card, I inked out: "And remember to be kind/when the pain of another will serve you to remin—"

Another screenful of texts, disbelieving, accusing me of lying about the documents. I could not fathom why he kept accusing me of not insuring Paul when I made a point of walking out with Paul to his Yaris and tucking the insurance card in his glove box— in May. "You'll always want to keep these papers here along with your registration," I had said.

I returned to the card, writing out the part where Jackson Browne looks into his child's future, knowing that one day he will "find another soul who sees into his own," and I tell Paul that is my wish for him, that he builds a happy marriage. "Take good care of each oth—"

My ex-husband's texts escalated to the level of unhinged. "I am just trying to make sure our child is safe!" I read, hearing the text spoken in a familiar petulant, tortured, martyr voice. The screen bloomed with one blue balloon after another after another. The font size was tiny. Should I read it? I didn't.

We had a pattern, and if I didn't read the texts or reply to them, I could break it. I couldn't change his temperament, but I could break our pattern toward the good. It had taken me years of therapy, mindfulness meditation, prayer, long walks in the mountains, and lots of pouring my love into my children, but I break good now. Here was our pattern: He stirred up an issue that wasn't an issue, got me and all associated professionals (lawyers, psychotherapists, college administrators, athletic association board members, school principals, pediatricians – I think I've told you enough) in an uproar, threw out accusations that escalated from bitter anger until they peaked at blind rage. This tipped him into a litany of all past perceived wrongs, a tour through our greatest hits that was so predictable we could almost hire a tribute band. But when he was done, he was done. When I didn't engage, it was over more quickly. It didn't end with an apology or an acknowledgment, but we reached a point where he started acting like the rage never happened and responded to the solution I proposed at the outset. From there, we reached a compromise that was best for the kids. I learned that the faster we got to the "Are we done yet moment?" the better. I also learned that if I said, "Are we done yet?" that was bad—very, very bad. Obvious to you, but not always to me. It would fuel the fire and we wouldn't be "done yet" for three times as long. I had tracked this pattern over the years, and I had truly improved my time. This had been my triathlon of co-parenting.

The breakthrough for me was that I no longer got hooked into trying to prove to him that I was a good soul. My hard-earned insight was that the test was how I lived my life and how our goodness shined out through our children. His rage-filled words stayed with him, and our good lives spoke for themselves. Living well and living free may have first originated as my desire for revenge, or quite simply, relief, but quickly had produced the reward that living in love-not-fear brings. I preferred focusing on our love and not the messiness because it felt better. The practice had sustained itself.

In this particular episode, which I was now in the middle of and which I will now file under "The Malta Episode," it continued to escalate as I sealed the cards and started to write the address on the envelope. The package would go to my ex's house because mine was sitting empty in Albuquerque. As I printed the name of his street, I picked out words on the screen I was trying not to notice: one bitter "unfit mother," a lamenting "I guess I will have to be the savior here," followed by a pious "You are no saint." I was in admiration of his ability to have an argument with himself. I knew that when the noise died down, and the facts were sorted, I would have already taken care of it. No, I was not a saint, just a warrior.

As I dropped the envelopes in the slot and walked out of the post office, I felt it necessary to note that I'd taken care of this auto insurance detail while moving across the country, starting a new job, and getting fired from said job, a fact he did not yet know. I also noted that the auto insurance record in question was actually sitting in the glove box of our son's car, which may be parked in my ex-husband's driveway in Albuquerque even as the man texted.

As I hurtled down the Northway, I noted that seven days remained before the Second Judicial District of New Mexico said that in the eyes of the state, we no longer could argue about these things. The twins turned eighteen in three days, and at the end of July, the state believed we would no longer need a judge to have oversight on this family. We'd be on our own. We'd have to agree on things. We'd have to figure out how to talk to each other with dignity and respect. Which was what we could have done fifteen years ago. Which was what I had always wanted.

That's why the firestorm was today. When this month came to a close, there would be no imagined audience or forum for the one issue that could never be resolved, which was not about auto insurance.

I rumbled off the freeway and circled through the parking lot to Staples. I smacked the park button and jammed the emergency brake. I was gritting my teeth. Once again, my ideal that we could put the twins first and behave peaceably was shattered.

I was weak. I looked at the text. The mood had turned. He implored: "Please, for once, just pay attention to your children. Think of them." I wished I could just laugh at this. My friends wished I could too. They do laugh, knowing that what I'm great at is showing up for my kids and what I've struggled with is co-parenting with a father who had to be told what showing up looked like. I couldn't laugh. It was tragic.

I also didn't have the energy for it. I was vulnerable. I was mortally wounded, and my ex-husband was worried about auto insurance we already had. The series of raging texts was small potatoes compared to the battle with Saratoga, yet it was a known battle from which I strangely drew comfort. Wearily I finally texted, "Are we really doing this again? You barrage me with wild accusations, I provide documented facts, other experts validate them, and then you drop it like you don't remember that's what we did the last time. I consistently tell you the truth. That consistently gets proved. You keep doing this. For eighteen years."

And then I typed words that I'd been holding back for eighteen years. "You know, only a real douchebag would do something like this." It was the first time I'd called him a name, and even that was indirect. It still gave him room not to choose douchebag-ness.

I cannot tell you how much pleasure this text gave me.

An hour later—the Staples project did not go well, and I needed an attendant to painstakingly walk me through it—I saw the screen had exploded. The douchebag comment had not gone over well, to say the least. But I knew the rhythm of this particular battle, and the screenful told me we were hitting the peak. Maybe it had helped. We would find a resolution. We always did. It was just never pretty.

One hour later, I got the insurance agent on a conference call with my ex-husband, and the insurance agent told him for thirty minutes that Carolyn had squared everything away, something that would take two minutes to say but had to be said in thirty different ways. I waited through it. And, we're done.

I DON'T KNOW WHO IS DOING THIS, fierce and functional by day, tender and terrified by night. I don't even know who the Who is doing it for; it must be the twins. At night, a wildness arises that threatens to overtake me. I still fall asleep wishing for the sweet relief of death. But then I don't sleep. I wake up in the morning, and I still want to keep something intact. It must be the twins. Because I know it's not me.

I took my nights at The Writer's Institute readings at Skidmore or with boomer bands rolling into "Fortunate Son" at Lake Local where on television monitors, Saratoga horses hurtled through golden dirt and where a few feet away from our table, blue water gently wept at the shore, and a family in pressed-white nautical linens tossed horseshoes, throwing their lucky mark into the sand.

In just three short weeks, I had rooted myself here in a way that if I didn't yank out these tender shoots, something could grow here. Judy sat back with her chardonnay. One year before, she'd lost her husband after a long illness. She swept her eyes to the forested hills rising from Saratoga Lake and told me she could see her way forward to buying a house there, maybe a year from now.

"Are you staying?" she asked.

"Every day, it goes both ways," I said. "I could stay or I could go."

If my day job was wholeness, then I had tasks on my list. I could wake up to a purpose, even though I didn't want the goal. The goal was not wholeness at this point; the goal was to live in a space beyond this immense sadness, so I didn't have to feel what I felt. So, the morning after the night at Lake Local, where the lake's genial white clouds on the horizon suggested I was somewhere and not nowhere, all the tasks became necessary. I could pretend that I once was fortunate, and I knew how to be fortunate again.

ONE NIGHT ON THE PHONE, in an anguished whisper, Paul begged me to tell his father I was returning from Saratoga. I assured my son that I would, but I knew I wouldn't breathe a word to my ex-husband until the settlement money was in the bank. "Do it soon," my son said, and I heard the constriction in his throat as he imagined his father's rage. "But not on his birthday." Monday, then. The money that said these people in Saratoga were honorable, would keep their word, would make me whole. Surely it will have arrived by then.

THE NEXT MORNING, a black pool of oil spilled across the Northway exchange. A silver tanker was splayed on its side, bleeding a river of onyx onto the green grass just a few hundred feet from the drive-through window at Panera Bread with the "you are beautiful" sign. In my mailbox, a package arrived, the twins' birthday presents, returned. It seemed that while I was doing such a great job of being all zen about the text storm, I wasn't so zen. When I wrote my ex's address on the envelope, I used my zip code, not his. Imagine that. I filed this under "forced error." It was the day before the twins' birthdays. Their presents would be late.

Because of the oil spill, I was forced to take another route to the Albany airport, where I would pick up Roma. The detour took me through a new discovery: forested hills and knobs of black rock, marking a place where the earth buckled between New York and Vermont as the lava flowed, and a mountain range was born, creating pillows of basalt.

Roma was cool about the delay. Her plane arrived late, anyhow, and when she walked out of the Albany airport rolling her luggage, it was like we'd just met up at Flying Star in Corrales.

I CANNOT SLEEP. All night I jolt out of a long, continuous dream to sudden long arcs of sound from the speedway, a black buzz saw that registers deep down in me like a scar. In the dream state, these unrelenting pulses of sound scrape a dark streak in my soul that resides in the place I never wanted to go, the place where I had failed as a mother. Today the twins turned eighteen.

THE NEXT DAY, Roma and I arrived at the Saratoga Race Course. At the gate, someone thrust a pink sheet in my hands, and

I paid a dollar to find out what horses were the best. Before me was a scene of my Kentucky youth, the hawkers, the green lawn before us, the clubhouse, the paddock inside the white fence. Only the red-and-white awning is not Keeneland. The peppermint striping, which looked like the artist's illustration that a few weeks ago we were warring over as to whether it would be the cover of the magazine, was now jubilantly on display in plastic racks all around the track. On page five, I had spoken to the readers of Saratoga in the same warm tone I used to write to my Albuquerque readers for sixteen years, inviting them into my life, our lives together.

The pink sheet said noneedtoflatterme was a top contender in the second race, a Kentucky-bred horse with a pedigree that dated back to Derby winners Seattle Slew, Secretariat, and Northern Dancer. The bay gelding came from Hinkle Farms in Paris, Kentucky, a mile or two from where my mother was born. I borrowed the Racing Form from Judy and confirmed that noneedtoflatterme came from a long line of winners. It noted that the second race was named after the Saratoga magazine. I looked up at the betting boards where the odds flashed in golden dots of light, and it occurred to me to stop nursing my worry about when the wire transfer was going to arrive. It will arrive during the two minutes of this horse race. I will place a bet on noneedtoflatterme, and that horse will win.

The bell clanged, the horses sprung out onto the track. Noneedtoflatterme jumped ahead, and my eyes followed the aqua silks as he streaked around the outside rail and rounded the turn into the home stretch, leaving all the others behind.

In one minute and fifty-eight seconds, noneedtoflatterme had won. I collected my winnings at the betting window. I checked my bank account. The wire transfer had arrived.

I'm not whole, but I have money.

IN THE DAYS THAT FOLLOWED, Roma and I were on a lucky roll. For twenty years, I had known her as a calm and steady comrade in feminism, first as two rising corporate stars, then as two solopreneurs. I had no idea she had the magic touch at the track. We scored on every race, rolling our winnings into the following race, and I flirted with a man at the rail. Afterward at Siro's, we met a Scottish horse owner she decided to name Shrek, and he invited us to his clubhouse seats the next day. That night, she and I arrived at the fruit and cheese at the end of the table at the same time that Paul Harding did. Only Roma didn't know this was Paul Harding. His reading was two nights ago, and even if you read his book *Tinkers* you wouldn't know what he looks like. I had the home-field advantage, plus I'd seen him on a panel at AWP, where he was with mentor Marilynne Robinson. It turned out that it was great Roma didn't know she was talking to a Pulitzer winner. Because on this night, Roma made a great wingman, something I remembered from when I was editor-in-chief of *Sage* magazine and I got two VIP tickets to a private dinner with Gloria Steinem at the home of a Santa Fe art collector. Roma broke the ice with Gloria by asking her how she stayed so slim while on the road with book tours. It turned out that was just the regular-person question to get Gloria into a twenty-minute conversation. Different question, but the same thing happened with Paul Harding, and suddenly the three of us were talking about whether the art of reading was getting lost in because of technology. He said no, and his laboratory was his two children, who were as immersed in technology as any other kids but also read. "They read because they see me read," he said.

I nodded. "It is the same for me. My twins just graduated from high school, and I believe the reason they did well in school was because they are avid readers." It felt like I was having a regular conversation with another concerned parent, not the man who wrote one of the best opening passages of a work of fiction I've ever seen.

I asked him how his book rose to the prominence of a Pulitzer even though *The New York Times* missed it that year and hadn't even reviewed it, a faux pas it noted with "every now and then a good book passes us by . . ."

"Easy," he said. "I can tell you exactly." He told us about the West Coast publicist who wouldn't stop talking about it…to the *San Francisco Chronicle* and all the media and bookstores up and down the coast. "It was one person. One person who believed in my book and wouldn't let it go."

I'M FREE TO GO. I'm also free to tell my ex-husband that I'm returning to Albuquerque. I wrote out the script, rehearsed it with Roma, and had it down so succinctly that she just nodded and turned back to setting up social media for her Etsy store for the day. I walked upstairs to the loft and delivered the news by phone. My script told him only what he needed to know, nothing more: I intended to continue to meet my commitment to paying half of the twins' college expenses. The situation in New York had ended. I was returning to Albuquerque. He asked me no questions and gave me no sympathy, which was exactly the outcome I wanted. All business.

Downstairs, I sank in across from Roma. "It worked. Beautifully," I said, then I told her about Rochester. This was the other suitor who had called last spring, hoping to lure me to Minnesota for a full-time position, the one that got Saratoga to act faster. Now the publisher wanted me to come in September to lead another consulting training with the sports staff. He also asked me if I would consider a ninety-day gig at his other newspaper in Illinois. Roma and I crunched the numbers of what it would look like when Carolyn returned to Albuquerque, reconnected with UNM, revived her book coaching business and led newsroom trainings across the country. Or moved to Illinois. Or

Minnesota. Or stayed here. Roma wrote numbers on a piece of paper and pressed it across the table to me. "Here, this is what your income will be for the rest of the year."

I am going to be all right.

I stood and looked around the room at the disarray of half-emptied boxes, a kitchen where the glassware and dishes were stacked because they didn't know if they were staying or going. "I have a favor to ask you," I said, moving to the kitchen island and clutching the returned box with the twins' birthday presents. "Would you give this to the twins in person?"

I showed her the sidewalk chalk. "I have a reason for including children's play chalk in their eighteenth-birthday package." She knew the story about the blackboard. "Ask them to leave me a message there. Something I'll see when I come back."

WHAT WOULD BE WRONG with staying in the solace of the blue gin lake and the red velvet mountains where Georgia O'Keeffe once glided out on a canoe with a sketchbook? When you move to a new place, you meet one or two kind souls and you make your way across the current from there. I had met Actual Real Journalist and I had met Judy. I had accidentally met two Pulitzer-winning novelists, their accomplishments decades apart. I had done this within a month of arriving. These seemed like stepping stones.

Walking back from the clubhouse past midnight, Roma and her daughter Willow and I stopped for Snowflake. "You know, I don't have to move back. I've thought about staying." This wasn't the first time I'd thought it, just the first time I'd said it out loud to people. In my imagination, I saw the Adirondacks the way Georgia O'Keeffe must have seen them, burnished with the glow of crimson and persimmon and gold leaves. "Everyone told me I would hate the winters here. It's just as well that I won't be staying through the winter." I looked to the glowing yellow window above the loft where my writing desk was. Autumn lay ahead. Track season ended on Labor Day. Siro's would be shuttered. An unlived life lingered in the air. "But I wouldn't have minded a bit. I would just hole up and write."

"I completely get it," Willow piped up. "I would love that too."

"I mean they shovel the snow here," I said. "I would go out for Thai carryout and live on it for days. And just write. Colm Toibin says . . ." I slowed down to make sure Willow and Roma nodded to the reference to the Irish writer who wrote *Brooklyn* ". . . that what a writer needs is not a flat in sunny Barcelona. The best thing is a long Irish winter with immovable gray skies. Solitude."

"Yes! Yes, yes!" Willow said, and we all watched Snowflake prance along in the tall summer grass, imagining the deep blanket of snow falling here six months from now.

"I'VE BEEN THINKING you'd come to Providence," Liam said on the phone.

That one hadn't been on my radar.

"There aren't that many weekends left," I said. I mean, if I'm leaving, I didn't say.

He parked the conversation right there in a blessed space, changing the subject.

I started looking at the days and weeks remaining before I had to decide something. Providence. I thought of it as a fun weekend to see the Atlantic Ocean before I returned to the desert. But I realized later, after I got off the phone with Liam that he could have been talking about relocating to Providence. He didn't promise a job, anything. If my life was shattered, why not a new city?

That afternoon, Peg asked about our road trip to Albuquerque. I hesitated just long enough that she filled in the pause.

"You can't go back to Albuquerque," she said. "You've gone too far."

DUSK FELL, and I headed to the Inn at Saratoga for Irish acoustic jam night. Songs flowed seamlessly, one to the other and another. From here, I could go to Providence or Vermont or Montreal or Maine, where I remembered once sitting on a rock at sunrise point in Acadia National Park and watching for a long minute as waves crashed against the crevassed peach-and-jade granite. I had watched the ocean, imagining the other shore, Ireland, and under-stood that once, I had belonged there. As the music swung into a slip jig, I sensed that something washing up on my shore, some-thing that once had been mine. Something I had never known belonged to me. What if Peg was right? I had gone too far to return to where I had been. Because if I did that, went to Montreal or Maine, then I could just keep going up the coast to Nova Scotia. And if I did that, I could go to Ireland.

Marty at The Lofts had suggested the altered state. But music was my altered state. It had altered me into truth.

In Ireland, they call musicians travelers. The travelers are sto-rytellers who hold the culture, knit it together with their sharing. We tell our stories for survival. I'm falling, but I haven't fallen. I had already shed my things, half of what I didn't ever need in the first place. From here, the horizon stretched out to the ocean. What if I just kept going?

nineteen

You've Gone Too Far

AS A MATTER OF PRACTICALITY, I was not in a position to make any decision at all. Anton Leir still had not signed the actual agreement that governed everything. True, the wire transfer arrived five days ago. I had focused on that achievement and not noticed the absence of a signature. Two more pieces wouldn't fall into place without it.

All I knew was that today was August 1, these things were not settled, and my children headed to college in seven days. Whether I returned to Albuquerque or not, I'd need to get Paul settled in Arizona and Grace settled in Denver. If I was returning to Albuquerque, I'd be teaching at UNM in twenty days. I had a small window to pin down Anton Leir and get my furniture to Albuquerque. Albuquerque was becoming the default, but . . .

To Roma, I was fragile, no longer so daring. She had seen me up close. To Actual Real Journalist, I was uncannily kind, a creative friend to cultivate. To Judy, I was solidarity, someone who helped her see a life beyond widowhood. To Samantha, I was valiant, the older sister who once imagined ten impossible things before breakfast. To April, I was the free spirit she shored up because I fueled her free spirit. To Portia, I was the one walking arm in arm with her. To Maureen, I was the unbridled one who both delighted and worried her. To Deborah, I was what the Japanese call *omoshiroi*, interesting. If I really were all those people they thought I was, I would be someone.

To my children, I was what they needed me to be. To Grace, I was a lodestar. To Paul, I was the one person on this earth he could be tender with. Even though he thought I was fucking stupid.

To Liam, I was a specimen. I don't think he'd ever met a woman like me. My self-sufficiency had vexed him, but he'd never allowed any other choice; now my vulnerability frightened him.

I frightened every one of them.

Slivers of me were everywhere, but I was nowhere. Except here, standing at this pearl-gray wall in the loft, staring at sticky notes for my novel. Here, the days in Saratoga dwindling to countable, still no destination known, I read my writing on the wall. Here, it seemed that every atom of blue light from the doughnut store, every leathery grain of dirt kicked up from the track, every leaf and every swatch of blue sky, every bit of stardust that spun in the galaxy, all of it had collected in and around these boxes, my writing desk, and the light that fell here at all times of the day, where the words were. All of it seemed to reverberate from this center, this place that greeted me every morning, where the dead and the living seemed to find me but not one of them knew my name. I was reduced to this: ink and paper. Words, and a voice.

I could stay here, then.

I could stay or I could go.

I could stay here.

My house in Albuquerque was ready to rent. It was also ready to sell. I could call my real estate agent right now and I could say, "List it." It could sell in a week. Mortgage freedom felt delicious. My skin tingled at the thought. House repair freedom sounded good too. My body felt lighter already.

I could call her. It would be easy. Just one phone call, done. I tapped the contact for my real estate agent on my phone, and her face bloomed in a circle.

Only a few times in my life had I ever felt this tingle, the sense that I was at the brink. Once, in the Caribbean, a man who loved me unutterably presented me with a choice I couldn't make. The Tingle wasn't the same as arriving at a fork in the road and choosing a pro or a con. The Tingle was an unexpected arrival. One small gesture, one lean right or left would decide everything that happens next, and you won't be going back. He and I wore snorkels and fins as we glided beneath the surface of crystal waters. The bottom of the ocean fell out to reveal a coral cove. Below us, rainbow and blue parrot fish darted through crimson sponges, salmon-pink anemones, and dusty ginger coral. The promise of all the colors had not been spoken. It had not been said. It had not been acted upon. I could not choose something that was not there. But The Tingle, that had been there. Both lives, both possibilities, both had been there.

Something stopped me. Roma would say yes, stay in Saratoga. She and I had already worked through this. Judy would say yes. She wanted me here. April had told me I must. My boundlessness had always saved her. "I'll be disappointed in you if you go back to Albuquerque," she had said, knowing how I like to please people. Maureen would agree with only half of this, the part where I didn't go back to Albuquerque. She would say no to Saratoga Springs and yes to Phoenix. The twins would say yes to reinvention. Who better to understand it than two people who were inventing themselves? But Portia would say . . .

I didn't hit call. I called Portia instead.

She heard me out but only so far into the details before she broke in. "I know all of those things are true, and you are resilient. You can be happy anywhere. But what I do know for sure is you are going to be happier if you are near your children."

Portia painted a picture. The twins may be preternaturally self-sufficient, well-launched as independent, self-reliant adults. (I may have overachieved.) Great for them, but it was hurting me now. If I got myself back on the other side of the country, I would be able to hop in my car and drive to Denver or Phoenix in a flash. "You're not done yet," she said. "They're still going to need you."

I would go, then.

IN THE MIDDLE OF THE NIGHT I startled awake, vigilant for the next threat. I saw that Grace had invited me to play Game Pigeon. It was 3 a.m. here but 1 a.m. in Albuquerque. We shot Game Pigeon pool on our phones together like we were down at The Lofts clubhouse. She slaughtered me at Knockout, and I left her in the dust with Word Hunt.

THERE IS THE MATTER OF PRECIOUS THINGS. A wooden box that contained mementos of my pregnancy. A butterfly angel sculpture I made in birthing class. An amulet from Medjugorje. The senior portraits. And two prints of the twins, at four years old, each in seven spirited poses, the ones I call the Wild Child photos.

"That is irreplaceable," Portia said, holding it before her, wearing a beatific smile. She had rushed herself up to Saratoga Springs to see me, the consolation she offered after she told me to go. She, too, had fallen in love with the town and realized she couldn't bear to not see it before I left. She was here for five days so we could go to the track and the yearling sales. In the Wild Child photos, Paul wore an olive shirt and Buster Brown suede shoes. He was leaping like an Olympic triple jumper; his arms spread wide like he was singing the hills alive with the sound of music; his tiny fists were clenched yet he smiled through his mean face; he hunched and clutched his shirt in the famed Puss in Boots simper that once compelled so much "aww . . ." that I bought the twins a white puppy; he pointed a finger to his temple and winked like he had a good prank in the works. Grace wore a turquoise floral sundress with her hair in a waterfall. She propped her hands on her hips to say, "What of it?"; she danced a salsa slide; she raised her arms like a gymnast landing it; she crossed her arms in the "I'm so mad at my brother" stance that she couldn't help smiling through. She balled her fists together in a wind-up to smack him. She half turned with a sweet face that was all petals and peaches. "In fact, I want a copy," Portia said.

To accomplish this, we traveled to the UPS store in Clifton, where before we sent them off with tracking numbers, we would have two color copies made. One as backup, one because she insisted, "I need my own copy of sweetness."

But when we arrived at UPS, they said, "We can't do that. Not soon." I was going to have to ship them on faith, along with the senior portraits. Then came the next twist of the knife: the items would arrive before I returned to Albuquerque. Now I didn't even know if they would be delivered or if UPS would attempt and attempt and attempt to deliver, then send the package back to New York at "no such address" and the best memories of the twins' childhoods would enter delivery purgatory. Or, the items would sit on the front porch of a clearly abandoned house, subject to theft or flood. Not one of the delivery options hit a window when I could be there to receive it or intercept it. Nor did it appeal to me to think about the items sitting in the back of a UPS Store in Clifton, New York, waiting to be shipped by the person on the next shift, who would know nothing of this conversation and the care the items required. Two workers began to package the items as Portia and I stood at the counter batting about the various options. When I saw one worker wrapping the twins' senior portrait in cellophane, taping the front of it where the emulsion was unprotected, I died a little inside.

This was more than I could bear. Everywhere I turned, another cut of the knife, nicking away at every memory I ever had.

"I have to . . ." I was choking on my tears. " . . . Portia, I have to just get some space."

Sitting on an iron bench looking into a soulless parking lot of a big-box store village, I felt the sting of tears. This seemed a brutal price to pay for taking a chance at a better job. It felt precarious and punitive. It had felt that way all summer. The battle had been to not just lie down and die. I wanted relief but I had no choice but to keep fighting. I despised these people and their dysfunction.

I was horrified to think about how this series of events had threatened to death- spiral a life and an identity in which I had invested for years. My career in journalism. My life savings. My house. My children's childhood.

I had willingly given all to my children. I had invested all in my children on the good faith that it was safely invested; the love had been transferred. I had given my loyalty to my children, not those other opportunities I passed on. But now someone was threatening it all. Even the good opinion of me that I hoped my children had. It astonished me that our relationship now felt so fragile. Though I'd lived with the sense of fragility from the day they nearly died, I counted every day they were alive as grace. Never did I think that the story of us could ever be erased. But here were these people in all their political machinations, their self-interested jockeying, about to destroy a life.

I could not do this alone.

I had done so much of it alone.

When I reemerged in the UPS Store, Portia had softened the entire room. Workers were packing the five boxes now with the most loving of touches, with the same reverence that I would give these items. "It's all taken care of," Portia turned to me and said, noting the well of tears that encased me. Her voice grew stronger, more certain. "Your neighbor will receive the packages on your behalf—I've called him for you—and everything is packed with extra care." She leaned to wrap her arm around me and whispered as I turned, glassy-eyed to watch the Wild Child prints get wrapped. "I'm-here Grace" and "look-at-me-I've-arrived Paul" receded behind bubble wrap. "The real ones are alive," she whispered. "And you'll see them soon."

ONCE I HAD BEEN BRAVE FOR MY FRIEND. I had been twenty-eight, Portia twenty-five, and one twilight night we had stood under oak trees outside on my street. "I'm going to take the job in Arizona," I told her. I didn't have children yet. Our parents weren't old yet.

"Aren't you afraid of the unknown?" she said.

The known world was Lexington, where I would work for my hometown newspaper where an ancient pre-corporate-acquisition rule lived on that the sports pages must publish a photo of a thoroughbred racehorse every day. The known world was dogwood trees and carefully cultivated roses, gardens crisscrossed with cardinal song. In that world, I would have children soon. It would be time to begin a family.

Arizona had been the unknown world, the place of wind-carved cliffs, a flute line of ancestral melody calling me to the lives of those who had inhabited the place before me. Arizona was the land of towering saguaros, arms held high like a holy-ground preacher calling me into the tent. Arizona was where the promised job was.

"It's all the unknown," I had said. "We just think we know how the Kentucky story will be lived. But we don't know anything, really." And so I went to Arizona, though like my son, I knew nothing about what awaited me there.

Goodness. That was what my friend had brought me in the Yaddo garden, where that afternoon after the Wild Child crisis, we walked arm in arm, she saying hello to another adventure I had dazzled her with, me saying goodbye. Goodness sat apart from the piggishness of acquisition and sat tucked in the place where you desired what you desired because you desired it. Too many roses had had the scent bred out of them so they could resist disease. Once fragrance has been bred out of the line, it is difficult and rare to get it back. On Portia's face, drawing breath from the scent of that rose, I could read now the whole story. Our lives had been two experiments, running parallel to each other, one staying in the known, the other stretching into the shadow of the unknown. Yaddo, it was the opposite of shadow.

twenty

The Birth Chute

ONE HOUR INTO PACKING, I stood, coffee cup in hand, amid a clamor that seized me in a red squall of reluctance. I was not ready to click my heels and say there was no place like home because home was no place like home. One packer punched tongues of cardboard down into the shape of boxes while the other rolled my glassware in blankets of unblemished newsprint. The box assembler tossed my Acoma pot into a carton like it was a red Lego block. I reached to pull it out. "This is sacred pottery from a Native American tribe," I said, examining the pot's fluted edge and thin walls, the hash pattern of black-on-white that told the story of long-sought rain. For the first time in decades, I looked, truly looked, at the geometric patterns of persimmon and black dancing through rainclouds on white kaolin. The pot had been a Valentine's Day gift when I was dating the twins' father, a romantic memory I suddenly was seized with preserving. "It's made by the Acoma people who were massacred at Sky City by the Spanish . . ." I wanted to continue, telling the story about how the Acoma held off Spanish warriors for two days before they stormed the settlement. I fought the impulse to tell how Oñate cut off the hands and feet of the Acoma he conquered, and how in 1998 on the 400th anniversary of Spain's founding of the New Mexico colony, Acoma activists cut off the right foot of Oñate's statue in Alcalde, New Mexico, in history's most patient sweet revenge. When the packer looked at me blankly, I decided to just get to the point. "Each of these is worth about $400. Some go for $1,200." I pointed to the list of rare and precious objects I had filled out for the moving company. "Didn't you get this?" Did you not know that what kept this style of pottery alive were four mid-twentieth-century women determined that tradition would not die, the Four Matriarchs. I looked at her and thought, she must be a matriarch. Does she know it? I'm a matriarch. Do I know it?

THE NEXT AFTERNOON, Judy and I, the lost girls of summer, a widow restoring herself and an empty nester who was empty before she was emptied, sat on a patio near Round Lake. Judy pointed to a high bridge with a biking trail and told me come fall, she would ride that path. The sun had reached its peak in the summer blue sky. We headed to Saratoga Springs Spa State Park, where Snowflake led us through a circuit, innocent of knowing this new place and its smells would not be home after all. We stopped at the windbreak of tall pines, and at that moment I knew I could not tell Judy the truth about me: I was down to one pulsing light.

It was time to go. I stole a glance to anchor my memory of her kind face, then turned to look back at the fulsome butternuts and crisp, green firs. All I could feel was a desperate yearning. I was a song slowing to a monstrous still point, a breath taken and held. A breath, nearly the last one, released. A note sounded through the trees. We turned for the airport. I had arrived saying goodbye to this place. But I don't know what place will say hello.

HIGH IN THE FIRE TOWER, I can stand tall and pretend we are the neighborhood lookouts. My friend, her older brother, his friends, and my little friend Portia sometimes, when she was allowed, if the capricious rules of my friend squared with the stars. Like any real front-range view, we scan out to layers upon layers upon layers of mountain, searching the far hills for stray sparks.

Only we are on an acre of grass in suburbia. We see treetops and squirrels and shingled roof after roof as far as the eye can see. If I have found favor with my friend, I am allowed to walk the perimeter of her fort in the sky.

But so many days I am out of favor. Perhaps it is something my little sister has done, or perhaps it is the too-earnest look I seem to always wear on my face. Something about me says that I am the someone you can do that to. I'm demoted from the fire tower, sent back across the lawn to my own backyard of chipped, green swing sets and rusty, red whirly birds. She enlists the other neighborhood children in the Game of Leaving Me Out, for no other reason than I have red hair and it is easy to make me cry. She and I have the same name, only hers is broken in two. Carol, then Lynn. "We're like sisters," she proclaims. "We're twins, even. We have the same name." But I say, no, yours is two names, and you have two *L*'s and two *N*'s, we're not the same. Plus, I have a middle name, Dawn, so that can't be the same. In her mind, this no longer makes us friends but rather rivals competing for the scarce resource of a pretty name. My mother insists the girl's name is not the same as mine as though hers had violated a purity code. When my mother gets wind of the bullying, she speaks to the girl's parents. When the girl suddenly moves to Illinois, my mother breathes a sigh of relief.

One day a letter comes, falling out from a tiny square card, blue-lined paper as soft as a first-grade worksheet designed to hold a shaky alphabet in place. The girl apologized in her own words with squat, looping script. When my mother hands me the letter, the girl's snow-white forehead and wave of black curls bloom in my mind, and I hear not the shrill, jealous voice sending me away but a quiet voice telling me she was truly sorry. I would never know what had prompted this gift of closure, only that every time after that when I visited my mother in my adult life, she reminded me of this apology. My mother was trying to tell me something. We must apologize for the harm we have done. When we forgive, we restore each other.

ON THE PLANE, churning through night clouds shrouding my country:

I am flying out of danger.

I feel white with pain.

The blood is drained out of me.

This was nearly a mortal wound.

What city awaits?

I closed my eyes and felt the shining wind that mounts before a monsoon rolls in, the double bands of rainbows that emerge after. I saw the foothills of the Sandia Mountains that held the burgundy light of the sun before it slipped beyond. I summoned to my heart the river of autumn gold that would burst into song, come next season. I had not forgotten the scent of piñon, the howl of coyotes through the black. I had not forgotten that here, I gave birth.

THEY ARE PUTTING ME OUT. I sit up in a dim room, and I feel a coolness press into my sacral point as they swab alcohol on my skin. I feel a bee sting, come to numb me. "Hold still," the nurse says and lets me lean my forearms on her. She tells me the epidural needle is going in. I lose all sensation in my abdomen and my hips. In fifteen minutes, the twins will be born.

My conscious world is here on one side of a curtain erected to mark the operating theater. My unconscious world lies beyond it, where the surgeon raises her knife to make the first incision, a transverse cut across my belly. The surgeon peels back my skin, pushes my bladder and intestines aside and, thirty-seven seconds in, slices open my womb. Within fifty- three seconds, Grace's head emerges in a rubescent tempest, emitting a crushing wail at the shock of being born. Her tiny stick fingers grasp blindly for the stethoscope.

"One baby born," the surgeon announces.

My baby girl is lifted, wiped, settled, and swaddled in a snowy blanket. My husband holds her to my head, so I can see her face for the first time. Her eyes are smeared with a gorgeous white stripe of vernix. I can't decide if it looks like war paint or diamonds.

Forty-five seconds later, the surgeon announces, "Second baby born."

Grace is whisked away, and my husband lifts another swaddled baby. Mellow Paul, laying out his long torso, wide shoulders, and lobster skin like he just washed up on a white sand beach. I feel the quiet force of him, my son.

They zip me to a recovery room while my husband follows the nurses and two bassinets to the nursery. An attendant explains the morphine drip. "You'll want to stay ahead of the pain."

WING FLAPS WHIRRED, HINGEING DOWN. The plane lightened as it hit the corridor of air ringing the city. This city that held our story as mother and twins splayed out below, burbling with light. How neatly organized we were, along the great aorta of a river, a road of gold, gridded out in quadrants of NE, NW, SE, SW one mile between major streets and a half mile between substreets, rising into the foothills. As the plane lowered in the sky, I felt the resistance, the band of air that held this city in an elastic embrace. Then, at last, the small opening. There was a full-on roar as we zoomed to the ground. Engines screamed. Who was that screaming? I was the one pressing now.

GRACE FELL INTO MY ARMS, smelling like orange blossom and ocean. For a moment, we hung on to each other for dear life, then we broke away. To any other eyes, this could appear to be an ordinary hug between mother and daughter, but we understood we had leapt into each other's arms from the brink. We stood in the foyer of an empty house.

We must go. The purpose of this late-night meeting across the river was to hand off Snowflake to Grace, who had been living at her father's house until she left for college in three days. Tomorrow I'd fly to Phoenix to settle Paul at ASU. I just had to lay eyes on the place. I did the walk-through. Light bulbs, towel racks, working faucets. Ceiling mended in Paul's room. Woodwork added to Grace's room. The house smelled like paint and plywood, not like dinner. I locked up.

twenty-one
Desert Vision Quest

OMW, PAUL TEXTED.

He and his father were loading the Yaris and crossing the desert. With his father tonight, Paul was driving across Navajo and Hopi land where other young men had gone before, fasted for days, sweated in lodges, let themselves be filled with the bright sadness that connects us with the sadness of all beings. In seven hours, father and son would arrive at ASU and father would settle son into one-fourth of a dorm room on a campus that used to be an air force base.

In any other culture, any other time, my son would experience a rite of passage, a series of tests of his character, a wise elder to instruct him, and a ceremony with fire and sage to make it so. With the ancient mysteries gamboling through his head, my son would walk alone into the desert under a blanket of stars to a bare, jagged rock and spread a wool blanket in the sand. He would build a fire in a pit of lava rock. He would wait in the desert for what seemed like a thousand years until the Eternal Desolation found him. He would experience the immensity of what he was to become and be struck with a dagger of insight that this could never be borne alone. He would realize that I am not fucking stupid.

In the endless stretch of sunbaked days, perhaps aided with peyote, he would see visions of hero warriors who have gone before him, and spirit animals would come to walk beside him. He would face his shadow and stand in his powerlessness. He would face God and death head-on—ahead of time, ahead of life—so he would know for himself that he could do his True Self no harm. Where he had thought he would be alone, he would find his way to be with all the world.

None of this happened.

Father and son rattled along in a prison lockdown silence because Paul had come to the point that he found his father insufferable, something he would unleash on me within minutes of meeting me at Wildflower Bread Company in Tempe days later. As I listened to the story of what actually happened, I pictured the sun-crackled Yaris packed in a Chitty Chitty Bang Bang sort of eccentric tinkerer bound-for-a-college-dorm disorder, father and son staring straight ahead, their mouths flat-lined into frowns, not speaking for hours at a time, passing through the Painted Desert.

"There's nothing I have to talk about with Dad," Paul told me in the parking lot at his dorm on a spur of a road called Twining Lane. "All he wants to talk about is wine varietals."

BEFORE THEY ARRIVED AND I ARRIVED, I took off early morning from Albuquerque to Phoenix on a plane that swooped up from the eastbound runway, tracked north along the Sandia Mountains, then leaned back into the western sky, which allowed me to capture a view of the full mountain range, Sandias and Manzanos, the white grid of the Northeast Heights, the green pulse of the Rio Grande Valley, the linty almond mesa and eerie volcanoes. In a rare moment of social media consciousness, I took a photo and posted this aerial shot to Facebook. "My city," I typed in a digitized sans serif font that failed to capture that my tone was not a proud proclamation but lament. Nevertheless, I had just announced to thousands of followers that I was returned to Albuquerque.

I AWAKENED IN PHOENIX to the grace of a morning that didn't seem to remember the temperature would spike to 102. Just like when I lived here years ago, the morning whispered assurances that if I could just stay with this, just work with me here, it wouldn't be too harsh. For three seconds, I was young again, starting a life here, believing that could be true.

At the sound of a ringtone, I turned in the bed to my phone. Ah, a text from my ex-husband. The screenful of blue balloons multiplied before my eyes. Apparently, the trigger was I informed him Paul would need to have his wisdom teeth removed. We had dental insurance, and the problem was . . . what, exactly? "I am so tired of your bullshit," the texts screeched. "You are a fucking liar." Lying about dental surgery? I might have better ways to use my imagination.

Must I respond? I did not defend the logic that if our son needed medical attention, it made perfect sense to inform the other parent. Instead, I typed, "Your texts are abusive, and I'm not going to read them." I didn't look for the rest of the day.

When I told Maureen over breakfast and the newspaper, she said, "I'm sure you've done lots of therapy on how to deal with him."

"Yes," I said, and we turned to the headlines about Trump, who was saying that there were "very fine people on both sides" at the white supremacist rally in Charlottesville, Virginia, where one woman was killed and twenty others injured.

WHEN I ARRIVED to greet Paul at the dorm, I saw that he and his three roommates had negotiated an arrangement that would give them a living room and a sleeping room, a place to watch the wide-screen TV and a place to sleep. A place to invite a girlfriend for a movie and a place to . . . Clever. Four young men had quickly reached a consensus about the rules of seduction. Paul and I trekked to Changing Hands, where I once held a talk on my book tour, and we compared notes on books of classic literature, philosophy, and Buddhism. I finally pried out of him his ASU password, so I could pay his tuition, something I'd requested all summer but only heard—you got it—"You're so fucking stupid." This moment, then, was the true culmination of my desert vision quest. I felt like a warrior. Mission accomplished, we enjoyed vegetarian flatbreads at Wildflower Bread Company.

"Dad doesn't get it, Mom," he said. "I keep trying to tell him I'm a vegetarian."

It was my job to listen today. Not to advise. I was not here to walk him through the pros and cons or even bite on how he talked about his father. He was an adult and knew how to make decisions and live with them. I was here, actually, to be curious, be a journalist, listen to what it's like to be an adult. We'd spent the summer apart, long enough for me to understand I could approach him now as a fascinating person, not someone I had to protect for dear life.

"Paul, tell me why it's important to you to be a vegetarian," I said like I just met him. "Is it for health reasons, or is it more for the sake of the planet?"

And he proceeded in this bakery adjacent to a bookstore, where I once gave a talk about my book and my ideas and he and his twin sister sat in the audience taking notes on my interactive worksheet, to tell me all of *his* ideas. I felt the pleasure of just listening, not having to correct or comment or guide.

At Bed, Bath & Beyond, I bought him shelves. When we arrived at ASU, he laid it on me that the summer had been very hard. "I can't talk to Dad," he said. I heard the pain in his voice. He went on to tell me that he felt a constant stream of criticism from his father. "I'll never live with him again."

I searched my mind for the way into the heart of a man I once knew and loved. I steeled myself against the guilt of leaving my son for a whole summer with a father he could not abide.

"Paul, it seems to me that when you don't get the ideal father, there are two kinds," I said, measuring my words. "There's the kind of father who criticizes you relentlessly and doesn't love you, and there's the kind of father who criticizes you because he loves you. Only you can decide which kind you got, but I think you got the latter."

Then came the moment of truth.

We had more to haul up to his dorm than one person could haul. Either my independent adult son would make two trips, or I would help him. Before I could even walk him through this decision in my most diplomatic and gracious tone, he stopped me. "Oh no, Mom, girls like it when they see a boy who is nice to his mom."

I was no longer a liability. I was an asset.

The boy had become a man.

THE NEXT EVENING WE ORDERED Thai food, and his father was still on his mind. Paul and I were driving west on the Superstition Freeway bending back toward Phoenix when suddenly he said, "I don't know why Dad's so hard on me."

It was late in the afternoon, and the sun started to slide from the sky. I was driving. I did know why his father was hard on him. A reel unfolded in my mind, the event that unstitched me every time. The fear stabbed through my belly, aiming for my womb. We reached the on-ramp. I stopped the reel. I merged into traffic.

"I do know why," I said.

The mind reel advanced. I'm pinned to the floor holding Grace to my chest, and my husband is screaming before me, wildly drunk, weaving on his feet and barely able to hold Paul in his arms. Both twins were fragile six-week-old babies, just now achieving the weight of full-term babies. I have a surgical wound from the C-section—I cannot get up and he is barring me. But that baby is slipping out of his arms, and I will not let that baby be dropped. "Please, I beg you, hand him to me. Just for right now," I pleaded. He raged. I had no agility, no physical strength. My words weren't working. My emotional appeals were only fueling more rage. But drunk people let their guard down. I prayed for a miracle. The opening came. He shouted, "I'm not drunk! I am perfectly capable of taking care of a baby. See!" He thunked Paul on the wooden floor and maniacally demonstrated changing a diaper. "See I can change diapers too!" With a surge of adrenaline, Grace squeezed to my right breast, and with my body shielding her, I sprung from the floor and scooped Paul up with my left arm. He was safe now. I held his tiny baby self to my heart, his bum tucked against the belly of his twin sister, and waited for help. I bowed my head as though I could shield the babies from the rain of their father's fiery words. At last, April and her husband came up the stairs. Her husband escorted my husband downstairs, and April helped me get the babies to their crib.

But none of that was why. What happened between husband and wife was not why. It wasn't about me. It was not going to be helpful for my sorrow to stand on the path my son had before him. The why was more primal than that.

Here was the answer I could give him. "It's because you are his son."

I glided into the middle lane where I wouldn't have to watch for merging traffic. The lane was open now. "I wish I had a better answer, something you could change," I said. "I think it will just be something you have to accept."

"I mean, Dad . . ." Paul struggled to find the words. For several minutes, he spoke through the problem out loud, delivering a thought train about dynamics I knew well, the specifics of which I could gather and ponder and try to stuff in this sentence, but the fact was, I only had one job from this point forward: listen now and listen again.

"It's better now," he said, but his sadness and the sadness of all sons and all sons of sons echoed out into the dusky sky.

BY THE TIME MY FLIGHT TOUCHED DOWN in Denver, I got the text that the Wild Child portraits had arrived in Albuquerque. They had been delivered to neighbor Bob's porch. Dutiful and diligent Bob confirmed that he had stashed them in his garage, out of the wind, safe from monsoons. My wild children had traveled in the back seat of a Prius across the prairie to upstate New York and back again on a UPS truck. At any point along the way, they could have been damaged by sun or water or stolen, vulnerable at any rest stop. Now they had been packaged at a UPS store without my laying eyes on the bubble wrapping and address sticker placement, shipped across the country to my doorstep on a day when I was in Denver. They had been intercepted by a neighbor, something arranged by my sister.

I arrived in Denver before Grace and her boyfriend, who were driving from Albuquerque. I settled into my strangely northern European hotel in the middle of a town that seemed to be all about cattlemen and oil barons and questers for gold. I walked the streets and waited for my daughter to arrive in her new city.

We loaded out into Campus Village, then spent an ungodly amount of money at the Target in Lakewood to buy useful things for their dorms. We commemorated the bulging shopping carts filled with dorm lamps and sheet sets by posting a photo to social media.

Watching Grace as she tacked Tibetan prayer flags to the wall of her dorm room, I wondered, could I have lived on without that material thing, the Wild Child photo, seven moments that captured their exuberance? Something that one day might be their Essence of Grace photo, their Essence of Paul photo, the one image that would keep them alive through the heavy-laden middle of the murk of life?

Grace turned to me for the photo I was taking now and made her "what fun" smile, shoulders slightly hunched, hands framing her face, palms upturned. Here was my real wild child sealed to the digital emulsion of all that matters, presenting one immutable fact: in this moment, we were both alive.

part three

-

Songs of Becoming

twenty-two

Albuquerque 2.0

SOMEHOW, I REENTERED THE WRONG WAY. I accidentally overshot downtown and entered from the west, from Old Town through the Country Club area known for its Christmas Eve luminarias and a notorious gruesome scene in *Breaking Bad*. To get back to downtown, I drove the Old Route 66, weaving through white-curbed roundabouts and barricades baked bitter orange from the sun. How had I got tangled up this way? I couldn't even tell you. When I approached the edge of the city center, I found, instead of a ghost town, a pulsing city, lemon lights and throbbing pink beats, music in the streets.

Tonight, this town had skin on. Lampposts that have lined the sidewalks for decades and been invisible to me showed themselves in neon half circles, desert jewel tones of turquoise, purple sage, and chamisa yellow. As I accessed Central Avenue, I passed under an arch in the form of a lightning bolt. It was a tilted Route 66 sign, the second 6 dimmed out. I had arrived at the heart of The Mother Road at nearly 2 a.m. Streets thronged with people emptying bars. A vibrating haze lingered in the streets as though something had just happened and someone needed to be called. I wound my way back to Hotel Andaluz, where I would begin to reacquaint myself with this surrealistic neon city. Once I'd read that the inventors of neon had coined the word as the Greek neutral of neos or new. I left the ridiculous cherry-red Mustang convertible that was my randomly assigned rental car at the curb and went to check in at the desk.

THE NEXT MORNING I ordered room service, lemon ricotta pancakes, mighty elegant comfort food. I decided that I was in hiding, a fugitive from the empty nest, and fugitive certainly fit this room because I was sure I'd seen it in a *Breaking Bad* scene. At some point in the day, I would have to break this spell and gather Snowflake from the kennel like an ordinary suburbanite who just lived here. Until then, this would be my hermitage.

I could call it my hermitage, but that would be just fancifying my loneliness. I could call it a silent retreat, inserting a friendly adjective that impeded me from just calling it a retreat. Because that word retreat, all on its own, was too close to defeat. I decided I would luxuriate in having a whole bed to myself, no one needing me, ever. I would delight in not being needed. I knew I was giving my first official day as an empty nester a nice contemplative mystic wrapper. Why not just call it absence? Their absence from my life, my absence from my own.

MIDAFTERNOON, when I could not push it any longer, I proceeded up the mesa at the pace of the damned. After all the miles I'd traveled, I should be closing in on a destination, but it felt like a cemetery. The only thing waiting for me at the top of the geographic escarpment known as Loma Colorado, the colorful hill, was a 270-degree view from a house that may be more than I wanted to care for. What if I simply sold it? What kind of down payment could I then make? Now that I belonged to no corporation, would I even qualify for a mortgage? Numbers zipped around my mind like cave bats. What if I was stuck with the house and I had to live in a location that made sense for a mother raising school-age children but not who I was now, whoever that may be? I didn't know if I would sell it, only that I wanted to be nimble enough to sell it. I did not want to be force-marched to a neighborhood that didn't have neighbors.

After the subprime mortgage crisis in 2007, the place had become a ghostland. The four houses nearest me sat as empty shells for years. In the soccer years, a fire ripped through the house under construction on the lot next door, singeing my catalpa tree. That house was never built. Crews swept away the charred remains, and for years, the lot sat, clean as a griddle. One year, a flood ripped apart the sandbanks, charting a 100-year path, something no one saw coming. The state had built a flood-control area, which meant that the two acres north of me, looking to Santa Fe, remained undeveloped, giving me an unobstructed view. For the last few years of the twins' childhoods, ours was the only inhabited house on the street.

Neighbor Bob greeted me with a hearty hello as he emerged from the shade of his garage. He shook my hand and told me he worked full time as a self-supporting artist in Tampa before he took a too-good-to-resist job with a company that designed and sold T-shirts. The job gave him income for his family and the flexibility to maintain an art career. The room between the garage and the kitchen was his studio, full of outsized canvases. He'd written a children's book, *The Boy with the Mechanical Arm*, and in the story, the boy went on a spirit walk where he tested his skills and talents. "I'm a songwriter, too, like your daughter," he said, and then I remembered that the twins had gotten to know these neighbors and I had been the hermit, which must be what single mothers who are hunkered down look like from the outside.

"Come on in, you're a writer, you have to meet Katy." He waved me in, and before I knew it, I was standing in Katy's kitchen, where she was slicing limes for sangria. She was splattered with paint, a touch of sky blue sprinkled in her dark eyebrows. "She's an artist too. She has a studio out back."

They had converted the RV garage, which from across the street had reminded me of suburban consumerist culture, where it was all about storing and maintaining your material things, then driving around with all of them on wheels. As someone who was now worried about whether her most essential material things would make it across the windswept prairies of grain, I did realize the self-righteousness of this judgment. I also realized the redemption of this, that someone else had come along and reimagined the space.

"Bob tells me you're a writer," she began.

"Yes," I said with surprising confidence. I was something. I was someone. "I have seven books and I work as a book coach and writing mentor."

"We're both artists, then," Katy said, "and thanks to my dear husband, I paint full time. I paint while the kids are at school." I remembered they had two teenagers, slightly younger than Grace and Paul. All I could see when I tried to recall Katy's children were two future nest jumpers. "Want to see my studio?"

Katy's studio was lined with spacious canvases of deeply saturated color—turquoise and orange and pine green and coral—that shimmered on cotton duck surfaces. The room was a study in falling horizons. "I started painting these after we migrated here from Florida," Katy said. "They started coming to me while we were on the plane, flying through the slivers of clouds."

A tumbleweed hung from her studio ceiling, sprinkled with glitter so the thorny branches looked like they were holding stars. She followed my gaze and pulled it down. "I still feel a little like this, like I'm still gathering the seeds of this place. I let it hang out here until I figure out what I will paint next. I think it's something about the Dreamers." Katy, who is Hispanic and Native American but has not lived in a place where people helped that thrive in her, was referring to the young immigrants who come here with big hopes, to whom she hoped to give art classes.

My neighbors wanted to see my house, so Bob said he'd load two UPS packages in my car and bring the other three in his. We parked the contraband, also known as my memories, on the porch of my empty house. When Bob learned I didn't have a bed, he offered to send Katy over with an air mattress, sheets, and blankets. Soon enough, she crossed the street, her arms overflowing with comfortable bedding.

Tentatively, I swung open the hammered-wood oak door to the tall windows receiving the view of the mountains. The house had been stripped to its natural cream-and-honey and blue-sky beauty, flagstone fireplace and wooden beams and freshly painted walls. "I see blank walls and think art," Katy said, studying the pristine surfaces with the eye of a gallery artist. As we walked through echoing rooms, I briefly mentioned I'd moved away and back in one summer. She picked up on the magic of this house and my wish to be here, and not there. "It's a God thing," she said, "that brought you back." Katy held her eyes on the knotty pine beams, then rotated out to that place on the hill like she knew that was the spot where I'd whispered a prayer to return.

LIAM WAS HURTING worse than I was, he told me on the phone as I turned out of my driveway and headed back to my hermitage at Hotel Andaluz for one more night.

The battle for *Saratoga* magazine waged on. He was trying to complete the website design so he could exit from Anton Leir but mainly so he could get paid. The stack of unpaid invoices mounted into a significant five figures. Every firestorm that Nerilla and Regan unleashed threatened to torpedo his entire business that he'd built for seventeen years.

"You are the lucky one," he said. "This won't alter your life. You're made whole."

"My furniture's not here yet," I reminded him. "Or my car. I'm driving a red Mustang rental that, um, hovers."

"Cool," he said like any guy.

"I'm not driving, I'm hovering," I protested.

But this went unheard. Anton Leir could still not pay for the car transport or the moving van, and my furniture would go into the purgatory of storage and my car would disappear into the *Breaking Bad* junkyard.

DEBORAH CALLED to see how the first official day of empty nesting in Albuquerque was going, though I wanted to insist that the clock would not start ticking until I had furniture. One more night of the unlived life at a hotel surely didn't count. I described just how empty my nest was: five barstools that stayed out of strange loyalty to the granite, five parcels of contraband memories, and my diploma. "I could hold a soiree in my garage," I said.

"Here's to taking the medicine ball approach to the empty nest," she said.

In the Native American tradition, the medicine pouch was a leather bag covered with beads. The initiate carried the medicine ball on a vision quest, which involved fasting, prayer, and isolation—and sometimes if you were lucky, a shaman who dispensed peyote. Sometimes, during the hallucination, the initiate met her guardian spirit. Often, the peyote made you throw up. That's what Deborah was getting at. I must be purging. I just called it puking. Getting all the poison out at once.

RETURNING TO HOTEL ANDALUZ, I was struck by the great surprise of sensory delights, an aquamarine light infusing the casbah rooms, the flickering flame on the Ibiza rooftop patio where I watched a monsoon roll in and batter the glass with rain and wind. A sunset spilled watermelon light on the mountains in a variation of bold elegance that I was certain I had never seen before. On the wall in the lobby, murals of Native dancers performed the eagle dance. I had imagined that coming back to Albuquerque would mean coming back to nothing and to old. The narrative running through my head hadn't been so much as "Goodbye to All That" as it was "Oh, Hello to This Again." But I lived in a neighborhood with an artist's studio and in a city with a downtown that boasted a hotel that had a full wall of hanging stained glass. Behind the band was a curtain of iron-gridded amber, copper, moss green, and cobalt glass, a piece of modern art that hung between two thick wood columns with pueblo-style corbels. Here, the rustic and the humble met the ordained and enlightened. Somehow it worked. A man reached for his wife's hand and led her to the dance floor, guiding her into a spin. She stepped out in delicate sandals, light on her feet.

THE NEXT NIGHT, JUST PAST MIDNIGHT, I heard a crash from the utility room. I had been asleep on the air mattress Katy and Bob lent me, lying inches from the floor. All the air had leaked out. No more inches from the floor for me. I was just sleeping on a hard floor with plastic in betw— another crash. I froze in terror. Whatever made that sound was big. I could only imagine an armed human intruder. I grabbed my phone. I visualized snatching Snowflake, my phone, my purse, my laptop, and calling 911 as I ran out into the desert night. If the intruder was in the utility room, I had . . . how many seconds? All of this seemed doomed and stupid. Another crash. An intruder was banging around the vacant north side of my house like he was gathering pots and pans for green chile omelets and hash browns. Did the intruder know someone was here? If not, then when I was discovered, would I be shot?

I froze. Did I have a weapon? No, I had freshly painted walls with no scuff marks that show a family was raised here. I had a deflated air mattress and a white puppy. I scanned the empty room and espied my diploma. Which had sharp corners. I could go for the jugular. The intruder also could have an AK-47, obliterating my head in a barrage of bullets so swift that when they found me, I would only be a body from the neck down, a stem without a flower.

Why was I not calling 911?

After a long twenty minutes lying stiff as a board as if my life depended on my stillness in this stark room, I decided I must summon the courage to investigate. I crept out, brandishing my diploma like a spear. A blur of gray skittered from the kitchen to the utility room.

A mouse.

Who left a big frightened turd in the middle of my kitchen floor. The spear-like silhouette of my diploma must have scared the shit out of her.

My nest was not empty.

WHEN I TOLD DEBORAH about my night of terror, she said I could stay with her for two nights until my furniture arrived. Snowflake could come too.

Arriving with Thai carryout, I described my silvery rodent for effect because Deborah and I were storytellers if nothing else, she a lawyer, me a journalist. I described Mama Mouse as looping her tail around her like a mink stole. Like she was at the Santa Fe Opera and telling everyone she *belonged* in my house. "I call her Mama Mouse," I said. "But maybe she's a dowager, old money, like *Downton Abbey*."

Before the sun set, we walked from her North Valley home along the Rio Grande and arrived at the sandbars. It was late summer, and the river was low. Depending on its twists and turns, this river stretched nearly 1,900 miles, originating in the Colorado mountains about 12,000 feet above sea level, spilling into the Gulf of Mexico at Brownsville, Texas. We call it the Rio Grande, but the Spanish called it Rio Bravo del Norte, which means fierce north river. Deborah told a story about the couple on the sandbar as their black Lab frolicked, and suddenly I felt connected to this ecosystem, my friend's neighborhood that hugged a fierce north river. I looked north to the Paseo bridge I had crossed every day for two decades on a morning commute. I looked south, where the river bent out to a western cliff, glass houses high on the rim.

As we turned back, Deborah told me she fought insomnia. That's why she tried to go to bed by 8:30. "It's not a problem to lose three hours of sleep in the middle of the night if you block out eleven hours," she said over pad thai. "I try to just roll with it. I read that it's the psyche's way of restoring the quiet mind."

"Father Richard Rohr calls it the hour of the wolf, when the psyche is most undefended," I said.

"I've read that it's the custom in many cultures to allow for it, to see it as a time of deep reflection," she said. "Our psyches crave it. We can keep our souls at bay only for so long."

"Once I wrote a column for *Sage* magazine in which I gave new meaning to the so-called witching hour," I said. "In Marianne Williamson's book *A Woman's Worth,* she wrote about 4:15 in the morning as the time when women would gather in the woods."

"The only time they could be undisturbed," said she, also a mother.

"Or undetected," I said, because men have always feared the power of women when they assembled and compared notes. "So the witching hour isn't scary. This is how women kept the flame alive."

I AWAKENED in the middle of the night, and it felt like it was for good, like I'd never sleep again. Agitated, I haunted Deborah's kitchen, fruitlessly seeking a pattern of logic in the array of vitamin supplements and whole-grain chips. I opened the refrigerator and pondered food. I was not hungry. I returned to bed and hugged Snowflake to my chest. I sat up and held the sensation of being unsettled and with no answer for it. I felt the horror of how empty I was.

IN THE MORNING, I pulled on the royal-blue, empire-waist dress I found when Maureen and I went thrift shopping in west Phoenix, where all the older ladies send their clothes. I hoped this wasn't a dead woman's dress. I slipped it on because I thought it would make me feel better about the day ahead. I told this to Deborah, who was conducting a divorce mediation today. She briefly considered the dressy dress strategy herself.

When Snowflake and I returned to the Saratoga house, I lay on my back on the freshly shampooed carpet in the most-emptied empty nest in America. I stared at the honey pine beams and cried. Tears dripped into my ears. I curled in a fetal position because I could see how small I was in this big empty house on a big empty lot in a big empty desert. Snowflake lay beside me with her chin propped on her paw, holding me steady in her gaze as if to say, "Don't worry. My heartbeat synchs to your heartbeat, and that won't change. I've got my puppy eyes on you." I closed my eyes. Just one month ago, I had stood on the hill and prayed to be returned. Lying on the floor, I scrunched my eyes and tried to squeeze that rainbow out of my mind's vision, but the unrelenting promise of it wouldn't let me. It had been a double full rainbow. Its size had been monumental. I had returned a promise to its promise.

Someone needs to do something.

IN EVERY NEIGHBORHOOD there is a haunted house. No one will go into the haunted house, and if they have to pass by it in the dark, they will pass with great care. I am that house.

In the Webkinz game Home Before Dark, six little creatures—a pinto, a pig, an elephant, a yellow Lab, a hippo, a leopard—must get through the maze before the sun sets and the moon rises. Their mother is calling them. Only this time, the little ones are not coming home. They're off the gameboard. And everyone passes me with great care.

So this is the game we're playing now.

I gathered my frequent flyer miles and booked two nights at the Tamaya resort.

THE MELODY OF A WIND FLUTE greeted me as I walked the flagstones. Young men in white shorts and golf shirts stepped lively to open the door for me. At the check-in, the hostess turned to a hexagonal, hammered-glass beverage dispenser with two options. "Margarita? Or sangria?" she asked. It was three o'clock in the afternoon. I announced my choice with a note of pleasant surprise. "Margarita."

Later on the patio, a wedding party gathered. As the sun started to set, the music stopped and the reception was over, just like that. A fire burned in the pit as two vested workers closed out the cash bar. As the tiki torches were lit, a thought burned me. It hurts to have skin, be pierced. It hurts to die. It hurts to be born. It hurts to be chased by love. It hurts to have no refuge. It hurts to yearn for reunion. It hurts to have to die to self to be brought back into love.

FOR TWO NIGHTS AND TWO DAYS, I lived like a fugitive. The Irish philosopher and theologian Noel Dermot O'Donoghue wrote that contemplatives withdraw from the world so they may confront the monster in the lair. For two days, I moved about the resort at glacial speed like I'd just had surgery and the stitches might break open. From my room, I looked east to the mountains from an angle at the extreme northwest edge of the city. For hours, I watched white clouds pass over the peaks of the Sandias. The light here was different every day. It had been different every day since I first came, twenty-five years ago. Still, what I needed was not this astonishment. I needed an absolute reference point, a fixed point where the clouds didn't move.

SOMETHING ABOUT ROOM SERVICE was like a sick day from school when your mother was completely attentive to you and no one else, a day when you could have her back. I ordered migas, scrambled eggs with red and green chile, corn tortilla strips, bacon and chorizo mixed through. I ordered a carafe of coffee—after all, I was writing. My plan was to journal, apply for jobs in Denver and Phoenix, apply for Father Richard Rohr's Living School as I read his book *Immortal Diamond*. I would not tell anyone I was here.

As night fell, I left the sliding screen door open, and the full moon moved over the mountain as I slept. I sleep and sleep and sleep. Stars shoot across the sky.

THE NEXT MORNING, Louisianne called. She'd been watching bits of my story unfold on social media and she wanted to invite me to stay a few nights with her until my furniture arrived. "And Snowflake is welcome too."

When we get stuck, we get separated and isolated. All those years of being a single mother had stiffened me into the act of solo survival. The antidote was to enter into conversation again. Two minds and hearts meeting, that's a conversation. I was going to have to start one. It seemed that without trying to start one, I already had. If I drew a map of the city, I would place dots on all the conversations I'm having: Route 66 (me and The Mother Road), Hotel Andaluz (me and downtown Albuquerque), Rio Rancho (Katy and Bob), the North Valley (Deborah), Corrales (Roma, Whitney), Tamaya (me and God and the wind flute), Placitas (Phyllis and Arthur, who invited me to stay Saturday night, also including Snowflake) and now, the East Mountains (Louisianne and her family).

All spring and all summer I had been engaged in a conversation I hadn't understood, which hadn't been so much about the emptiness as it had been about how to be spry, begin again. Dots on the map stretched across the landscape, all the conversations I had entered about where to start: Providence, Louisville, Lexington, Phoenix. Santa Ana Pueblo, North Valley, East Mountains. Placitas. Or here. Just here.

WALKING THE PATH overlooking the pool at Tamaya, I heard a sprinkle of raindrops, a drizzle and the almost-breaths of air, then a downpour, the recorded sound of a rain stick through the resort's continuously looping soundtrack. In the elevator, the white-clad attendant told me that in the high desert, rainstorms come at night. Yes, the monsoons. Once I did not know this. "We only get about ten inches of rainfall here," he said like this might be my first visit. "Most of it comes in July and August."

I managed a smile and pretended this was a revelation, not the familiar meteorological rhythm of my adult life. I closed my eyes as I listened, really listened, and remembered a line from Seamus Heaney's poem "The Rain Stick": "What happens next is undiminished for having happened once . . ." goes the line as the rain stick is upended. "You are like a rich man entering heaven through the ear of a raindrop. Listen now again."

SNOWFLAKE AND I HEADED to the southern edge of the Sandias and passed between the gap between the Sandias and the Manzanos (the watermelons and the apples). We drove deep into the forest of the East Mountains and arrived at Louisianne's homestead, a Dutch colonial her scientist-husband outfitted with solar power years ago. Louisianne had two sons, one who was born in a miraculous fertility moment the same year the twins were born. When the twins were little, our kids had gathered for birthday parties with piñatas and chocolate cake. Once her son Danny had cracked a fresh egg from the chicken coop on Grace's head just to see how she would react, which was not well. Tonight Louisianne was preparing taco salad in tortilla cups shaped like floppy hats.

THE NEXT MORNING, Louisianne set aside breakfast dishes to play a song on her guitar. She told me she was singing on stage again after many years of setting music aside for her children. I showed her Grace's music school audition video, playing Grace's cover of "Song for Zula." I'd dwelt with this song all spring and summer, and only now did I understand that Zula was an African word for "brilliant, ahead." It had come in the disguise of a love song, but the pining, all along had been for this. "Brilliant" and "ahead" had defined this year.

Louisianne heard what I heard, the ghost of loss behind Grace's songs, this young woman's profoundly felt sense of grace and strength and joy. How unfiltered it was, how compassionate, how fierce. "Oh I see now," Louisianne said, turning to me and beaming her marveling face into mine. "Your daughter's voice.

This is how I imagine the angels sing." Because angels cry for us. Angels know. Angels are tender when we have to be steely. Angels hold burdens for us. Angels need our love so they can love us through.

The delicate work of preparing our hearts and wombs for these children who came to us had begun long before conception when Louisianne and I had first met as spiritual adventurers in A Course in Miracles circle group that met weekly in a metaphysical bookstore near the UNM campus. In A Course in Miracles I had found a spiritual study that aligned with what I knew to be true about my native faith but, more importantly, a way to be fearless in placing my faith in love. In A Course in Miracles, it is said that the opposite of love is fear, but what is all-encompassing can have no opposite. Only love is real. Through A Course in Miracles, I had lived beyond the scary pulpiteering of my Southern Baptist roots into a space where every test was love. Love, not fear. Love, not money. Only love.

Love was the default, the whole operating system. It was what was already installed in us and could not be uninstalled. In our ACIM circle, we had spent hours and hours on the lessons of love, when the questions on my mind then as a young woman all centered on searching for the way to begin a life with a husband and children. I had treasured the relationship between Louisianne and her husband because they had presented a laboratory on the power of forgiveness in real time with real struggles. "Your task is not to seek for love but merely to seek and find all of the barriers within yourself that you have built against it" was the passage we returned to again and again. I had done the work, and my husband had come into my life. He had joined the group because I had told him I wanted to be with someone who could join me on the spiritual path. He had come with me every week, and we had seemed to be talking the same language about the practice of forgiveness. I had married him. Once, during a bitter marital fight, he had complained, "You have all these rules," and I had said, "I only have one rule: My rule is love."

Louisianne had found her way back into Christianity, and after the twins' near-death at day care, I had been tossed up onto the shore of the Episcopal church, which had offered a blend of contemplative practice and centering prayer, social justice work, and a Celtic nature-based spirituality wrapped in a genuinely wholehearted church.

"I knew the Episcopalians from the inside out," I told Louisianne as we sat in her kitchen and the August sun stretched the day into limitless time where our children's arriving adulthood sat so near their fragile beginnings.

Days after the twins had *not-died*, my babies and I had shown up for portraits at the studio, for the twins' eighteen-month birthdays. I had brought the stuffed Blues Clues chairs with the red swirls, thinking they would make good props. In the photo, bright-eyed Paul bantered with an air that already suggested rock-star scientists like Steven Pinker or Richard Dawkins or Neil deGrasse Tyson. He turned to Ukrainian princess Grace, the unwavering neuroscientist working at the cutting edge of emotional intelligence, the one who could tenderly hold you through your sorrow with active listening and a song that pierced your soul. But they were only eighteen months old, becoming what they would become, and Paul was discussing something lively and relevant with his cohost such as "The Truth About Breast Milk" or "Do Parents Play Favorites?" The journalist in me loved how subversive they were, though I understood they were critiquing me. Grace delivered on the benefits of breast milk for optimum brain circuitry, then cut to an interview with a pediatrician. Paul wrapped it up, sharing a chuckle with Grace, who announced in a clear, high voice, "Don't go away. When we return, we'll have a preview from the exciting new *Clifford the Big Red Dog* movie."

They wouldn't go back to that day care. They mustn't. I would need to find a better place for them. Finding a placement for two not-yet-potty-trained toddlers at the same time in this city had seemed an impossible task. I could easily find one opening, but two? I looked at them under the studio lights, and I thought, "Three days ago, I almost lost you." And every day, they almost could die. Because that's how fragile life was. The beings in front of me were full of light, so light they had that just-now-arrived look like they were still stars, dust and gas and sparkle, a comet streak arriving from the frontier of creation. Like they had materialized into these beautiful shrouds, the new pink skin of the atoned, mere seconds before airtime.

St. Michael and All Angels Episcopal Day School called. They had two openings. Two other twins, also a boy and a girl, were leaving. I knew the parents, friends of a friend. They were leaving Albuquerque and moving across the country to Columbus, Ohio. They had created just the right space for us at just the right time. I had shown my gratitude for our admittance by serving on the board of All Angels Preschool, where I had watched the rector navigate through a listening tour of all the constituents, including the lowly preschool board, to wrestle with conflicting ideas on how to administer the food bank for the homeless. In live time, frame by frame, I watched these strange Catholic-lite people arrive at a win-win solution that had come from Third Force thinking. This was not the organized religion I had known. This was love in action. I had found a way to do active Christianity that was aligned with my native faith but did not require me to do the Sunday School posturing of a hyper-religiosity that seemed so far from authentic love that it was very nearly anti-evangelism. This Christianity at All Angels was not defined by how good of a poser you could be. In fact, when I entered the community with vapors of my old Sunday School poser ways still trailing behind me, they simply gave it no audience. Zero. Which convicted me. This Christianity was defined by how much you could love, how you could steer yourself into a contemplative discipline, so you could help other people love more.

"Plus, my children were safe there," I added as I narrated this to Louisianne. "And they loved ringing the bells."

Louisianne's path back also was led by her children. I smiled as she told me her story because all the boy energy in this house delighted me. Her sons go skiing and hang gliding and mountain biking. The evening before, Danny had invited me to the garage so he could show off the cherry-red British racing motorcycle he just bought from a dude in Durango. I watched his eyes gleam in admiration for the way the shiny silver engine would propel him through the long curving road through the Rockies while his dad provided the steady calm advice any young motorcyclist needs, and his mother tried not to freak out. After many years of the thrash, she and her family left the new-age world, then the Christian world because, as she put it, shaking her head, "We had to go. We had to find truth again."

"There came a day . . ." Louisianne told me this as the sunlight fell through the conservatory and her green parakeets twittered in their cages. She beamed the full light of her face to me. ". . .when I heard, 'Are you done yet?'" Which meant: Are you done doing it alone?

twenty-three

Music for a Broken Piano

THE FIRST SIGN OF TROUBLE was the voice message informing me that the driver was in Santa Rosa, New Mexico, two hours out. I registered my complaint: twenty days of delays, all the stringing me along. It was absurd. As a consolation, the company offered to have the crew unpack for no extra cost. Did I want that? "At this point, I think you owe me something," I said.

It was clear more trouble was brewing when another pickup truck arrived along with the moving van, and the agent and another man walked the length of my driveway. All the boxes on the van are smashed, the agent stepped up to tell me. "I've never seen anything this shoddy," he said as the general manager pressed his card into my palm like a communion wafer. The agent got busy snapping pictures of collapsed boxes. "We don't know how badly the contents of these boxes have been damaged," he said, "so I want you to take pictures of anything that's not right." He shook his head. Five crew members eyed me sympathetically as he cued them to load out.

Shortly after, we found a dead baby mouse in the garage under the plastic shelving. I puzzled for a minute about how to dispose of this tiny creature. The dark-haired crew member nodded toward the garden-implement corral where I had left my shovels for imaginary future renters. Right. He offered to scoop up the little critter and take her to the trash. She was tiny, not more than an inch long. A baby. Not long after that, we found another baby mouse near the garden-tool area. He was tiny too. I scooped him up and sent him away. They were so adorable that I forgot the word "infestation." I wondered, why did the small ones have to die but Mama Mouse live? They were cherubic, small, silver creatures. They looked like they were just sleeping, certainly too cute to poop and pee and chew paper. Had Mama Mouse been searching for them, worried about their safety? She had lost them. We had departed. Their spirits had departed. My own babies had departed. And I had left too. Only this stubborn mama had kept showing up this summer, even after her babies lay dead in the garage. She continued to forage the kitchen in my empty house, seeking food for them. The whole summer I had been in New York living it up at Yaddo and The Writer's Institute and the track at Saratoga, she had been popping her silvery head out from the stove every night, searching for her babies to bring them food. Her dedication was impressive. I had just been out-mommed by a rodent.

THE REAL TROUBLE BEGAN WHEN the crew unloaded my grandmother's Art Deco waterfall vanity. The wood had been stripped off on the right side of the vanity top, leaving a pale dagger of exposed unfinished wood. We settled it against the east wall of Grace's empty room, and I snapped a photo.

My distressed-oak writing armoire arrived without the iron-ring handle. I snapped another photo. More small damages: the latch on the music cabinet, the cross panel on the CD cabinet, split wood on another CD cabinet. And then, a huge gash in the brown leather loveseat.

"Nobody even *tried* to protect this," the crew supervisor with the gray-streaked Harley Davidson beard said. "We would never load it up this way."

On that same sofa, I had vowed to be emo-diverse this year, to fully live this love and be present for all the ugly pain. Now, even that precious vow was ripped right before my eyes, white fibers sprouting from the leather. I would look at it, see it all. I wouldn't flinch. I would see the ugly. This ugly was part of the story too. I snapped a photo in the harsh summer sun. In the live video, the wind lifted the tufts of fiber, taunting me.

My writing desk arrived, the one I had bought with the Rick Bass prize money for "Pretend," the story featured in my TED talk. I saved that prize money for two years before I found the perfect desk. This was it, gleaming reclaimed wood, now with a gigantic scratch across the surface. It was so egregious that it looked like it had been keyed. It was not in an accidental place.

As dents and dings accumulated, the crew became hypervigilant, calling me over for photos. The file cabinet, bashed in two places. A blue glass pitcher, cracked. The juicer, shattered.

The sense that a force was out to get me mounted. So when the dark-haired one called me, my heart sank. "Ma'am," he said, "you need to come look at this."

"Is it the piano?" I said.

He solemnly nodded.

The right-side spindle had been twisted off. Like someone had wanted to break a bone. Like someone had been intent on dismemberment.

"How does someone do this?" I asked him.

Six men and I stood looking at the damage.

This piano had been treated like a strumpet. Had she disobeyed? Had she displeased someone? How dare she.

But that was not to be the final blow.

It was *The Annunciation*.

The glass cracked from top right corner to bottom left corner beneath which Leonardo da Vinci depicted archangel Gabriel arriving to bear the news to Mary that she would conceive a child. You are to be a mother, Gabriel told her. How Mary must have felt when her son was crucified, puzzled she might have misunderstood the plans of these men with wings. Sure that blessing of

Gabriel, when he first alit before her, his white wings fluttering still, meant *something*. Mary sat before a white marble table sculpted with a scallop shell, ionic scrolls, ferns, and flowers. On it was a tilted bookstand, not the New Testament, it hadn't been written yet. She was about to live the writing of it. As Gabriel lifts his forefinger before her, her two fingers remain pinned to the words on the page. She was not sure whether to listen to him or whether to stay with the text. She wore a salmon-pink dress, draped with the blue robe of fidelity. "No, wait—what?" she said. "You're an angel?"

In the background, Italian cypress trees floated like candles. In Da Vinci's rendering, Gabriel's wings were muscular, the color of white mushrooms, an engineering marvel. These angel wings weren't mere fluff or decoration. They transported him. They were aeronautic. Gabriel knelt before Mary, two fingers raised now. "Hear me," he said.

And so she let him talk. Gabriel took inventory of who she was, why God found favor in her: *You are the daughter of . . . You are the granddaughter of . . . You are the one who . . .* is willing.

THE AGENT ASKED ME to fill out an inventory of the damage:

I am the granddaughter of a woman of indomitable spirit = my grandmother's Art Deco waterfall vanity with the round mirror.

I am the daughter of a man who wrote a novel two weeks before he died = my father's desk.

I am a writer who won a prize = my writing desk.

I am the daughter of a woman who poured her soul into her discipline and her art = my piano.

Once I was a wife = Turkish bowl from honeymoon.

I am a mother = *The Annunciation*. I had prepared. I was found worthy and difficult but yet faithful.

For months, I had been mounting my courage to fight that this not be dismantled. It seemed at every turn, I was opposed. Not just blocked. Targeted. Singled out.

Crushed. Pummeled. The Annihilation.

It *was* about me.

Standing in my foyer with the door open to the setting afternoon sun, I let it register with me that my furniture arrived, scarred, twisted, and disfigured. The only message I could hear was: this has come to nothing. Motherhood, career and livelihood, mother, father, grandmother. This shattering was threatening to wipe out not just fifty years of a life, it was sweeping deep down into the roots, erasing my lineage too.

It seemed too high a price.

It was more than I could bear.

Why not just accept the message? I felt the twinge of this thought. I had been getting this twinge all summer. I'd resisted it. Today I could not. The idea that I was no one had been brewing in me like a storm for years. True, now in this light, it appeared to have been a desperate leap. The hope for something better seemed silly. My struggle to fight it seemed fruitless. Daunting. I was simply exhausting myself trying not to disappear.

Why continue, then, to struggle against the thought?

Fifty-six years of not wanting me here? Fine, Universe, you win.

Why, I demanded to know from God, would you give me such a desire to love and serve but not give me the means to do it?

In that instant, I realized the foolishness of my question. God *had* given me the way to do it all. I just kept choosing to do it my own fucking way.

twenty-four

Why I Don't Park My Car in My Garage

FOR MONTHS NOW I HAD WANTED TO DIE IN MY SLEEP. I had been saying it out loud to everyone, the painter and the carpet cleaner, Liam and old friends and new friends, and they had taken it as a bitter joke. But the idea had become a habit. It was more than a wish now. It was a constant inner scream for sweet relief. One night the thought came, "Why wait?" Why not do this faster? Liam had already told me that eating poorly and living with chronic crippling stress hadn't really sped up his process of dying. Not that dying young was what he was after, just that his habits pointed in that direction. If I was going to flip the switch at midlife and start cultivating self-destructive habits, I had a lot of catching up to do.

The faster way was a terrible thought. I had always felt confident I could never carry out an act of self-harm, even after the panic attack. All the methods seemed too terrible, too something I could imagine in brutal detail. Yet clearly my plan for dying was too patient. If all was being taken from me, why not take my life too? The thought pierced me like a jagged arrow and rooted deep in my vital organs. The thought caused me to tremble. Not necessarily because I was afraid of it but precisely because I was not. I rested in the assurance that I had no method in mind, none that I could imagine or execute.

The thought swooped up behind me like a motorcyclist who had been threading his way through a long line of cars. He arrived next to my window, wearing a bright yellow helmet with a smart chin strap, nodding in recognition, just inches from my elbow. "Of course, you could," the voice said like a honeybee, smooth, industrious, believable. "All you would have to do is park your car in your garage and turn it on." Would that work in a Prius? A partial zero-emission vehicle that earned me free parking on any street in Albuquerque? It scared me that it would. It scared me that it would be easy to try. I looked across to the motorcyclist, but his clever face blurred ahead, his message delivered. There, in my own emptied-out home had arrived a solution that had not been possible to see coming, and now, arriving so deftly as it did, I realized the thought had been tracking me, weaving in and out of lanes of cars, keeping up with me through the hairpin curves of the Mogollón Rim, the fathomless bridge over Glen Canyon, tracking me through Colorado mountains and windswept prairie and across the mighty river, the horse pastures of Kentucky, and blue hills of West Virginia. The thought had begun as a streak of red on the New Mexico horizon, disappearing as I rounded a bend or mounted a hill, hanging back distantly enough to appear and disappear and reappear until we both arrived at the same light. Do I know you? Do I want to know you? Don't I already know you?

The bean sí, the death messenger. For how many lights, how many miles, had he been following me? How many years?

In Irish folklore, the bean sí heralds the coming death of a family member. She wails, she shrieks, she keens. In most accounts, she has long streaming hair, wears a gray cloak over a green dress, and has red eyes from crying all the time. She is a woman who has made time to cry. She has perfected crying into a constant keen. She is a professional crier. Most of the time, she is old, crouched, and swift as a storm-bearing wind. But sometimes, she is the young woman, the sweet singing virgin, the one who died young. The one feature that is consistent is that her cry is mournful beyond all other sounds on earth. Her cries are so mournful that they drown out all other sounds. Her wailing lament is all you can hear. Most of us would know her as the banshee.

The banshee is the one waiting for you in the place in the forest, the one who will trouble you with requests to stop doing what you are doing, stop right now. Her lament asks you to make or unmake your life. Her questions won't go away.

This idea that I was unwanted had grown and grown. It now threatened to overtake me. Each day when I woke up, my anger accelerated. I demanded from God to know why didn't you just let me slip away? Did you not hear me?

Erasure seemed like the right choice, the direction everything was going. Maybe it was time to accept that. I had devoted every ounce of me to making sure my children were on their way. Now it was a big nothing. I had been deposited back into the same place I had been at seventeen when I wasn't a journalist yet. I wasn't a mother yet. I had no past yet, only a banshee howling that no one else could hear.

In *Through the Looking Glass* the Red Queen takes Alice by the hand, and they run full bore, feet pounding, hearts racing. When they pause, Alice gasps for breath. She looks around in great surprise to see they are still under the same tree. "Everything is just as it was!" she says. "Of course," the Red Queen says. "What would you have it?" "Well, in our country," says Alice, panting a little, "you'd generally get to somewhere else—if you ran very fast for a long time, as we have been doing." "A slow sort of country!" says the Queen. "Now here, you see, it takes all the running you can do to keep in the same place. If you want to get somewhere else, you must run at least as twice fast as that!"

In a previous newspaper life, an older and wiser colleague had taped this passage to his computer screen. I had been too young to accept his cynicism. The story had motivated him into a hippie-zen detachment from the furious deadlines we faced. It reminded him of the impermanence of daily journalism. We never knew what part of today's story would become tomorrow's history. We only told what happened today.

Yet now I had entered a slow sort of country. I didn't want to run twice as fast anymore. I didn't want to move across the country and back in one summer. A woman had run for president and won the popular vote by three million votes but wasn't president. A woman with a Yale law degree who had proclaimed in China that "women's rights are human rights," served as a U.S. secretary of state, and as a U.S. senator—was not enough.

In my slow sort of country, my loss was a failure, not of a career, not of motherhood, but of a life. It had been a waste. God had been wasting His time here.

I turned to *Immortal Diamond,* where my eyes landed on this: "We each set out trying to create our own hand-cut and handmade diamond, but experienced pilgrims tell us that the diamond was first made by Another, and it is uniquely drawing us forward into a brilliance that is now uniquely ours."

I wanted to believe the words I was reading. I wanted to believe that if Oprah believed those words, they would be true for me too. I wanted to believe that was true for each of us and I could be included in that. I was not a diamond. Carbon under pressure, perhaps. Another billion years and maybe the crystals would be crushed into a diamond. I didn't want anyone to see me this way. I didn't want anyone to come.

"This world does not want me," I texted to my sisters. "Don't try to find me. Don't seek me out. Don't talk to me. I need to disappear."

It was time to listen to what the world was telling me. It was time to stop being stupid.

But I didn't have a method. So I was okay.

THE NEXT MORNING, I had accepted the idea of the method. I woke up with the bright clarity that morning brings, and it seemed perfect. The bean sí was right, so clever. It was one method I could execute with no courage and no pain. So obvious. I could just park the Prius in the garage. Turn it on. Go to sleep. Easy.

No one would stop me.

No one was here.

No one would find me.

For days. Weeks, even.

The Prius was already in my newly empty garage. It was wide open in there like the Prius was on a shiny showcase floor. The solution was minutes away. I just needed to find my car keys.

The other night, I had parked the Prius in the garage for the first time in years, resulting in the most awkward of moments, something worthy of a *Family Circle* comic of my meanderings. I lined up the Prius so it was perfectly poised to enter the garage, then realized I didn't have a garage door opener like a normal American. To enter the garage like a proper suburbanite, I had to enter the house through the front door, wind through the hallway and the utility room to the garage, and push the button to open the garage door. Then I had to go out to the car, start it, pull it into the garage. So many extra steps. Ridiculous. Like a *Family Circle* plot, I could easily forget where I was going and what I originally set out to do.

But there it was, the Prius, expertly parked in the garage, so neat and clean.

It would be so easy. I looked at its green self, and it looked at me.

I texted my sisters and Portia. "Someone needs to call, and someone needs to come."

IN A FEW SHORT MINUTES, I heard from all three. "I need someone to lay eyes on me," I said to them. I asked Portia to call three Albuquerque friends who would see me in person, though I am a pitiful sight. She and my sisters were 1,200 miles away, so they needed proxies. I chose not to reveal to Portia exactly why in an explicit way. I knew she loved me and understood what she needed to understand. It was still possible to read this as temporary sadness and not hopelessness. By their love, the people who loved me didn't see that it was a life never meant to be a life, a mistake, a deformity, a birth defect, which is the way I saw it. They couldn't see that, and for that loving blindness, I was grateful. The presence of my friends would prevent me from thinking what I was thinking. Portia called Deborah, Whitney, another friend. I didn't know what they knew, but I think Deborah got it.

Next, I listened to the sweet sound of Samantha's voice. Her presence steadied me. She had always placed her hope in me and never failed to assure me that she believed in the prowess of my highest ambitions.

Then I spoke to April, who knew the depth and breadth of it because she'd faced these thoughts nearly every day of her life. "The reason you feel empty is because you gave it your all," she said. "If you hadn't given those twins all of you, there would be someone left. That's not a sign you did it wrong. It's a sign you did it right."

For the next two hours, she walked me out of the woods into the light of who I could be now. I promised her that I would not park my car in the garage until I was on the other side of this. Or ever.

HOW WILL I INHABIT this empty, open garage that is a showroom to nothing? What can go in it that isn't my carbon-emitting car that could choke me into a forever sleep?

That evening, I stepped into my garage, launched open the great rattling door so that it slid open to the view across the mesa to Katy's house and a burnishing sunset sky. Her studio door was open, so I knew she was painting. I turned to the blank chalkboard wall. I could map a story here. I picked up a piece of sidewalk chalk.

twenty-five
Spiritual Chemo

AT FARMERS MARKETS ACROSS THE CITY, dark green chiles tumbled as they roasted in cast-iron cages, sending the scent of char into the air. Mornings arrived with a crisper edge, and the light on the mountain was sharp and unfiltered. Still, nothing had changed for me, only that I was willing to hold myself in place until someday it would be better. Deborah came to restore me. We would get the kitchen arranged, and then I'd be functional. I chose drawer liners, chocolate mesh that seemed smart and stylish. Still, I counted it as a decision. A choice, a preference—and preferences indicated there was a self inhabiting this place.

Deborah and I were breaking open boxes and finding a place for each small object, but what I was really doing was listening. She told me she was mediating a case in which a boy with autism was getting lost in the war between his parents. I couldn't help this boy, and she was only able to do so much. But I could listen. Sadness had located itself in me, found its harbor here. My sadness had a story that was mine, and I had chosen to participate with it and found every other sadness in the world. If my saying yes to this sadness helped the Syrian refugee/the sexually assaulted woman/the mother who lost her child in the Sandy Hook massacre/the tree consumed in flames and ash to die quietly in the Pacific forest, then I will live in it. So that we may bear the suffering together. I've made a profession of listening. That is what Actual Real Journalists do. I've been listening a lot lately, to Roma's grief in anticipation of her father's death, to Louisianne's dark night of the soul, to every story told to me over a dinner table or at a wine bar, what we're vigilant about, what keeps us up at night.

I found a small, cubed box that I didn't recognize. I sliced through the tape and cracked open the box. Deborah sensed I'd discovered something and lifted her head to see what I would pull out. Wrapped in newsprint were two crystal claret glasses. Waterford crystal.

"My goodness," I said with a gasp. "These are from Ireland. From when I was studying abroad during college." From before I was a journalist. I barely had had the money to buy anything in that store on Nassau Street across from Trinity College Dublin, where we had seen the Book of Kells and learned about traditional Irish music and the Tuatha Dé Danann. I had bought the smallest glasses in the store. Now I held them up to the skylight so the sun caught the deeply etched lines. The light bent into bands of color, scattered across my kitchen tiles.

"They surely have been sealed in this box all this time," I continued. "At least since I first came to the Southwest. It astonishes me how preserved they are."

As Deborah admired the Waterford crystal, I felt like I had just opened a portal to my twenty-one-year-old self, who had none of my troubles. I set the two glasses on the counter and vowed not to keep my twenty-one-year-old self sealed in a box for another thirty-five years. I would not cart her around the country from Kentucky to Mississippi to Kentucky to Arizona to New Mexico to New York to New Mexico again. That twenty-one-year-old self had ridden a green double-decker bus every day into An Lár, the City Centre, listening to U2's electrifying "Sunday Bloody Sunday" and reverent "Forty" on a Walkman. On Ireland's west coast, the Wild Atlantic Way, she had stood on the shore of Galway Bay as dawn broke the light into rippling threads of pink and blue. She had taken her first excellent photo with a professional camera. When she returned to her home country across the ocean, she would become a wife and a journalist. But before that, she was already a someone.

I turned to Deborah, who had been watching my face. How do I explain? These Waterford claret glasses transported me to a liminal space, where I had lived between my childhood and my future adulthood, the tender space where my children lived now. I cracked a smile before tears could form.

Deborah raked her eyes around this room I had left and come back to, where all my things vanished and then they returned.

"Carolyn," she said, "I've got to admire your pluck."

THE FURNITURE NURSE ARRIVED the next day. He arrived with the gentle efficiency of someone used to taking pulses to monitor the underlying operating system while precise surgical slightly invasive things were done to accomplish repair. Using heat, he seared the ripped leather of the espresso-bean loveseat, erasing the wound. The scratches on my grandmother's furniture, my father's desk, my desk—vanished. Within less than twenty minutes, four of the five most-damaged pieces were restored like this man was wielding a Skywalker laser sword. When this man looked at wood, he saw bone and flesh and skin, something that for him was alive. He turned to the piano, examining the ridges of exposed natural wood in the twisted-off leg.

"You can repair that?" I said, twinging at the violence of the dagger-like projection from the body of the piano. How many years it had taken for that tree in the forest to grow, for the fibers of wood to interconnect, rise tall from rich soil, become lumber, become a piano.

"Yes, miss, I certainly can," he said. "You won't even be able to see where the break was."

He delicately united the pieces like he was attaching two waves in the ocean. He placed a vise clamp to hold the leg in place.

"That needs to set for a week. I'll return and," sensing my sadness, his voice grew softer, "then all will be well."

TO MY FRIENDS, I issued a desperate challenge disguised as fun so I didn't sound so desperate: Take me somewhere in Albuquerque you think I haven't seen before. What I didn't say was: I feel like I'm supposed to die now but if I see something I haven't seen before I might glimpse a beckoning toward life and not death. I am that self that is no self at all. It was my way of asking them to help me restore myself to myself. I don't know how to just say, I'm gone. Is this place gone from me?

Whitney arrived to take me to M'tucci's on the West Side, where her college-age son worked. "This is my way of scheduling social time with him," she whispered conspiratorially as she leaned in to examine the clamp on the piano leg. Her eyes fell on the senior portraits of the twins arranged atop the piano. "It takes about six weeks to recover from the empty nest," she said, and I should say here that Whitney has always been a practical and fiery prognosticator. She had predicted that the twins I carried in my womb would be a boy and a girl and that I would move to the house I am in now.

"Look at Master Paul with his goatee." Whitney lightly tapped the frame. "And look at Miss Grace, ready for her road tour." She lifted Grace and turned to me. "Six weeks, I'm telling you. That's how long it takes." And this seems doable. "Don't get me wrong." She placed Grace back on the piano. "The empty nest hurts like hell."

Whitney had known my ex-husband longer than me, back to his college days, so long she considered him her errant brother. I had told her the latest drama, his demand that the twins keep spreadsheets that will document which parent is providing more financial support. It's more of the same. By paying health insurance, car insurance, and cell phone bills, I was already seven thousand annual dollar-laps ahead of him, but this new judge-and-jury plan was amusing in all the ways it would never happen. The twins had executed the overruling superpower of the teenage eye roll and would never start the spreadsheets. This would heat up, hit its peak, and we'd do right by children. Because Whitney knew him so well, she had steadied me through all these storms.

Every time Whitney saw me, she told me what has become our tribal story as two matriarchs. Weeks after I left my husband—six months after they had *not-died*—she came to my condo. She watched me scoop both babies from the floor and balance them, one on each then-petite hip. "My heart poured out for you," she said. "I wanted to throttle him. I just thought, my god, what have you done?" How could he not step up to this? How could he not man up? That is what she meant and what she never held back from saying to him. I never have an answer to her question, only the one she witnessed that day. I had scooped them up and held them close.

"You did it, though," she said. "And you know I love your children like my own."

At M'tucci's I told Whitney that out of the blue, Paul had asked me to come to Phoenix for a concert. "After a whole summer of hanging up on me…" and I don't even finish the sentence.

"You see, they come around," she said, because had heard her fair share of "you're so fucking stupid."

Just then, her son served our appetizers. He was sporting a Billy Idol look and had muscled up, now a chick magnet. I remembered holding him as a baby, the night after my first miscarriage, wondering if I would ever bear children. Tonight, Whitney and I shared a toast, holding between us that pure place, the fertile before-time.

GRACE IS NOT COMING HOME for Christmas. She's not coming home for Thanksgiving. She won't be here for my birthday, which is on winter solstice just four days before Christmas.

She might not even be here for fall break.

"It's not because it's my plan," she said with the strangled voice of a hostage. If we were Facetiming and not just on the phone, I possibly would be able to capture the Morse code of her eye blinks, crying for rescue. "I have to stay in Denver."

She told me Paul already had a plane ticket purchased for him to go straight from Phoenix to Denver the second he hit send on his last final exam. This means: Paul is not coming home for Christmas. Paul is not coming home for Thanksgiving. Paul will not be here for my birthday. I won't see my children for the rest of the year.

"It's not me, not my choice." Her voice grew tenser. "It's been decided for me."

As I have been moving across the country once and back again, as I have been watching my media career burn to ash, as we have been completing the wondrous task of raising two great people and launching their lives, as we have been approaching the relief of court-directed parenting, the father of my children had made a plan so far ahead of what I could see on the calendar that it has ambushed me. He had scheduled all the holidays from Thanksgiving to January 6 for himself. He had excised me from the lives of my own children.

"Talk to Dad," my daughter said in a voice that now strained toward anger. Anger toward him, to be sure. But also anger toward me. If I'd stayed in New York, I would have been in a separate, safe bin with new rules, a place with fir trees and fireplaces and freshly fallen snow. But now I was back in the same old orbit we'd known before and all hated. If I didn't exist, she wouldn't feel pulled. This conversation could hang out in the territory of seething anger at her father, or it could teeter into spitting anger at me, the other person tugging. She didn't want to be in the middle. She and I won't ever speak about the naked aggression of this. I'm tempted to name it for what it is. But we don't have to say it. She knows.

For hours, I lived in torment that in reaching for an opportunity to better our lives, I had left an opening for my children to get snatched away from me. I'd just been exiled. It felt like the surgical scalpel had been waiting to cut, and cut deep. It felt like I didn't have anesthesia. Now every nerve would have to feel all the pain. I was back in Saratoga, the place where I felt all the raw edges and I ached again. The place where I learned how to give every last thing away.

I called Deborah and she promised to help me write a letter that would "shame the shit out of him."

"Do people keep going to court when they have adult children?" I asked her. "I mean…"

She shuddered at my naivete.

Friends counseled me that he could not do what he was trying to do. "Your children are adults," they said. "They are eighteen, they love you, and they aren't going to stand for their father blocking you from seeing them over the holidays."

Everyone acknowledged that this act assured bad karma was headed his way, but when I talked to Deborah two days later and she couched her legal opinion with an echo of the same spiritual opinion, I asked her impatiently, "So when does this karma kick in?"

"The only way to answer this challenge is: How do you want to feel about this a year from now?" she asked.

I wanted the twins not to be in the middle of it. I wanted to stop the shenanigans so this battle didn't play out every year. I thought when they turned eighteen it would stop.

"Some ex-husbands don't stop," she said. "You got that kind."

The twins were so beaten down from this that they would rather forgo seeing me for the holidays if it meant they wouldn't have to be in the middle. I composed great, eloquent speeches on the consequences of letting the bullies on the playground win. For a brief moment, I felt a consolation that I could choose to operate this as a tai chi maneuver, move out of the way of the force of my opponent, and let him fall. After a full summer of his father's bitter medicine, Paul had come to his own conclusions about how he wanted to spend his time, which was "not there." I fantasized about going to Niagara Falls over the holidays on an insight meditation retreat, letting them have their father 24/7, and letting me have pure silence.

Let them be worried about me because I'm in some state of bliss.

Let them be curious about me because I'm immune from storm outs and text tornadoes. Let them feel compelled to quest for themselves how it can be possible I'm free and living beyond. Let me carve out the new path.

I could be happy and let that shine forth. I could let it glow.

Let it glow, let it go.

Let go of my own children?

Thomas Merton says, "We gain only what we give up, and if we give up everything, we gain everything."

I'd already died. I'd been living without gravity. Without death or fear of death. I'd already been practicing. I'd lived through a summer stripped of material possessions and divested of an identity that had been buried in work and kids, work and kids, and what I had discovered instead was kind humans, my writing, a lake with ghost pines at the shore, a wellspring of jubilant water through a rock. Now I'd entered a new season where I did not need to own things, even my offspring. The poet Kahlil Gibran wrote, "Your children are not your children/They are the sons and daughters of life's longing for itself." I would give my children, then, to that longing.

I read the words of Thomas Merton but I was not there. My children were certainly not something I could just give up. Let me just say that in all caps: I AM NOT THERE. I was only just now arriving at the part where I have been forced to give up everything and I'd gotten used to it. I hadn't yet chosen to live this way, just gotten skilled at enduring it. Surely, I was thinking, it will end. This would have a short duration and we could get back to real life, like I was in Oz with flying monkeys chasing me, but of course that wasn't real. I'd just click my heels and the flying monkeys would be gone.

My friends, bless their hearts, thought it was just a bad movie too. They had rushed into the vacuum because they didn't want me to be without things. Like a mattress to sleep on. Like kitchen drawers lined with chocolate-brown mesh. Like that mattered.

WE WON'T TALK ABOUT THIS. That will be his decision, not mine. He won't answer my calls. I leave business-like voice mails about setting up a time to talk. There won't be a call back. I make a case by email. My inbox remains empty. I send a short text asking for a time to talk. I know I risk a text storm. Or silence. I get silence. I realize how I drew comfort from the text storm. At least we were engaged. At least on some level, he cared about what I cared about. At least he recognized me as their mother. Now I get silence.

I know now where the conversation must take place. In another realm. Where the things I've left unsaid still live. Where the things I've left unheard can at last be heard. On the soul level, which is the only place any of this can be solved.

I settle on my meditation cushion and take in one breath that is deeper than the one I took the moment before. I let that breath wash out of me and I take another even deeper breath. I fill my lungs and feel the breath spreading, nourishing my shoulders, my arms, my hands, my rib cage. I sink in to my breath, and my whole being is tingling with life. I enter the meditation.

In Phoenix with my son, I had chosen to equip my son rather than burden him. There was no need to carry this on. In that moment, I realized, I had forgiven Paul's father. I had stopped the line.

This man had colonized my mind and soul. It was time for him not to live here.

Under fire, I had offered words to my son that changed everything that would happen next. I would show up that same way to myself, in integrity, raw and authentic, for it is said the True Self can never be harmed.

I was ready.

In my visualization, I arrive unbidden.

I approach the edge of our bonfire, the place of our last authentic conversation. I feel calm and mighty and shielded with love. I've come to the other place where my two angels burned, the place from which I was exiled. Immediately I see this will not be easy.

"You're unstoppable," I say. This is not a statement. It is a question. Because after all this time, I still don't understand what the battle truly is.

"You're not pure," he says.

"You needed me to be pure." This, too, is a question. It is a question about why.

"There is no seeing of you," he says. "I don't see you."

"You're not right about me. You're not right about the twins," I say. "You're not right."

"No one else will ever have you."

Arrow after arrow after arrow had pierced my flesh. These were not fresh words. These wounds were old. Some arrows had fallen to ashen ground. Others had lodged in my flesh, though. He would get to those. Those were the poison arrows, the ones that had traveled through my bloodstream, circulated in my thoughts, deposited their venom in the dark capillaries of my life-giving organs.

"You had no right," he says.

"No right? No right to what?"

"To leave me."

I had had every right. And every reason. You gave me one

every day and every night. And after I left, you gave me more. This is not what I say.

Instead.

"We still have the same question we have always had placed before us: What will we do to save this?" I let my question settle. Still, the problem remained that we must. We would always be returned to that.

I toss a stick on the fire. I would be his ghost now. Sparks rush skyward in a fiery wave. I don't have to be his ghost. We can let it be a hearth, not a bonfire. Let it be the secret earth. We could say, "I release you."

I turn to him. "I've done nothing wrong. My 'sin' was that I loved the twins, and I only once loved you."

Now I have told the whole story from beginning to end.

"Your 'sin' was that you loved them, and you wouldn't love me," I say.

Love had become our court of law, though my husband would not grasp that. We would have to act accordingly.

This love was burning him. This love was burning him but not like it was burning me. It was burning me brighter. It was burning a hole through his pocket. It was burning him to have to put them first. It was burning him to have to love me in order to love them.

"You don't have to love me anymore," I say.

The stars turn in the sky.

"You are no saint." As he stands, a log falls, throwing up a hiss of sparks.

So many times, oh so many times he's said this to me. This time, I am not stabbed when he says it. Inside, I laugh a little. Only in this moment do I realize it is a false argument. I don't have to be a saint to be a wife. It isn't in the average job description. I don't even have to be a saint to be a mother. For a long time, this argument threatened me. Only now do I know how unattainable that is. I have devoted plenty to the effort. I'd tried to be a saint. I'd felt like I had to be. Had he wanted to be married to a saint?

I draw in another deep breath. I take in a series of three breaths and let my mind settle.

I lift my eyes. I am not a saint.

Now that I am shed of any obligation to sainthood, new questions can bloom in my mind. Was the problem really that I was trying to be better, or was the problem that he was not trying to be better?

My eyes meet his across the fire. I feel a sharp pain in my left rib just beneath my breast. The same pain had kept me awake all last night. The father of my children, whom I once loved with all my heart, had stabbed me, using the beautiful creatures we had created in love as the spear tip in a battle I could never understand.

His eyes finally look into mine. I let him see me in my unsaintliness. "You're falling apart," he says. "You're fragile."

"I already know how fragile I am," I say in a strong clear voice. Becoming a parent will do that to you. It's supposed to. If you know you're vulnerable, you know you aren't all-powerful. You realize you're interdependent. You realize it's all on the line, all the time, and you need love. "I am a mother," I say and as I stand, I surprise myself when I say it. I finally am seeing myself through the eyes of no one else. I have stopped playing the role of anyone but someone who loves and deserves love. I am shed of being the someone who solves all the problems, does all of the protection, shores everyone up, pretends it's all good. I only have need to be my True Self.

I look into his eyes, those eyes that always look away. "If you think I'm fragile, then it's not because you actually see me or know me. Because you don't. You never made the effort."

I look up at the moonless night sky. We really do live far out from the city.

I turn to him. "It's because you believe you are fragile. You're terrified. You're off-loading."

For years, I've let the father of my children off-load his most unpleasant emotions on me. It is poison to me now, a cancer. His rage, his bitterness, his palpable terror at the magnitude of the task that had been ahead of us that was now behind us, complete, dusted, done. Any sort of emotion he didn't want to feel, he had rained all that down on me.

A chemical imbalance has existed between us all along. I'm not speaking about addictions or fixations. That's the story of someone else's book. I am speaking about his not having the ability to metabolize emotions unless he dumped them on me. For so many years, I've tried to metabolize them, simply because I am accomplished at it and I believed the twins needed for me to do that. I'd said, "I know how to do that" before I could have the thought, "But is it my job?" Here I was, the woman whose accomplishments no longer mattered because stellar resumes and feats of spinning plates don't matter, don't solve the problem, just solve the appearance of the problem. I'd made it look fine.

But it was never fine. The deluge of off-loaded anger and bitterness had been swift and relentless, of such a volume that I couldn't metabolize it. I'd stored it. In the moments of let's-just-take-care-of-the-children please-let's-put-them-first rant-all-you-want-but-I'll-still-be-there-for-them-no-matter-what-you-call-me, mine had been a game of triage. Only so much of it could be felt at any given time. There had simply been no time to cry. I had stayed strong for the twins.

I'd made a promise.

In the distance, the dark desert sky falls to full black, leaving only a narrow band of city lights to define the edges of things. "We did something sacred here," I say. "That's why, no matter what we do, we're still tied together." Schools could fill up gymnasiums and march young faces across the stage to collect scrolls of achievement. Judges could say it was over, free our children from court oversight, proclaim them capable of recognizing they belong to us. But it would never change the essential truth.

When the moment comes to say it, I make a place of prayer. I find one pleat in the fabric of the life I began here, a fold where I must have tucked a prayer eighteen years ago when I lived here by the bonfire and I prayed for my lost babies and the babies to come. I must have cupped a small cradle between the embers and sparks of this fire pit and banked it here. In that cradle of prayer, I find no stirring. No bustle. It's a space of breath, two breaths, and there is no fuss now. I lean into the white brilliance of the fire, and I say to him what I have needed to say all along. It surprises me how few words it takes. How simple they are. How right. The words themselves have their own sweet power. Like fireflies, they seem to hold within their abdomens light-emitting organs, and when said, my words grow lighter and lighter, lilting across the desert sky. I watch him watch the lights as they rise higher and higher. I stand up. When I turn from him, I will not look again. I walk away.

I ARRIVED HOME. That is, home to my meditation cushion. I lit the candle before me. I brimmed with the light of someone who has spoken and now allowed herself to finally hear. My face was washed with tears. I'd forgiven him and released myself. Only now could I feel the heaviness of all the old leaden thoughts I carried in my belly. With shaky legs, I stood and fell to the bed. Dark cells leave my body like lava. Each time I hit a contaminating thought, I nodded. I recognized it. I sent it up. *Take this out of me. Let me have space in my body for You to dwell here.* All the while I had been storing the dark, there hadn't been space for anything divine to live in me. As I had been trained in mindfulness meditation sessions with Jon Kabat-Zinn, I scanned my body for any part that was not settled. I scanned for all poisons. All the dark places. Where had I stored protection for the twins? Protection they no longer needed. Protection that enslaved them. Where had I stored the idea that I must be both father and mother, both provider and nurturer? Where had I hidden myself from myself so I could be all?

My garage, now empty and echoing except for one death-giving vehicle, had long been crowded with all that was unresolved. Beginnings, hopes, creative impulses, promises—no endings. It could be the place where I ended all of this. Where I ended that game.

Or I could stay here, run the scan again until it was clear and light. The more I scanned my body, the more I uncovered all the stored feelings that could never be brought to light because any or all of them would have shattered the twins. I had had to hold those emotions in a delicate balance of a two-household family, giving them over to the only stability that was possible. My stability, cultivated fiercely and fearlessly—and the half-baked phony stability their father offered, just enough to do something with. We had had to take him at face value. He said he wanted to be a father, so we pretended he lived in the role. He said he wasn't drinking and driving, so we pretended he wasn't. He inhabited the shell of the archetype. We had had to pretend that forgiveness and healing were present because court-ordered custody had asked us to be nice. I had meditated. A lot. I had written a book on mindfulness meditation. When I was editor of *Sage* magazine, I had led a seminar on mindfulness-based practices. Thomas Merton calls the work of the contemplative the work of inner disarmament.

I had become a fort.

"Take this *OUT* of me," I pleaded.

Beyond my window, the city lights of Albuquerque shimmered. I stood and refused it, all of it. I'd said my words. I would not carry his because they were not mine. I stood with my hands before me like a warrior wrestling an opponent to the ground. I pinned the physical dark energy mass between my palms and spun it. I held it off, preventing its force from pressing closer into me. I grappled with its unwieldy force. I braced my legs and I shoved it with all my might in the direction of that bonfire, his house, this city. Yours, not mine. *You* must carry it.

Exhausted, I dropped to my floor. The weight of darkness

was palpable—it pressed unrelentingly on my full body. I cried and cried until the dark presence lifted from me—all the cells. As I felt them lift, I vowed I would accept nothing less than all. Cells ripped out of me, making the sounds of splitting threads. They rose like torn bits of fabric, collecting and undulating in a current that swept out of the room. Each time a curtain of dark rose, a rippled past, a silence, settled. I rested my mind and scanned my body. I looked for any dark tatter lingering in any pocket of me. When I found more, I lifted my words. *Take this from me. It is not mine. I have carried it for too long.* Now I watched as, visibly, a dark curtain ripped and rose out of my belly. I felt the space of lightness it left in the cavity of my body. And as it accelerated, chunks spewed out of me like ash.

I stood. I looked out to the distant city. I saw to the horizon where the twin peaks of the Manzanos waited beneath the stars. Though I counted each twinkling star, I did not know their names. Lightning flashed high above in a deep sea sky. I saw with a subtle but transparent clarity. My eyes fixed there, on a word: Love. That's the name.

All that is not Love does not remain.

Only Love remains.

I brought myself back into the room. What I saw around me was no longer separate from me. I had the unshakable conviction that I was in the presence of God. But God was not outside me, above me, or out on the city lights on the horizon. God was all around and in me. I hadn't died—I'd been engulfed. *This* was the death I had been resisting, the death I had been running from. God and death can seem like the same thing. I'd melted and melted and melted until I had no option but to melt. I'd dissolved. It felt sweet. The One I had been looking for had found me.

THE NEXT MORNING, I arose with a fresh gaze. I looked across the room at my writing desk, and I felt a presence. The presence fully inhabited the space of my chair, the window to the south, and the mirror that caught the light of the sun. "Why do you cry?" The voice whispered my full name. "I'm here."

"I know," I said.

twenty-six

Halo

FOR ROMA'S FATHER'S MEMORIAL, I decided to wear the same dress I'd worn to my mother's funeral, the one with a pencil-thin red belt and a black knit sweater with an elegant Michelle Obama ruffle. Straight from the funeral, I'd go to the airport, where I would fly to Rochester, Minnesota, to lead a newsroom training.

I slipped into the next-to-last pew at San Felipe de Neri during the rosary. When the coffin entered the church, the priest gathered the family in the vestibule so he could prepare them for the departure to the cemetery after the service. I stood steps away from a re-creation of the moment when I, as the oldest and the first, had walked behind the coffin of my mother, my sisters following as we exited the church. I had walked behind my mother out into the brick-walled vestibule with the immense paned windows and stepped into summer sunlight. I had turned when the pallbearers steered her left to the door where the hearse awaited.

Once I had been a five-year-old innocent, entering that Kentucky church clutching the hands of my mother and father. I had gazed at an immense mural, a Greek-lettered *A* and *O* floating up from blue and white tile. Those grand tiles couldn't be a humble Galilean carpenter speaking to me, the one with the calm face and the long beard. It seemed to be a message about the eternal mystery of matter and spirit. How we even come to be or why. What we were before, what we will be after. It whispered the message of the Universal Christ, someone I could only name later. The *A* and *O* said, we were told, "I am the Alpha and the

Omega, the first and the last, the beginning and the end," a ripple of such cosmic dimensions, I couldn't grasp it and no adult could explain it to me. Yet my eyes had risen to it every Sunday through my childhood, seeking to understand, sensing all the real answers undulated above the pulpit where a white man banged his fists and cried out we were not pure. When as an adult, I tried to comprehend the Alpha and the Omega, I began with language, the stepping stones I knew. Alpha and Omega were the first and last letters of the Greek alphabet—in between stretched the whole utterance of every thing.

My mother, my father, and I had entered that church, the beginning of a family. Now their four descendants were exiting, the end of a family. My parents would be gone, and I would remain. I would be an orphan.

In the vestibule of San Felipe de Neri, Roma stood at the coffin of her father amid her sisters and brother and mother. A priest told them about what they would walk through. When it had been my turn to walk through, I felt like I could not walk. My parents had led me to the threshold of a faith in things they could see but I could not yet see. How was I supposed to exit with this empty space in my palms where their guiding hands should be?

As Roma's father's coffin proceeded up the aisle, my ex- husband's friend Barbi scooted in next to me, whispering a hello and hugging me to her shoulder. Barbi and Roma had become close friends after erupting into a heated political discussion at my wedding to the twins' father, something we all laughed about now, and they had been fierce allies in liberal feminism ever since. Barbi had served as a guardian angel of sorts for my children, tempering my ex-husband's excessive behavior, keeping a benevolent eye on the twins, and loving him like a sister. I knew she'd always had their best interest at heart. I'd been grateful for that and for the 2016 election party she'd hosted when mothers and daughters and friends arrived to what we thought would be a celebration of the election of the first woman president of the United States.

From the lectern, Roma and her brother alternated reading passages from their father's memoir. I'd helped Roma prepare the obituary, which told the tale of being the son of migrant farmworkers, losing his father at age seven, his mother at age fourteen. Yet he earned an MBA and worked for thirty years at Sandia National Laboratories, raising Roma and her siblings. His was a Dreamer story about the will to overcome whatever misfortune may throw at us.

High above to my left, most natural to my gaze, was Station VII of the Stations of the Cross. The Galilean carpenter had nearly fallen under the weight of the cross. His knees had touched ground, and he pressed himself up with his left hand, his face only six inches from the sand. A muscular centurion in a silver helmet had grabbed the upper arm of the Galilean carpenter from behind and above, straining to lift him. Behind him, a white-robed man tried to lift the cross, so the speaker of spiritual truths could struggle to his feet. Yet further back in the crowd, a man with a face contorted in bitter rage cursed the man with the calm face and the long beard. Streams of blood ribboned from thorns piercing the temples of the One Who Taught Love. As I tilted my face up to view this mural painted on plaster walls where the midday sun beamed down, the halo around the Serene One was a perfect glowing orb, embracing more and more light as if accumulating every ray of sun.

The homily began, and my eyes leapt to the east side of the church, ticking forward through Stations VIII and beyond. The Galilean carpenter was back on his feet, bearing the cross on mighty shoulders that had built shelters for people. Two women kneeled before him, one fallen to her knees, raising a child to him. The Serene One gently held out a hand to haven them, bring them into sanctuary. "I've got this," he seemed to be saying, and then his halo glowed brighter. What was the Assailed One trying to show us about all our wrong ideas about God? Not how bad it was. Not how he bled. Not how he struggled to stand. Not how invincible he was. Not how sacrificing. That halo. Why, the more they wanted to dim him, did it glow brighter and brighter?

Jesus had fallen. By Station IX, he teetered at the edge of consciousness. A soldier poised a spear to his flesh. Someone held the carpenter's foot in place for the nail to pierce through. Behind him, a religious scholar raised a palm to renounce the One Who Taught Love, make him vanish. The halo glows brighter. On the other side of death, his body has been lifted from the cross and gently cradled in a deep blue robe, handed to Mary, his mother. Now she wore a halo. As their heads bent together, one alive, one not, their haloes merged. You see, it is true, spoke the blended halo, love is stronger than death.

Wrong ideas about God become wrong ideas about everything, says Father Richard Rohr. When you fall into the bright abyss, all the weighing and counting become unnecessary.

I'd forgiven the man who failed me as a husband. I had been scanned and wiped clean of any of it, all of it. I had no burden. I had forgiven myself for choosing something that hurt my children. I had forgiven myself for all the times I did not love enough. I was holding hands with Barbi and the person to my left, and as I did so, a gathering strength flowed through my arms. Forgiveness brimmed out of my heart. I understood that *because* the father of my children renounced me in bitter rage, I had been tested. I grew in fortitude and I grew in virtue. I hadn't known where to turn but love. Love was a beacon to better. Because I loved my children, I had always chosen better.

Every time, the dart of "you are no saint!" flew, it drew blood. Let's talk now about saints, really talk. How does someone succeed in being loved, having impact, creating meaning? How does someone succeed in triumphing over obstacles, transcending that which would do you in, pulling themselves forward? Naturally, you would look to those highly evolved people who had done it. Living role models and archetypal figures. Rohr says only then can it constellate in our consciousness that it is possible for us too.

Only in pain had I leaned deeply into the imperative to live into better. I hadn't set out to be a saint. But now I knew, I had been to saint school. I had died to that old self my ex-husband kept persecuting. That old self was false, and nothing can be stripped from what was always false.

The louder the Roman centurion screamed, the wider the halo of the One Who Loved Us glowed. From icon to icon to icon, on the road to the crucifixion, September light filled the church. Jesus had not been falling. No way. I had had it wrong all this time. It was not a demonstration of falling; it was a demonstration of loving. Love brought him to his feet.

It had taken great love and great suffering to see. For too many years, I had not believed I was doing anything but persevering. But here it was, painted on humble icons lining a humble church, in this white church with the robin's-egg blue altar and the gilded statues whose saints held palms upturned to the light, undefended and vulnerable and, therefore, powerful. We don't want to see how that works. It feels weak. It's the opposite of weak.

Barbi lifted our hands to the windows that spilled with azure sky. She leaned to me and whispered, "I grew up Catholic, and I just love all this shit."

"THEY'RE BEAUTIFUL!"

The sound of the bassinets rolling through the door is joyous music. They are minutes into this life.

I hear him before I see him, my husband and our new family. When the bassinets round the corner, they have gathered every voice in the river, an interplay of birdsong and forest song and people song. The writer Anne Lamott once said, "Every sound is by definition a stop, which is how we can hear it."

Here, we stop. I listen now again. I listen for the love in the pauses where the river current nudges stone. I listen as it bends, flows in a bundle of tendon, muscling now, gathering speed. Again. He says it with my name, attaching my name to the joy. "Carolyn, they're beautiful!"

My husband stands between our two babies, overcome with tears of gratitude. He hands Grace to me. He lifts Paul to his heart.

No matter what has come before and will come after, I will always remember him this way.

After I feed the twins, he spreads out newspapers—*Albuquerque Journal, Wall Street Journal, the New York Times, Investor's Daily* and the *Ukrainian Weekly*—and he takes photos of the twins on the day's heralds. Grace is swaddled in a yellow blanket, slightly turning her face to Paul. Paul is in a white blanket, whispering today's news in her ear.

I forgave. And I forgot anything that had ever happened, anything that had ever been said. The father of my children was reincarnated into a man who was innocent. I love our children, he loves our children, therefore, he is innocent. From this day forward, the only story I will ever tell the twins or any other person about him is this one.

And you, dear reader, you must forget everything I have told you about him in this story. I have told you so you would see how I transfigured my sorrow and confusion into love. I have told you so you could see how ridiculous we were not to forgive each other sooner and let each other be. I have told you so that you can laugh at us and maybe see yourself. I have told you so you see how very possible it is.

What did I ever learn by dying? asks the poet Rumi. This summer, my adventure in going beyond myself had been a lesson in dying before I died. Father Richard Rohr says that people are only afraid of death as long as they do not know who they are. Once you know this, you can begin living, instead of climbing, proving, or defending. I had been transfigured. Everything I had resisted had become ash. Even as it burned off from me, it regenerated me, became something newly reborn. Having faced the first death, I had lost nothing that was real. The second death can do me no harm, as Saint Francis said in "Canticle of the Creatures."

Roma and her father are leaving the church now. Now the center was everywhere, and the circumference, the edges that hold us, was nowhere. What if the road to nowhere goes everywhere? I stood with mourners on the sun-drenched steps of San Felipe de Neri looking out at the white gazebo of Old Town plaza. For four years now, I had been walking point behind a coffin. Now it was time to walk to nowhere.

I hugged Roma twice. I love her so much. I apologized that I could not go to the cemetery. "I have to fly to Rochester," I said, and she nodded knowingly. I walked around the corner and suddenly I was dazzled by this town, the warm apricot adobe and the pristine white crosses against the azure sky. I turned down Church Street, where an exposed-adobe wall swept out to embrace a patio with strings of Christmas lights and turquoise doors. I noticed them. I noticed it all. I swung into a handmade-soap shop and decided that this would be my first college care package. I smelled every single square of artful soap before I settled on one that captured the rime of watermelon light at the base of the Sandias, an ocean wave of crimson against an almond-coconut sky. I dropped in two squares of soap and two bath bombs and I decided to mail them once I landed in Minnesota.

While I enjoyed a pear salad and a midday glass of pinot grigio at Artichoke Cafe before hopping on my plane, I got a flurry of texts from a worried client. "You aren't leaving me, are you?" she texted. "Don't let Rochester take you. You belong here."

This was worth a voice-to-voice call. "Don't worry," I said. "I won't be tempted again." I've paid for the pearl of great price. I don't tell her this because she is Jewish and I am . . . beyond a category. My category is Love. My category is the True Self. I invoke the ghost of Thomas Merton and every other teacher who led me here, no matter their labels or their paths. I will not forget what I have paid to find treasure in the field, the one Jesus said was worth selling everything for.

twenty-seven

Useless Things

THIS WEEK, the top dermatologists in the world gathered at the Mayo Clinic, and now after a day of delivering their important conference talks, they came to Pescara to unwind. I came, too, after a day of brainstorming with newsroom reporters on all the ways they can tell the story of the diversity of this city, where twenty-eight languages are officially interpreted at the Mayo Clinic, including American Sign Language and Tigrinya. Many students at Mayo High School were here because they were children of doctors summoned to practice at the Mayo Clinic on H-1B visas, and many are here because their parents have fled Somalia and they have refugee status. I came to lead a diversity news project targeted to the earnest and skilled sports writers, a group that was completely and unilaterally populated by white males. One of the codgiest found it so refreshing that I had elegantly and tenderly lifted him out of his box of interviewing the same old mansplaining white male coaches that he had chased me around the newsroom to show me his revisions. The sports writers and I have talked all day and all night about how to cultivate the trust of both the elite populations of the sons and daughters of world-renowned doctors who play soccer and the newly arrived refugees from Somalia who have placed their sons and daughters on the same soccer fields. Each have separate cultures that despite the good intentions of the newsroom, reporters cannot break into.

Two women joined me at the long marble high-top. One was divorced, the other married, as she quickly let me know, to a Trump supporter. "I voted for Hillary," she chirped, confident I was of her tribe. The wife winged her shoulders back like she was shaking off a cloak and explained in a conspiratorial voice. "I still haven't told him."

Three generations of family networks had woven themselves around her and this husband whose vote repulsed her. They had four children together, sons-in-law, daughters-in-law, grandchildren. Threads of raw silk, whistle sleek and soft nubby have woven themselves together through the years into a bolt of cloth that she would not unravel. She shuddered, clearly struggling to tease out how her network got so tangled in something that is such an ill fit. Her Trump-supporting husband blustered about his right to status and lamented about threats to his privilege. He had become the burr in the fabric, the strange nub that she wanted to pick out. She was out here tonight so she could breathe. So she could find me and talk to someone.

Sometimes she knows the true collateral damage lies in all the ways she has worked into that space of seeing things from his viewpoint so she could hold her marriage and family together. "And never the other way," she said, "never any curiosity about the way I see it."

I had wondered why 53 percent of white women in red-voting states had voted *for* Trump. On Election Night 2016, after the inevitable had become clear, I had stepped outside into the cool November night with Roma and Barbi. Someone had wailed into the night, "Will the world *ever* be better for our daughters?" When I learned days later that my own tribe had betrayed me— and women of color like Roma and Barbi had renounced him—I fell into disillusionment.

And now the answer to my question was sitting before me, like an answer to a prayer, like God was actually listening and like God actually cared about American politics. Like God understood that the patriarchal mindset of conquering and colonizing and leaving the beings of this earth in a wasteland was not good for us. The patriarchal wasteland was about greed and fear and power. It was long since past the time to talk about love or how we can be better. This woman sitting in front of the shimmering fish-wave lights was asking me because she wanted her family to be intact, "Do you believe in love? Do you believe in something better?"

I swallowed hard. For my children and this planet, I would continue to practice the best criticism of the bad by living the better. Yes, I said. I do.

THE NEXT DAY, I got word from Liam that he had Saratoga news.

"You won't like this, I'm sure," Liam began. "They're doing a national search for an editor now. But—" here it comes "—Nerilla and Regan have persuaded Anton Leir that the search should only consider male candidates."

"Because why?" I heard the edge in my voice.

"It is believed that men don't do drama," Liam said in a measured tone.

"Professionals don't do drama," I said and I'm grateful he let me say it.

"Yep," he said and sighed.

"There's more that you don't want to tell me."

"I'm probably not supposed to tell you."

"But you will."

"So they brought in this editor who had kind of been a complete disaster at a high-profile national mass-circulation magazine," Liam began, and I heard his frustration and contempt and disgust. "And he demands a higher salary, of course." I'm convicted here. When I negotiated a higher salary, I was told that I had "spooked" them. Nevertheless, this narrative is too entertaining for me to break in with that. "But also an apartment and a car allowance. He's lived in Manhattan all of his life. He doesn't know this is a small town in upstate New York. This would bankrupt the magazine, of course. The revenue they're getting, especially with us out of the picture, won't support a salary like that."

"Define 'like that.'"

"Oh . . . uh . . ."

"Just tell me," I said because I've covered hurricanes and earthquakes and forest fires and 9/11. Because for the first time in my life, I had been fired. "The worst has already happened."

His salary was $100,000 more than my salary, Liam revealed. Plus, it included an apartment in downtown Saratoga right off Broadway in those new condos and a monthly car allowance. Not to mention bonuses for when you deliver what-everyone-else-is-going-to help-you-deliver because-they-get-bonuses-too. This was how white male privilege worked. I knew the patriarchal mindset.

"This editor, he's known for his dramatic exits," Liam concluded and described a few scenarios, some of which have been displayed on social media. They are vivid and visceral and vindictive.

"That really takes the cake," I finally said.

"Yep."

My mind flashed on the Saratoga job interview dinner at Max London's, when Nerilla drew me to her end of the table, so I could sit across from Anton Leir. "We're just in love with her," she said, presenting me. After we got settled in, the wine poured, Anton Leir said, "You know why I love Saratoga?"

"Why?" I said with the avid interest of a job candidate. I wanted to know what made this self-made billionaire tick.

"Eye candy," he had said, leaning across to me. "Saratoga has the most beautiful women in the world."

Nerilla had smacked her thigh like a trainer pats a favored thoroughbred. Then she kicked her ankle-strapped foot out suggestively toward Anton Leir as she laughed at his joke, which was just a joke after all because he certainly was not viewing his whole life through the lens of whether he was sexually attractive. He was not seventeen. He was seventy-eight.

And so here we were, two seasons later. The man with the dominatrix mistress in Miami and a sweet spot for a blonde fifty years younger than he was was hiring a man because men are not dramatic.

"But you've got this opportunity in Rochester, managing editor. Or Illinois, editor-in-residence," Liam said. "I promise you it's good."

In the media business, I had sought success and equality in a male-dominated world. To do that, I had played by their rules and done pretty well. Some women don't even get within range of the glass ceiling. I had gotten close enough to bash my head against it early and often.

I had set myself up to be judged by the masculine criteria for success. I had not seen that, inevitably, I would fall short for one simple reason: I am not a man. By those rules, the best I could ever hope for was to be a successful not-quite-man, not quite good enough.

And live with that. I had been living in a culture where most women are doomed to fail. For fifty-six years, I had been under the illusion that it was not like this, that feminism had wiped that away. When long-held illusions fall, they fall hard.

Get over it, I wanted to say to myself. But I didn't, and plenty of other women didn't. When U.S. Senator Kirsten Gillibrand announced her 2020 bid for the White House, the first story she told to *The New York Times* was about her reaction the morning after the election of Donald Trump. She was crying. No, bawling. But two months later, she experienced the most inspiring day of her political life: the Women's March. We'd thronged the streets. We weren't going to "just get over it."

AS I WRAPPED UP IN ROCHESTER, I saw that the owner would not be in a financial position to bring me on for the editor-in-residence role in Illinois or the permanent managing editor position in Rochester—and that was okay. I walked the skyways, the enclosed pedestrian bridges that link the Mayo Clinic and downtown in an interlocking climate-controlled village of tile and glass, where you could always be at a remove, one floor up from the street, where down there is weather. And where there was a tiny newspaper office that sat in the shadow of the Mayo parking lot, earnestly and capably every day asking questions, being curious about the people here, looking out for them.

In Saratoga, I had nearly become what I was not. I had colluded with patriarchy. Walking through the corridors to the Rochester Art Center, I encountered the vast lobby named after the Mayo Clinic, where they were setting up a banquet. When people arrived to at this place, they looked out to Zumbro River and Mayo Memorial Park. Behind the tall windows, I felt cut off from the river and the green fields, from the wild mystery and freedom that made my heart sing. Couldn't Liam see that?

Couldn't I?

This was the wasteland. I had already spent much of my life doing work that didn't bring me alive just so I could feel secure. I had defined myself by work I did for others, and when the time of fruition came, when the opportunity came to just say what I was and what I wanted and who I would become, I didn't say it. And I wondered why my heart was breaking?

It was time to catch the shuttle. On the bus, I opened my laptop, and I kept typing, finishing my application to the Living School like every next keystroke would save my life. The third question was, "Describe an experience of failure and what it taught you." I began to type. "This summer, I moved across the country—twice."

My fellow travelers and I transferred to the shuttle that would take us to Minneapolis, and I added: "This summer, my twins graduated from high school and left for college. I emptied the nest. I am a single mother, so they were my all, my whole family. But I found another word for emptiness…" By the time we arrived at the Minneapolis airport, I was on the final question, which asked me to describe an experience when a shift in my perspective enabled me to let go of my ego and allowed a more Spirit-centered self to emerge. The True Self was the self who lived here now. It had doubts about the unknown too. But it was not afraid of death. I had been there and back. I typed my answer: What died in me was not all that. What remained was Love, which needs not hide or be protected. Instead of sacrifice, I lived in a new economy of grace. The True Self was the game changer. It had shown me the absolute freedom to love. I was transfigured.

From the plane, I turned my face to the sunny wide-open skies of the prairie. I could say goodbye to all that. And say hello to this horizon. It is boundless.

AT WALMART, I knew where the chocolate-brown drawer liners were, exactly the best kind and exactly the right shelf. I had now been here, to this store on Albuquerque's river's edge, enough times to disqualify it from the Walmart Challenge. Though I knew my destination, I wandered up and down the aisles, marveling at the array of things.

My inventory:

Scarecrows with plaid patches, long strands of straw for fingers and toes dangling to the floor, orange-triangle noses and orange-blush cheeks, hyperextended smiles.

Pocket folders and snap-top crayon boxes.

Candy melts in pastel colors and ice cream flavors.

Party-favor bags. Elsa. Spider-Man.

Straw bales in case you're having a hayride party this week.

Fabric bolts in shimmery chiffon and cotton duck print in Disney princess patterns, Jasmine and Mulan, in case you have time to sew a costume.

Fleece in neon colors, because that makes sense if you are out in the wild and you want to tell everyone that you are not a deer.

All the back-to-school merchandise, No. 2 pencils, felt markers and spiral wide-rule notebooks, tossed into bins and marked down. Everyone is back to school now.

In the toy department, the Fisher-Price stack of ring toys sported a unicorn touch, because what? We are hoping for something magical beyond belief? I smiled, though. Count me a believer in the wisdom of the wild child.

In the toy aisle, the Fisher-Price chatter telephone was the same, comfortingly, friendly eyes on a wheeled telephone with a rotary dial. This classic roll-along pull toy and its insistence on cultivating genuine toddler chatter, that was real.

Globes and picture frames, bike helmets, and plush-toy minions.

Room fresheners in pumpkin spice garden spa orange buttercream lavender sugar.

Because this was Albuquerque, one whole segment of the candle section featured Sacred Heart Jesus candles.

Cookie jars and shoe organizers, laundry baskets that were cones, laundry baskets that were rectangles, aqua-oil pillows, a *Toy Story* blanket. A *Frozen* lunch box.

For people who were still packing lunches, a bright green insulated cup with a built-in straw. For people who were still setting tables night after night, plastic place mats. For people who were still cleaning up after people, plaid dish towels and teardrop pot mitts with images of blue owls. For people who were expecting a crowd, foil roasting pans.

There were light bulbs and garden hoses, Keurigs and cold-brew coffee stations, bath scrubs and tampons and hair clips and grill brushes. Plain clear totes with white lids or gray totes on wheels or mint-green totes with pull handles. For people who were hauling things from one living place to the next living place.

Only now could I see this as the on-ramp to frantic accumulation. In the world of quantity, we were always haunted by competition, writes poet John O'Donohue. In the world of the soul, the more you have, the more everyone else has.

There was nothing here I needed. This store was filled with useless things.

I had constructed a persona as mother and journalist and author and defended it with all my might. I had started in life as an ambitious and talented young writer who wanted to marry, bear children, live in a house with a view. These were good containers for a life. To begin on that path, I had made myself an endless self-improvement project, some of that fueled by ambition, the unadulterated joy of success, but honestly, some of it fueled by fear of failure, the constant companion of "if you want to get somewhere, you must run twice as fast as that."

My particular illusion, a white Western woman, educated and empowered to a point, was that I was separate from what I wanted because I am a woman, and women must always come in second. But that was just the way the lie came to me, the illusion that told me I was separate from power, trapped here on this side of the glass. The deeper illusion was that I was separate from the Source of all my good. We, each and every one of us, have a story about it, and that had been mine.

A combination of great failure and great suffering, a combination of great love and a great severance from that love, a combination of spiritual practice and an interweaving of all the friendships, old and new, that had nested in my life, a perfect storm of small-town politics and fragile egos and greed and my own wailing grief—all had ended my game.

The aisles were full of ways to start a new persona, build a new home, start the game again. I heard the unrelenting invitation to jump in. But this time, I could hear that consumerism was the yawning grave. I had forged my way through a summer of living without things and living instead with the invisible fragments of love I'd tucked into the fabric of the whole universe. I'd lived without things and lived with people, who were unpredictable and multidimensional and endlessly twisting into a braid that vibrates rhythmically, beating out the law of love.

With joy, I surrendered these useless things. I walked out of the store.

(I did buy the drawer liners.)

twenty-eight

Divenire

NO ONE SEES THE CHANGE. It is invisible. I continued to do the work of being me, empty-nested mom, journalism professor, book coach, author. I graded young journalists on AP style and inspired them to probe for the truth. I described narrative arc to emerging authors. I kept telling this same story on social media. Because I was still living in a body, I limited my carbs and never got on the sugar train. I craved roasted green chile and smothered burritos, and when Balloon Fiesta came, I craved them more. I noshed on manchego cheese, stuffed green olives, and quince paste; I drank rioja and I listened to live flamenco guitar. I hiked the foothills and went to sacred hot yoga. I still applied mascara to my nonexistent eyelashes, hoping they'd be seen.

But that was not because I believed these preferences were still me. It was because I understood that a functioning ego was a necessary vessel for an incarnate soul. I accepted the terms. I believed that God chose this particular functioning ego for a purpose, though I'll devote the rest of my days to standing in the presence of the Holy One and asking what that is.

I hiked into Domingo Baca Canyon, and a pounding storm rolled in. When I turned back to look at the city, a rainbow had formed out of the mists from the foothills. I was *in* the rainbow, looking out to the ragged, ashen clouds over the city. Here, it said, you are the person who is *here*.

ABOUT FOUR O'CLOCK, Paul texted: "On my way." I imagined him pulling out of Mesa in the Yaris, up into the Superstition Mountains on Beeline Highway. I knew he'd be driving by the light of the full moon across the trackless desert. A seven-hour trip.

"This is not what I would have chosen for my precious son," I said to my California friend Diana on the phone. I was thinking of the near-catastrophic near crash on the Utah highway. I was thinking of the long stretches of lonely desert road between Phoenix and the descent from Nine Mile Hill into Albuquerque. I had hoped he would cross the desert through daylight. I walked out to my peak and looked at the starlight. "Talk to me a little while longer," I pleaded with Diana.

I felt calmer delivering details about Paul. Networking on LinkedIn, he'd found a connection with a connection of the author of *GEB*, scored a grant for computer science research, and got paid in bitcoin, which in fall 2017 was the best time ever to receive bitcoin, ahead of the mega-growth of cryptocurrency. By Christmas, it would quadruple, and Paul would stash it away for future research trips and grad school. "He's got the touch, Diana," I said. "This boy of mine is going to do well in life."

What I understood now about my son that I didn't understand before was how much he wanted the room to figure out his life for himself. Even if he made mistakes. He craved and demanded the thrill of it. Except for the way he drove on California mountains and in Utah canyonlands, he'd been more ready for adulthood than I knew. Because he just wanted it so bad. Adulthood and independence energized him. "Not every seventeen-year-old is that ready," I said.

"And you have *two* who were that prepared," she said. "Your twins seem to be gliding into adulthood."

"That's true," I said. "I see the others who aren't." I had a good data set on college freshmen after five years of teaching at UNM. "Some of them are lambs being led to the slaughter. Life skills are the No. 1 skill to have to be successful in college. I'm happy, Diana. My kids are happy. I am not worried about my kids."

"That's gold, Carolyn," she said, and we signed off.

Out on my hill, I watched the moon rise over the midnight edge of the mountain. This same moon guided my son's way. He must be out of the Mogollón Rim and past the Painted Desert, nearing Holbrook. I let out a deep breath.

I prepared his new bed for him with flannel sheets and a luxuriant blue fleece blanket. When I knew Paul must be somewhere between Gallup and Grants and getting tired, I snapped a photo of a bed and a book and a puppy. The book was George Saunders' *The Tenth of December* and the puppy was Snowflake. "Warm bed and a book await you," I texted.

Around midnight, I heard a soft knock at my front door. My son stood in the glow of the porch light with his guitar case, smiling broadly. He gathered me in a brave, bold hug.

Though it was late, he wanted to talk. He'd been learning Ludovico Einaudi's "Nuvole Bianche" ("White Clouds") on guitar. When he played it for me, the swirling chords worked through my heart. He was playing our life together as mother and son, soaring, wing-beating, gliding, landing, all of our rough miles.

THE NEXT MORNING, we sat on the back patio and watched balloons rise on the blue horizon. I made him a vegetarian breakfast. They called it the Mass Ascension because 800 balloons rise at dawn. It was a sky square-dance of dazzling color. Beneath "the box" that produced the ideal conditions for flying, the city rested in a pronounced calm.

"I'm just now getting to the point where I'm okay," Paul said as he turned his face to me. "It took me a long time to get over it, not getting into MIT."

"Oh, honey, I had no idea it hit you that hard," I said.

I could say a lot of things I'd said before, about how competitive it was to get into those "reach" schools, about what a privilege it was to be gifted with the intelligence, the parental support, and the possibility to aspire to such a thing in the first place. But I didn't need to say this anymore. He'd worked his way through. It was here that he would find the courage written into all the songs that had ever been written.

"Mom," he said, "it's good to dream, though."

One year from this moment, another memory will layer on. My son will return from his second year at ASU, ecstatic with his choice and what he has made of it, and we will sit on this same patio as the Creamland dairy cow balloon rises from the Balloon Fiesta field and balloons in jewel-tone colors pass over our hill, steering toward the flat, open lot below. And he will say, thinking of his hero Douglas Hofstadter, who won the Pulitzer but whose physicist father won the Nobel, "Mom, a PhD is not enough. I'll do that before I'm thirty. Then what?"

He will turn to me with searching eyes, and I will say in a sturdy voice because the answer always begins with a question to the unknown. "You'll ask yourself, 'What wondrous new life do I want to live now?' "

After I cleared the breakfast dishes, we made plans to meet at the Greek Festival. I announced I was meeting a friend there and he could meet up with us later, and he appreciated the freedom to decide the terms. When he joined us in the tent where they hold the traditional Greek dancing, I thought he was so handsome, I had to tamp down my pride. We bumped into his history teacher from Sandia Prep and her husband, who used to be his soccer coach, and it seemed like a million years since Paul was a child. Uncannily, at the same table, was a friend of Paul's father since college, who had been like an aunt to them, but also happened to know the history teacher and the soccer coach. She told me she just happened to be in Denver last week and took Grace out for dinner. All these years I had relied on the eyes and ears and hearts of loving angels to watch over my children in Albuquerque, and here we were under a white tent with a bouzouki strumming and a line of dancers snaking across the floor, and I was understanding that the network of us has expanded to immense territory beyond this place. We'll keep watching out for each other. We are an infinite network of stars.

The day ended with a twinge of agony. Paul wanted so very badly to be here when Grace arrived next weekend for her fall break, but, ultimately, he decided it was too much driving. The next day he packed his car and headed to Arizona. He'd miss his twin sister by a week.

WHEN SHE ARRIVED, Grace and I jammed together. I played piano accompaniment to "Hero," the signature song from "Boyhood." She sang, "Everyone deserves a chance to…"

"I love this song because I see this is the conversation we've been having, about you becoming what you will become and my letting go, letting you be free to go," I said as her easy long desert road oohs faded out. "It is beautiful to love someone so much that it hurts when you say goodbye. I try to remember that when it hurts."

"That's interesting," she said, "but that's not what the song means to me." It was about what happens when you can be free of protection. It was about autonomy. It was about loving it all— the beautiful, the ugly, and the uncanny. It's about deciding for yourself whether your hair will be virgin ashen blond or strawberry blond, about not having to live up to anyone's expectations. About bearing witness to the courage of our songs, about how the light of our melody carries on endlessly even after death. She was singing me the story of deathlessness. Because she'd already been there. Now that I had, too, I could hear her. Her song strummed across my soul. When she sang her next song, she was explaining to me the infinite, how rare and beautiful our love for each other is.

Next, she played a polonaise by Chopin, an assignment for her piano class.

I played "A Time for Us," the theme song from "Romeo and Juliet," the one I played for my mother the day I was fifteen and we bought music for the new piano, the one I played every time I came home, my offering.

My daughter and I had a new tradition now.

The next evening, Grace and her boyfriend left too soon and too late for the long drive to Denver. I stepped in from the porch and closed the door. I approached the piano, alone. I slipped to the cherrywood bench. I played the song again, "A Time for Us," the last song I played for my mother. She had gasped between breaths on the nebulizer and said she must take a nap now. "But I want you to play for me," she had whispered as I braced her through the six steps to her hospice bed. Facing each other, we laced our arms together. Her frail fingers clasped my forearms from inside the circle of my embrace as she paused so she could work to gather the next breath. "I'll be able to hear you, from here," she said in a wisp. Her blue-veined willow china hands slipped away from my arms as she lowered herself to the edge of the mattress. "I promise you, I'll hear every note."

When I touched my fingertips to the ivory keys in the outer room, I anchored, A minor, 3/4 time, moderato. From the first yearning note, I knew I would not stumble. Every note was crisp, precise, imprinted forever into the pins and tendons of this instrument because it had been placed there so many times. Each time I neared the end of the song, I wove myself back into the repeat. I repeated the plaintive verses, the roiling bridge, the stabbing climax where Juliet falls to the floor. Every time I looped through, new variations emerged. Perhaps Juliet is still alive and this time Romeo will see her slow breaths. I dropped the melody to the left hand. I played it in a higher octave. I could not let the song end because now there was only one outcome.

Now, here at this new place in my home where for many years we would gather, I played Grace home. *I love them more.* The song doesn't end—it mounts in intensity. The more I play, the more I love them. I love them *because* they left. I love them *because* they want to become who they are.

Entering the kitchen, I came to the refrigerator, where my eye caught on a photo of four-year-old Grace. She wore a corona of laughter and lemon curls as she snuggled next to my mother. Now comes the ability to reel the line into my history and cast it forward with hope. All those years, I'd brought the twins to my mother, and they'd witnessed her devotion. My mother had drawn herself to the piano like someone draws to healing waters. The photo was one of the last photos I had of my mother in Albuquerque, because after that, she could no longer travel. It must have been nearing Halloween, the same time of year it is now. In the photo, Grace was a beacon of joy, her delight so contagious that my mother lit up. The electrical surge between grandmother and granddaughter was palpable. I hovered my fingertip above my mother's face, "She," floating to my daughter, "touched her."

Grace was singing. She was writing songs.

"Because she…" and I touched my mother's face "…touched me…" I touched my heart … "she…" I touched my daughter's face "has a song in her heart. Because of me."

A midnight text arrived. "Home now" bloomed on my screen in a green bubble below Grace's face. "Guess what song came up on my Spotify as we were logging the last miles?" "Hero." The last miles are the hardest. The wee hours when you need some protection.

ONE WEEK LATER, I arrived in Phoenix, to these tobacco mountains that form silhouettes of sleeping camels against a cobalt sky. I sat with Maureen at breakfast over *The New York Times*

and *The Arizona Republic*, we talked about the #metoo story under the chandelier above her dining room table. Women were protesting in the streets.

"I wish you would just live here," Maureen said. "We're secretly hoping that Grace ends up here for grad school."

I looked out to the patio, the roses and bougainvillea against the wall. Dennis had already migrated to his writing hut. In my memory, I saw Grace and Paul, age six, tossing skeins of white yarn through the lush trees and Christmas lights, creating a lattice of cat's-eye strands over our heads, laughing with delight on the lawn. In my memory, I heard teenage Grace playing a song lamenting about what they had done to her song.

Maureen's home felt like home, and my home felt like home. Louisianne's home felt like home, and Judy's loft apartment felt like home, and Deborah's and Phyllis's and Whitney's. The lake at Wiawaka, the morning sun on the Pino Canyon trail. Paul's dorm room with his mint-green electric guitar. Grace's dorm room with its Tibetan flags. It's all home.

IT COULD HAVE BEEN DIFFERENT. I could have stayed in Saratoga and I could have not been here on a patio in a Thai restaurant in downtown Mesa, listening to my son talk about his plans and his visions. I could have listened to him from afar, maybe on Zoom, me in the loft looking at the butternut trees (which would be golden now), him in his dorm looking east to the Superstition Mountains. I could hear it just the same but not see the self-assured way he sits back in his seat. In the concert hall, the stage was being set with Ludovico Einaudi's black grand piano, where this white-haired Italian composer with the thick square eyeglasses would play as the screen would spin scribblings of ancient symbols that told us what was true before we could talk.

In the sweep of two seasons, my son had not gone to Stanford or MIT. He was not dead on a Utah highway. He did not die in an ambulance racing down the spine of Albuquerque under a blood-red sky. He had not "just gone to UNM" in a fit of fear or pique or weary surrender to his father. And he had not abandoned me or pushed me away because I was stressed and flawed and looked upon him as though I was a strange giraffe mama poking her head high above the treetops, scouting the forest for her calves, looking to see the danger ahead for her children.

Paul ordered fried ginger tofu. I chose yum yum soup. I brought him news of Grace's trip back home, and he hung on to every detail. When I was finished, he sat back and sighed. "Ah, I fear I shall never see my twin sister again." They had been apart for nine weeks, the longest stretch of their lives. It would be Thanksgiving before he saw her again.

He told me he was taking human development and cognitive science to lay the groundwork for the artificial intelligence classes he'd take when he got deeper into his major. He was reading another Douglas Hofstadter book, *I Am a Strange Loop*, and he talked to me about what a self even was. How do we know we are a self, and how can a self emerge from something selfless as a stone or a puddle? (Or a mother?) Each of us is an individual point of view, and our perspective can exist outside of the brain. "The score of a Bach fugue can contain the composer's essence," Paul explained. "A folio of his sheet music is a notation of his sensibility, what was happening in his brain. So the experience of his music brings us into Bach's subjectivity—into his mind."

I checked my watch. The show would begin soon. I signaled for the check. "You're talking about immortality," I said. "The essence of a self can live on."

"No, Mom, a self is more alive than that, more than notations. Yes, we can know there is a self because there is a narrative the self leaves behind, because who *is* the storyteller?" Paul continued as the server set down the check. "In other words, each of us is more than a self. We are a collection of selves. We each contain a set of neurons in symbolic models that mirrors and reflects the other people in our lives. That's kind of what the book is about." He looked out at the distant horizon, the sun falling beneath a roof of blue clouds. Then he turned his face to me. "But what really struck me is what he wrote after he lost his wife. He said that after she died, he felt 'soul fragments' of her consciousness in his."

"So this self, it's relational," I said and signed the check. "When we receive each other, we are planting a part of us in another. We can live in others, and they can live in us."

"Maybe," he said and stood. "I've been playing guitar more. My roommates play. We are thinking of forming a band."

"That's cool," I said and joined him on the sidewalk, folding the receipt. "Have you thought about this? You and Grace are both studying the brain. And music. She's a music major, and you're forming a band. You're pursuing cognitive science, she's pursuing neuroscience."

As we turned the corner, the sky filled with brilliant pink. Beyond toward Phoenix, a wide crimson band marked the far western horizon.

"Yeah, I'm top down, she's bottom up." He stopped and considered his gaze lingered at the brink of the sky. "I think someday we'll write a paper together." I smiled as he turned to me, his blue eyes bright. "Remind me of this in twenty years."

I nodded as I took in this young man. "That," I said, "is going to happen."

IN THE CONCERT HALL, as we slipped into our row, I asked Paul which song he was most waiting for. "'Experience,'" he whispered. The piano pulsed, then a melody laced through, gathering speed. A violin entered, the sweet fluttering of wings. The circling beat of a bodhran came in, gaining altitude. The story of a whole life was lived.

During intermission, when Paul turned his face to me, he was so happy my heart nearly swelled out of my chest. "I keep thinking about what it must have been like to see a great composer like Bach or Beethoven or Chopin in his time. I think we're seeing that kind of genius now," he said. "What's the song you're most looking forward to?"

"What is the song you most enjoyed?" I asked.

"Experience," he said, and I nod, because now I know how much he wanted that.

"What's the song you're most looking forward to?" he asked me.

"'The Olympics song,'" I said. "The one Procter & Gamble used for the Moms/Pick Them Back Up campaign." My mind flashed on little skaters slipping on the ice, moms lifting them up, the downhill skier soaring over a hill of white powder, the mom's eyes tearing as she sees it's her child who is leading. The song began with a slow planting of seeds, long measures in 6/8 time. Then ever-accelerating lines of melody reaching into higher octaves. "*Divenire*," I said the name. "It means 'to become.'"

FALL HAS COME TO THE BOSQUE and I live alone now. It is autumn, the season of radiant invitations. I turned my car south down Rio Grande, entering the North Valley. Come with me now, come down this road named after the grandest river, the one that carries stone and sediment from the Sangre de Cristos, lifeblood. Come with me now as it settles into a nook between the Sandia Mountains and Mount Taylor, cutting now, gathering speed before it makes its turn at El Paso and heads to the Gulf of Mexico. Ride with me as I turn right and slice into the North Valley like an autumn pear. Past horse farms and adobe compounds. Past the farmers market with the clock post, the lavender fields, over the canyon of Montaño Road, past the corn mazes and the Italian vineyard with the ceramic-tiled roof and long reflecting pool. Come with me to the open fields where snow geese gather, arriving from their long journey from Canada, chattering as they describe what it was like there, once, in northern climes. Imagine what they see from above, when they first spot the open field by the river, landing in the dry bronzed grass, their excitement when they recognize it from the pale blue sky. Imagine for how long, so very long, they have been traveling, how they have been guiding each other, taking turns navigating. Float down as they bank right and descend to the river. Imagine the first touching down to soil.

Epilogue

MONTHS LATER, I MEET LIAM at Tamaya, where he is speaking at a newspaper convention. I walk past the kiva of stacked stone. A wind flute sounds in my ears, the haunt of a signal sent out from one red sandstone cliff to the next to the next, seeking to hold life and call rain and catch light, to say, are-you-there-I'm-here. As two attendants swing open the doors for me, I see Liam standing, his eyes soft and waiting.

"Like it never happened," he says, his voice choking a little.

He circles me in his teddy bear arms. I feel the great rush of his relief press all through me. Only then do I understand he had worried about me the way someone greets a warrior emerging from a battlefield.

We walk down into the golden cottonwoods, their rough bark amber in the blazing late-autumn light. Above us, snow geese have arrived at the blue gleaming vein of this grand river. Their black beaks cut swift arrows across the sky. They chatter with the sense of here, here, here. Here we are.

Later, we sit at the firepit, clutching ourselves to its orange glow. Looking out at the net of black branches by the river, he says it again, lifting his face to me in the firelight. "Like it never happened."

The glass ceiling question bids me to answer. I don't.

The soul question bids me to answer. I hear it.

Now, in the words of poet David Whyte, comes and lands and sits inside me the ability to read all of my life backward and understand, and read it forward with hope.

"But it did," I say. "It did."

SOMETIMES WHEN I THINK ABOUT SARATOGA, I vibrate with a sadness I can't explain. It is dawn, and I have emerged from the northern woods to a battlefield of terrible beauty. A hush hangs over the scene I enter. Embers float down from treetops, touch my hair, my cheeks. My eyes search through a charred village, hoping to detect one living pulse. What was the story here, in this place?

The last minutes I lived in Saratoga, Snowflake and I circled the walking path. I knew the sun and warmth and lushness wouldn't last, yet the force of summer seemed to lie to us like it could settle in here for good.

In some turns of the season, I stay. I don't get on the plane. I stay and let the night fall. I stand at the edge of the woods by the spa, near the Roman porticos that lead to the baths, where the healing waters lie.

Light leaves my body, the remaining small sparks of me. Carolyn. My daughter. Grace. Her songs. Her kindness. My son. Paul. The eternal braid of his code. My words. My outpouring. My lights flurry into the high trees. Aimless wanderers, beautiful crystals who know they might melt. My lights are pulses, then only flickers. My last light, out of me, but rooted in the spiral of me I feel a thread, can track these tiny dancing beams far into the forest. They don't die, these last fireflies of me. They dart and loop low through the tree trunks, lacing them with light. They soar to the high branches, swoop deep into the thickening wood, catapulting ever and ever and ever into the distant hills. I am nearly losing sight of my lights. I know they search and search. They are going farther than I ever knew.

And then I know. They aren't leaving me.

They're leading me.

Acknowledgments

Writing only seems like a solitary endeavor. If ever you would see me writing, you may see me sitting at my laptop, accompanied by a swirl of insight, an active imagination and an army of words. It may look like I am alone, typing out a story. Maybe I have a window with a view of a mountain, maybe a hearty fern in a blue pot, maybe a white candle.

But I am not alone.

Writing is always a collaborative act. I don't write TO the page—I write THROUGH the page.

To you.

Writers always write in community. We're always in conversation—with wise, kind and super-skilled people who become our mentors, our advocates, our inspirations. Our Muse.

I am deeply grateful to and humbled by this process. I'm in awe of the magic that can come forth. This is my love letter to all who accompanied me on the journey.

This book found me more than I found it. Many times, I asked, "Why does this book unstitch me?" When you ask a question like that, well, you know you have a book. You know you need to go, keep going and not go alone.

So many people have cheered for me, wept with me, encouraged me, listened to me, recommended books to me that sparked more conversation, talked it through with me and led me out of the pure confusion of how to lay down sentences on these pages.

So many people have been my steady and noble witnesses along a path that made it possible for me to find rejuvenation after the loss of seemingly everything. They watched me reinvent myself. They helped me regain an emotional agility that many of us think vanishes with youth. I now hold the "pearl of great price," the one worth selling everything for.

I'm grateful to live in a thriving literary ecosystem that sustains me—and equips me to sustain others as a book coach/developmental editor/writing retreat leader. I see your faces all around the hearthspace of this work and nod to you. In your quest, you ground me. From the wild beauty of my heart to yours, I thank you.

Several of you, I want to name specifically:

Erika Krouse, my first developmental editor on *Boundless*, who first made me believe I could fast-track this memoir and shape a life story into art.

Emily Rapp Black, my second developmental editor on *Boundless*, who knew my sorrow as a mother and kept believing in this story.

Jona Kottler, who kept saying, "Hold to your vision. Your vision is your vision. Keep writing." Thank you for writing with me. (And thanks to Flying Star Cafe and Satellite Coffee in Albuquerque—not sure we could have done this without you.)

The Lighthouse Book Project, which gave me a literary booster shot when I was eight years out from finishing my MFA in Writing and I needed structure again. You have become my second literary family.

To my first literary family at the Naslund-Mann School of Writing at Spalding University, where I earned my MFA in Writing, thank you for the gold. I say everything about Spalding is gold because all my writing from that point forward has been spun into gold, and it will keep on being gold. Thank you, Sena Jeter Naslund and Karen Mann, for seeing that a creative writing program that was intellectually rigorous *and* emotionally supportive was possible and necessary.

Thank you, Sena, for all the times you said, "Welcome home," whether we were in London, Barcelona, Buenos Aires, Florence or Louisville. Thank you, Katy Yocom, who helped me get lost in all those places and find myself again. Thank you, Terry Price for leading our merry band of alumni for many years—your building of that literary community is why I say, "Spalding is the gift that keeps on giving." Thank you, Kathleen Driskell, for carrying on the vision, writing poetry that takes my breath away and rocking that red hair! And thank you to my mentors, the exquisite Robin Lippincott, the perspicacious K.L. Cook and the wise and passionate Jody Lisberger.

There have been many other writing mentors: Percival Everett, James Baker Hall, Ron Carlson, Valerie Miner and more. You came to me through my other almost-MFAs at the University of Kentucky and Arizona State University. And thank you to the late Lisa Lenard-Cook, who helped me love the beautiful mess of a manuscript.

To the team at Atmosphere Press, I'm so glad I found you in the lonely exhibit hall at the AWP Conference when a pandemic struck the nation and sent most literary types into forced isolation. I'm so glad I found you again in Seattle, when I got sold on the idea that with Atmosphere, I would be in good hands.

To my longtime readers at Sage Magazine and the Albuquerque Journal, which published my columns for 16 years, thank you for your eyes and ears on my life. Thank you, dear readers, for always asking, "How are the twins?" because you watched them grow up. The seed of this book came from one brave and poignant column written days after my two babies nearly died.

To *Fourth Genre* for publishing "Resurrection," an early version of the story of my twins' near-miss with death—specifically Laura Julier, for some mighty fierce editing that gave that story the one more thing it needed.

To *Under the Gum Tree* and *The Colorado Sun* for helping me tell the early parts of my empty-nest story.

To the Living School, the Center for Action and Contemplation and founder Father Richard Rohr, which have grounded me in acts of contemplative solidarity and enriched me with the teachings of the Immortal Diamond and Thomas Merton's True Self.

What, ever, have I learned by dying? That the False Self can fall away, and will. But you can do the True Self no harm. Thank you for helping me find another word for emptiness. It's: *Boundless.*

Thank you to the contemplative practice that has sustained me through our Circle 14 community—you are my spiritual family.

To Bill Ostendorf, you sent me on an adventure, and I got a good story out of it. Also, you saved my soul.

To Jane Walker, always prescient, always ready with the brave truth, always hilarious,

You get to be Maya Rudolph in the movie. I'll be Kristen Wiig.

To Roma Arellano, sorry about the Maya Rudolph thing, but can you be America Ferrera? I'm sure you've got a speech like that in you. Together, we have been fierce feminist entrepreneurs, writers and mothers. I thank you for your calm wisdom and the way you make me giggle at all appropriate and inappropriate times.

To Roma and all our mamas, Tricia, Wendy, Cindy and Danielle, just look at our babies! We did this together.

To Martha Kaser, don't we have the stories now? We can even make Costco fun. You get to be Melissa McCarthy.

To Peg Fiedler, there is a road trip in our future. You be Geena Davis. I'll be Susan Sarandon.

To Marianne Hund, we keep the faith together.

To Maureen, you are my light. I'm so glad we figured everything out about our lives in Venice. As the poet David Whyte wrote, **"Friendship transcends disappearance: an enduring friendship goes on after death, the exchange only transmuted by absence, the relationship advancing and maturing in a silent internal conversational way, even after one half of the bond has passed on."** I suppose we will keep keepin' on with that conversation.

To Portia, you are my angel.

To my dear sisters: Shirley Flynn Mitchell, you see my dreams and I hold yours. Together, we keep them alive. Linda April Flynn, you held me through this. You are one of the bravest people I know.

To my late father, Gene Paul Flynn. You made me a writer by

believing in me. One day I came home from school and told you I wanted to be a writer, and you gave me a Brother typewriter and a collection of Hemingway short stories. With that, you installed in me one true, abiding idea: "You can make it from here." Because of you, I have always had a creative birthright and an immeasurable inheritance as a storyteller. I relish family dinner nights laced with your family stories, jolly humor and passionately recited lines from Shakespeare. I am so proud that you became a novelist, too.

To my late mother, Bonnie Belle Flynn. You filled our home with faith and beauty and the awe of music. By the way you leaned into playing the movements of a Beethoven symphony on piano, you taught me narrative flow. Watching you annotate your music with fingering notes and dynamic prompts, I mirrored your devotion to discipline. In the ardent way you played, you taught me how to bring forth the motifs and interludes, harmonies and descants—all the nuances that are the subtext of music so that a song tells a story. One day I stood before you as you fought to catch your last breaths. I held the pages of my novel manuscript in my hands and offered you words I wanted to make sure you heard before the music faded out of you: "I knew how to write this because you taught me how to play music. *This* is my music."

To the father of my children, once you said, "Carolyn, they are beautiful!" Yes, they are.

To Emerald and Lucas, my little stars who are big stars now. I have loved having a front-row seat to your becoming. The promise of the future is what I've helped you to see, and yet…always see this: On this day we are alive. Let's keep holding the awe and splendor of that. Be brave, be light, be you.

27 July 2024

Book Club
Discussion Questions

1. **When you have become no one, how do you become someone again?** That's the question at the heart of *Boundless*. As Carolyn faces the impending emptying of the nest, she states that as a single mother of twins, "two-thirds of my family will leave at once." *Boundless* asks you to notice when you have become an empty shell and determine for yourself what you would do to become someone again. **What does that question awaken in you?**

2. *Boundless* opens with Carolyn holding her two babies in her arms as an ambulance races them to the hospital to save their lives. From the very first sentence, *Boundless* announces it is concerned with **the fragility of life**. How does holding this awareness inform how we live our lives in full vibrance?

3. In two places, Carolyn laments the dearth of life passages, one for the empty-nested single woman ("there is no life passage for someone like me") and the other for a young man about to launch his adulthood ("In any other culture, any other time, my son would experience a rite of passage, a series of tests of his character, a wise elder to instruct him, and a ceremony with fire and sage to make it so…."). **What is the significance of life passages in moving us out of old, stuck lives and into new chapters of life?**

4. *Boundless* jump-cuts from the moment when Carolyn's two babies are losing their light and hovering at the edge of death to—suddenly they are 17 and on the brink of choosing a college. **What does this say about the fleeting nature of childhood?**

5. There are a lot of road trips in *Boundless*—after all, it's called "a road trip to rejuvenation." From the very first trip—one last spring break to keep trying to be a family—to the reverse-Manifest Destiny trek heading back east across the country to the forced re-migration to Albuquerque, the road trip is a motif. There is the line, in Chapter 3, "clearly, it was time for a road trip," which hints that the road trip provides solutions. **In what ways does the road trip act as a change agent on Carolyn's life? On our lives?**

6. Grace fills this story with music, from the joyfully strummed Vance Joy song to the redemptive "Song for Zula" she plays to cool down her twin brother's teenage backtalk. **How does music connect us? Change us? Clarify things for us?**

7. When Carolyn talks about the future with her twins, she observes their exhilaration as well as the fright that can shut down conversations in seconds, She refers to them as "scorched earth" moments. **What does this tell you about what all three main characters—mom and twins—have on the line?**

8. With the pressure mounting for the twins' to choose their future, Carolyn refers to her home as the **"Be Who You Are" house**. Why?

9. At the outset of *Boundless*, Carolyn has hit the **glass ceiling** in the media industry. That she may never achieve that goal in her field, because print media is in a death spiral, is a profound disillusionment. Should she just accept this? What happens that finally allows her to accept this?

10. Carolyn makes a lot of mistakes in *Boundless*. **What is her first mistake? What is her worst mistake?**

11. Carolyn says we're not empty-nesters—**we are the wisdom teachers**. Why does the world need this now?

12. From the opening, when Carolyn's babies almost die in her arms, to the end, Carolyn has started **a conversation with God** that she may not want to have. How does this conversation change over the course of the book? In what ways does her relationship with God become less problematic? What role does forgiveness play? Surrender?

13. A lot of things get shed—or vanish—from Carolyn's life. Early on, not knowing what to do with her about-to-be-emptied self, she wonders where to go to get out of the house. "Not Walmart, with its plenitude of useless things." **How does this show us that she sees herself as "a useless thing"?**

14. Several moments of despair and suicide ideation are depicted in *Boundless*—Grace pounds nails in the wall that say "Try dying" and Carolyn whisks her to another school. After being fired, Carolyn has a panic attack and prays to die in her sleep. The thought takes hold in her, and it occurs to her there could be a method for ending her life. When she reaches out for help, she calls her sisters and childhood friend. "I need someone to lay eyes on me," she tells them. Her sister April knows this territory well, and bravely guides Carolyn out after the panic attack and suicide ideation. *Boundless* depicts situational depression and sympathizes with those who suffer from severe clinical depression and suicide ideation. **Why is it so hard to talk with those we love about this kind of despair? How can we shed the stigma and invite others to be vulnerable and find support? To be brave, be light, be you?**

15. On the brink of leaving Saratoga, destination unknown, Carolyn realizes that none of the possible places has to be the place. Her friend Peg says, "You've gone too far." Carolyn realizes, "Slivers of me are everywhere, but I was nowhere." **What if the road to nowhere goes everywhere?**

16. After a summer without a coffee maker, after giving up her house and her car, after a truckload of her furniture returns damaged, she has gotten used to living without material things and found something beyond that. In the chapter, "Useless Things," she says "there was nothing here I needed. This store was filled with useless things." She resists the on-ramp to consumerism, to be an endless self-improvement project and instead live in the rarefied space of an authentic identity not defined by roles or things. She comes to a moment when she stops being all the people her friends and the world see her to be. "All of life seemed to reverberate from this center, this place that greeted me every morning, where the dead and the living seemed to find me but not one of them knew my name. I was reduced to this: ink and paper," she writes. **How does this illuminate what Thomas Merton calls the True Self?**

17. Near the ending, with her twins settled in college, we have a scene with her son that takes us full circle from the conversation in Chapter 3 about becoming an adult self, inspired by Paul's favorite author, cognitive scientist and artificial intelligence pioneer Douglas Hofstadter. Perhaps the conversation all along in *Boundless* is about what makes a self be a self and why we have a self. "The essence of a soul can live on," Carolyn says to Paul, thinking of how the sheet music of a Bach fugue is an annotation of his immortality. Paul observes that it is more than that and mentions the Hofstadter book, *I Am a Strange Loop*. After we are gone, fragments of our souls live on in others' consciousness, lives we have touched, he says. **How does this answer the great question of the book?**

18. The title is *Boundless*, and you'll see hashtags on social media for #BoundlessAreOurDreams and #BoundlessIsOurLove. **What does the title mean to you?**

About Atmosphere Press

Founded in 2015, Atmosphere Press was built on the principles of Honesty, Transparency, Professionalism, Kindness, and Making Your Book Awesome. As an ethical and author-friendly hybrid press, we stay true to that founding mission today.

If you're a reader, enter our giveaway for a free book here:

SCAN TO ENTER
BOOK GIVEAWAY

If you're a writer, submit your manuscript for consideration here:

SCAN TO SUBMIT
MANUSCRIPT

And always feel free to visit Atmosphere Press and our authors online at atmospherepress.com. See you there soon!

About the Author

Memoirist, novelist and essayist Carolyn Dawn Flynn is the author of the memoir *Boundless* and seven books of nonfiction. *Boundless* was longlisted for the 2021 Mslexia International Memoir Prize and the 2022 First Pages Prize.

Her novel *Searching for Persephone*, shortlisted for the Elixir Press First Novel Prize, is excerpted in *The Write Launch*. Her work has been published in *Fourth Genre*, *Under the Gum Tree*, *Arts and Letters*, *The Colorado Sun*, *The Tampa Review*, *The Whitefish Review* (Montana Prize for Fiction), *Albuquerque Journal*, *Sage Magazine*, *Albuquerque the Magazine* and *Wilde Frauen*.

She is a single mother of Ukrainian-Irish-American twins and was the longtime editor of a life-giving magazine called *Sage*. In her TEDx Women talk, "Tell a Better Story, Live a Better Life," she has inspired countless others to live their sacred yes—even in a world that may split open, as the writer Muriel Rukeyser once famously said, if one woman spoke the truth.

She is a 2012 graduate of the Naslund-Mann Spalding MFA in Writing program and a native of Lexington, Kentucky, where she grew up near Red River Gorge. She now lives in Albuquerque, New Mexico, where she is a hiker and a pilgrim and a desert dweller who is an appreciator of horizons.

Find out more at carolynflynn.com.